SEX, POWER, AND PARTISANSHIP

SEX, POWER, AND PARTISANSHIP

How EVOLUTIONARY SCIENCE Makes Sense of Our POLITICAL DIVIDE

Hector A. Garcia

Prometheus Books

59 John Glenn Drive
Amherst, New York 14228

Published 2019 by Prometheus Books

Cover image © Jozef Micic / Alamy Stock
Cover design by Jacqueline Nasso Cooke
Cover design © Prometheus Books

Inquiries should be addressed to
Prometheus Books
59 John Glenn Drive
Amherst, New York 14228
VOICE: 716–691–0133 • FAX: 716–691–0137
WWW.PROMETHEUSBOOKS.COM

23 22 21 20 19   5 4 3 2 1

Library of Congress Cataloging-in-Publication Data

Identifiers: LCCN 2018041385 (print) | ISBN 9781633885158 (ebook) |
ISBN 9781633885141 (pbk.)

Printed in the United States of America

For my children

CONTENTS

CONTENTS

CHAPTER 4: EQUALITY VERSUS HIERARCHY 67

CONTENTS

CHAPTER 1
EVOLUTIONARY POLITICS

Animals eat one another without qualm; civilized men
consume one another by due process of law.
—Will and Ariel Durant, *The Lessons of History*, 1968

A nation's sinew begins to tear. Triumph in one group is met with fear and bewilderment in another. Old prejudices are reanimated; new ones are invented. The masses succumb to irrational forces, prodded to frenzy by politicians and the media. The nation is poised to devour itself.

The controversial election of Donald Trump as the forty-fifth US president polarized the United States more than any other time in its contemporary history. To those watching, it seemed remarkable, and yet the partisan division was a familiar enough scenario, even in the "United" States. The 1960s saw police and the right wing clash violently with the leftist counterculture and with the civil rights and anti–Vietnam War movements. In the 1950s, McCarthyism drove the nation into repression, fearmongering, and political paranoia. Panic over Communism destroyed countless Americans' careers, or saw them wrongly imprisoned for treason. A century before, the American Civil War drenched the nation's soil with the blood of over 600,000 people, greatly as a result of disagreement over slavery; even in the twenty-first century, bloody clashes between the Left and Right have erupted over the place of Confederate monuments in America. All of these schisms have been grounded in partisan psychology. Such Left-Right divisions are old, seen all over the world, and, in some form or another, certain to continue.

But why are these periods of conflict so common across nations and history? To truly understand the turmoils of today we must look somewhere most of us are unaccustomed to looking—our primordial past. Our current political struggles are ancient, rooted in a time before we even had nations, and indeed before we were fully human. What I will show you in this book is that the difficulties we face forming cohesive societies in the modern era reflect psychological adaptations with a simple, ancient purpose—keeping our ancestors alive in savagely dangerous environments. All too often these adaptations are at odds with the environments in which we currently live. This mismatch between the ancient and the modern is at the core of what divides us along political lines. While we will excavate far below the landscapes of our political parties in search of answers, political partisanship will remain a key framework because when nations turn against themselves, a reliable fracture opens between the political Left and Right.

To begin to understand this fracture, let's turn to an unlikely source for psychological insight: media pundits. American political commentator and talk show host Chris Matthews once described Republicans as the "Daddy Party" and Democrats as the "Mommy Party." Writes Matthews,

> Republicans protect us with strong national defense; Democrats nourish us with Social Security and Medicare. Republicans worry about our business affairs; Democrats look after our health, nutrition and welfare. Republicans control the White House; Democrats provide a warm, caring presence on Capitol Hill . . . it's the traditional American family. "Daddy" locks the door at night and brings home the bacon. "Mommy" worries when the kids are sick and makes sure each one gets treated fairly. This partition of authority and duty may seem an anachronism from the *Leave It to Beaver* era, but it's an apt model for today's political household.[1]

Similarly, in a play on John Gray's best seller on the differences between men and women, *Men Are from Mars, Women Are from Venus,* the meme *Republicans Are from Mars, Democrats Are from Venus* has recently echoed across the popular press.[2] Hardline conservative commentator Ann Coulter even boasted on Fox news, "I am more of a man than any liberal."[3] As it happens, these observations are far more empirically accurate than we might have imagined.

Naturally not all men are conservatives, and not all women are liberal. In fact, research suggests a link between partisanship and *gendered* psychology.[4] The term *gender* often describes masculine or feminine traits that may be expressed *independent of sex* and very often honed in their expression by culture. But even though gender can exist independently of biological sex, as we will learn throughout this book it is not independent of biology. Neither is politics.

To help us safely foray into this treacherous crossroads of gender, sex, and politics (as we move forward, religion will also cross this path), let us proceed with the understanding that in the grand scheme of human psychology, men and women, and liberals and conservatives, exhibit far more similarities than differences across innumerable psychological indices—daddies also worry when the children are sick, and mommies too bring home the bacon. Nevertheless, we venture into the slivers of difference, for those slim terrains abound with explanatory information about our evolved political psychology. The old adage that one should never discuss sex, politics, or religion in polite company would suggest that hazarding there could be fraught. Given the outlandishly controversial status of evolution, in America anyway, this topic may have a similar impact. But even a casual read of the history of political division reveals that the consequences of not understanding are far worse than the discomfort of knowing.

This book is about how Stone Age mating gave rise to our political orientations. More specifically, it is about how evolution programmed our minds with mating strategies to help us reproduce amid a fierce field of competition, how men and women employ different strategies to achieve reproductive fitness (i.e., representation in the gene pool), and how political partisanship arises from these sex-based approaches to perpetuating our genes. More precisely, I explain how all the hallmarks of political conservatism—its tribalistic flavor (us versus them), its emphasis on female sexual control, and its hawkish and territorial nature—are rooted in male mate competition, the ageless biological struggle for reproductive dominance. Far exceeding the scope of any government sex scandal, male competition for women turns out to be the core driving force behind contentious political issues as wide-ranging as affirmative action, social welfare, gender equality, contraception, abortion, taxes, criminal law, and foreign policy. Even the winner-take-all mentality of conservative economic policy is based on male competition for mates.

War, by necessity, is a critical focus of this book because it is rooted in team-based male-mate competition, and because our evolutionary forensics finds its crimson fingerprints all over our gendered political orientations. The risk of being annihilated by the outside tribe—and the potential gains of taking over the rival tribe's territory, resources, and women—forged the coalitionary psychology of men. Here I will show you how the militaristic logic embedded in that psychology maps squarely onto all the hallmark values of political conservatism. It is from the context of violent male mate competition, and its most heightened expression, war, that we are able to most fully understand the masculine tenor of conservative political psychology, along with the set of complex emotional responses that are roused in the conservative clash with the Left.

What I also reveal is that the roots of liberalism, too, are far older than we imagined, having arisen from the timeless effort to rein in dominant males and to prevent them from monopolizing resources and impinging on the evolutionary fitness of those with less power. More fundamentally, liberalism is based on the prodigious human task of rearing offspring, a critical survival enterprise championed by women, and provisioned by the "Mommy" parties of the world. We will review, among many other evolutionary dynamics, striking evidence suggesting that male competition has impelled some women to adopt conservative ideals as a means of competing with other females, making alliances with dominant men, and producing sons who are themselves strong male competitors.

And so the political insights offered by the commentators quoted above begin to acquire novel explanatory power when seen through the lens of evolutionary psychology, a field that rests on the understanding that we humans have spent 99 percent of our history in small bands of hunter-gatherers, living in environments very different from those in which we currently reside. Survival in those environments was harsh, with perpetual threats from predators, starvation, disease, and violence from outside tribes. These are the environments in which our political predispositions evolved. And because our current circumstances comprise only a blink of an eye in our evolutionary history, we retain psychological adaptations for that ancestral world. What this ultimately means is that the dark-suited men who represent us in government wield the power to steer the global economy, shift the parameters of human liberty, or unleash the devastating machinery of war, and they do so using Stone Age brains. This basic fact of human psychology is equally true for the women increasingly moving into positions of political power, and for the masses of people who elect our leaders.

But critically, having a Stone Age brain in the modern era poses certain challenges. Even though the risk of being massacred by neighboring tribes has drastically diminished since our perilous days as hunter-gatherers, our minds remain calibrated for ancestral environments that roiled with intertribal bloodshed. And as we grow into a vast, interconnected community of nations, bound by a global economy, our capacity to rain destruction on our neighbors grows commensurately. And so today we maneuver our way through precarious foreign and domestic policy arenas under the influence of these ancient and often volatile calibrations. But through evolutionary science we have an opportunity to better understand the primal workings of our evolved minds and to better transcend our most destructive political urges.

THE EVOLUTIONARY MODEL: WHY, HOW, AND CAVEATS

Disentangling the ravel of human politics may seem a daunting task. Today the political machine spans a vast, interconnected community of hundreds of nations around the globe, controlling billions of individual human beings. Adding vertiginous complexity to an unfathomable scope, politics are conducted with a stunning degree of bureaucratic intricacy, veined with deception, confounded by continuously shifting alliances, obscured by the conflicting commentary of partisan analysts, and steered by behind-the-scenes maneuvering of wealthy political stakeholders. This political machine is a colossal, dimensioned, dynamic web of human interaction that is often difficult to comprehend.

But evolutionary science is in the business of distilling complex processes down to their most basic elements. It does so by illuminating the ultimate *reasons* for everything that we love, abhor, think, and do, including the political policies we support, whether we are liberal or conservative, or whether we are inspired or repelled by the words of a president.

Understanding evolutionary science, though, requires an unflinching gaze in the mirror. Often revelations we find in evolutionary approaches can be surprising and, for some, a bit unnerving. There are those who worry that in accepting our evolutionary psychology we somehow concede freedom to our genes. However, there are endless examples of how we are able to reject the hand that nature dealt us. Eyeglasses, automobiles, computers, vaccines all reflect our ability to transcend our genetic limitations—here in vision, speed, endurance, mental computation, and resistance to disease—and the list goes on and on, from the simplest household items to entire fields such as medicine. And certainly, without an understanding of our evolved psychological impulses, we are *more*, not less, likely to enact them without consideration.

Using evolutionary psychology to understand human behavior can also require navigating tricky cognitive and emotional terrain, in particular avoiding common logical fallacies. One common pitfall is known as the *moralistic fallacy*, which occurs when we assume that undesirable qualities of nature simply cannot be true. Linguist and cognitive scientist Steven Pinker offers an illustrative description of how this fallacy emerges:

> The moralistic fallacy is that what is good is found in nature. It lies behind the bad science in nature-documentary voiceovers: lions are mercy-killers of the weak and sick, mice feel no pain when cats eat them, dung beetles recycle dung to benefit the ecosystem and so on. It also lies behind the romantic belief that humans cannot harbor desires to kill, rape, lie, or steal because that would be too depressing or reactionary.[5]

Political liberals may be more likely to commit the moralistic fallacy, which may sound like the following: gender equality is desirable—therefore any psychological differences observed between men and women must be *a priori* false; war is morally wrong—therefore we cannot have instincts for it. This fallacy is partly what makes conservatives dismiss liberals as ignorant or naïve about the way the world really is.

But the inverse of the moralistic fallacy, the *naturalistic fallacy*, assumes that what is natural must be moral or desired, and it is equally to be avoided. Writes Pinker,

> The naturalistic fallacy is the idea that what is found in nature is good. It was the basis for social Darwinism, the belief that helping the poor and sick would get in the way of evolution, which depends on the survival of the fittest. Today, biologists denounce the naturalistic fallacy because they want to describe the natural world honestly, without people deriving morals about how we ought to behave (as in: If birds and beasts engage in adultery, infanticide, cannibalism, it must be OK).[6]

As you may have guessed, political conservatives are more likely to commit this kind of fallacy. Examples may sound something like the following: men are naturally physically stronger than women, therefore women should be subordinate to men; warfare is instinctive, therefore it is acceptable. This fallacy is partly what makes liberals see conservatives as coldhearted and cynical. There are evolutionary reasons for adopting one or the other of these fallacies, as I will later explain. But for the time being, the goal is to avoid either of them.

The other challenge is in seeing psychological impulses that are usually hidden from conscious awareness—for example, becoming aware of the powerful drive to reproduce our genes, which we normally take for granted as simply the desire for a sexy partner, or love for our children. Eminent evolutionary psychologists Leda Cosmides and John Tooby refer to this phenomenon as *instinct blindness*.[7] We are often blind to our evolved predispositions, which are so ancient that they work seamlessly in the background while directly affecting our foreground behaviors and ideologies. The evolved *reasons* for our political behavior can be counted among those difficult-to-see processes. We can observe examples of *political* instinct blindness in media interviews where voters holding fervent party, leadership, or policy stances are stutteringly unable to articulate reasons for their strongly held positions when queried. This reflects more than just deficits in political literacy; it also reflects politics' deep channels into primitive emotion centers of the brain that operate below the level of conscious awareness.

In order to overcome instinct blindness, American psychologist William James suggested in 1890 that we must make "the natural seem strange."[8] In other words, we must strive to achieve reflexive distance from processes so natural that they're usually taken for granted. Others have suggested we take the perspective of an imagined Martian anthropologist studying humankind, with no preconceived notions of how human beings should think or act. These are great suggestions. Empirical research is another means to overcome instinct blindness because it can isolate in the psychology lab what may be difficult to see in the flow of everyday living. Because political views are so prone to bias, with political bias often being a form of instinct blindness, using the objective lens of science to understand our political selves is even more crucial. In examining the evolutionary psychology of human politics, we will therefore draw heavily on scientific research and also examine parallels between political behaviors among humans and other species, which can help to illuminate evolutionary processes that are difficult to see in ourselves.

But don't our politics simply reflect the values we're taught as children or the political ideas we were exposed to? Aren't they a matter of where we grew up or where we live? Most people tend to think of their political views as carefully considered choices they have made—perhaps reflecting the influence of particular experiences or people in their lives. There is no question that parents serve as important filters of information to their children and that they impart (or try to) their moral, religious, or political perspectives. Equally, there's no question that our cultural surroundings profoundly influence how we think, what we teach our children, and how we publicly express our political views.

Yet the picture is not as simple as we once thought. An increasingly large body of research is finding a genetic component to our political natures. Twin studies are one such branch of study. Identical twins, who share nearly 100 percent of their genes, show high concordance in their political orientations and more concordance than nonidentical twins, who share only half their genes.[9] Even more revealing, however, are studies of twins reared apart. Research has found that monozygotic (identical) twins reared apart have virtually the same likelihood of sharing a political orientation as those reared together.[10] In other words, the influence of upbringing doesn't seem to matter among identical twins—genetically similar individuals hold remarkably similar political views despite having grown up in different households and despite not being influenced by one another growing up. When political orientations of nonidentical twins reared apart are examined, concordance drops off dramatically.[11] Overall, meta-analytic research suggests that *30–60 percent of the variance in our political preference is due to genetic factors.*[12]

This in no way means that we are genetically programmed political automatons. Simply put, our ability to adapt to environmental circumstances would seem to underlie at least 40 percent of the variance in how we normally behave politically. This adaptability is what makes human political psychology so complex; it's also what allows the possibility of modifying our political stances when they no longer serve us.

Moreover, political parties themselves can and do shift over time. For example, before the 1980s, the Democratic and Republican parties in the United States were less ideologically polarized than they are today, which means that not only did the parties share certain characteristics but also that there was greater *within*-party variation—i.e., a wider liberal-conservative spectrum within both parties. Several historical factors have been identified that have been pulling the parties apart, for example, the rise of ideologically driven media interests (like Fox News) and conservative talk radio networks in the 1980s and 1990s, and the rise of coalitions between economic conservatives and religious fundamentalists in the 1970s.[13] Also influential was the civil rights movement of the 1960s and 1970s, which spurred mass defection of white Southern Democrats to the Republican Party.

And so in our efforts to understand the psychology of political orientation, we should not place excessive weight on party affiliation—political parties are subject to shifting and realignment. However, parties fall along a Left-Right continuum that is itself exceptionally stable; the ability to identify oneself on the Left-Right dimension has been reliably demonstrated across nearly every human society. As one example, the World Values Survey Association (WVSA), which is run by an international team of scientists and scholars, collects a mammoth amount of survey data on values and beliefs across the globe. Between 1981 and 2008 the WVSA asked over 250,000 people from ninety-seven countries to identify themselves along the Left-Right political spectrum with a question: "In political matters, people talk of the 'left' and the 'right.' How would you place your views on this [ten-point] scale, generally speaking?"[14] Across this ethnically, geographically, religious, technologically, and politically diverse sample, nearly 80 percent were able to place themselves along this dimension. When graphed, the results of this enormous survey show that endorsement of Left-Right political orientation forms a natural curve.

Like other variables of the natural world, the universality of the Left-Right dimension and the fact that orientation falls along a natural curve suggest that survival adaptations are at the core of our political leanings. If we look for these adaptations, as we will throughout this book, we discover the bones of our ancestors undergirding the modern body politic. In order to understand these adaptations, a deep dive into the biology of being liberal or conservative is in order.

CHAPTER 2

LEFT, RIGHT, AND MOTHER NATURE

HOW NATURE SHAPES PSYCHOLOGY

Every year something spectacular happens on the Serengeti, something that exemplifies the eternal and binding relationship between life on Earth and the natural environment. Following the nutrient-rich grasses brought to life by rolling, tidal rains, 1.5 million wildebeest—with countless zebra, impala, eland, and antelope in tow—sweep across the African plain to form the largest movement of land mammals on the planet. The unfathomable herd of horned, hooved, snorting, bleating wildebeest marches across the savanna like an unstoppable army, driven by an invisible, unswayable, instinctive force. Until they come to a river. For good reason, the onslaught halts here. Floating in wait beneath the muddy brown flow are one-thousand-pound crocodiles—green, coldblooded terror machines carried over from the age of dinosaurs, with spiked teeth, and jaws capable of 3,500-pounds-per-square-inch force (about the weight of a Volkswagen bug).

Understandably the wildebeest stop here, peer over the edge, snort, stamp in place, look nervously at one another, and then stare back into the muddy river. One can almost imagine one saying to another, "Well, *I'm* not going first; *you* go first. . . . No, *I'm* not going; *you* go," and so on. Turning back is not an option—those grasses have already been eaten, or ground to dust under the hooves of the swarming millions. On the other side are stretching plains of fresh, green, lush grasses, so necessary for life. The clogging continues until finally something remarkable happens, as it has for many millions of years. Amid the indecision, one among them seems to make up its mind and say to itself, "Screw it, I'm going." Several others follow, leaving a line of hesitators on the bank, waiting to see what happens next.

An important point that I wish to emphasize here is that the decision to surge ahead through that dangerous river is not completely random. The ones that go first tend, on average, to have an inborn predilection for taking the first step. This trait, which as shorthand we can call *risk-taking*, has its benefits. Those who make it across will have less competition for the lushest, most nutrient-rich grasses, as well as the freshest drinking water. However, you know what happens next. Submarined green monsters zero in, clamp down, and drag the intrepid gnus under, where they are drowned, twisted apart, and consumed.

Yet, some of these bold river-crossers make it to the other side and feast first on the greenest grasses and drink the freshest water. It's not hard to understand how this would have its survival advantages. Those born with traits coded for risk-taking probably reap the benefits for survival and reproduction as often as not in other ways besides access to the choicest greens. But why then aren't all gnus risk-takers? Because these same traits coding for risk-taking also land some wildebeest in the stomachs of crocodiles.

Back on the other end of the herd, queuing last in the rush across, are the lingerers. These wildebeest are less often food for crocodiles, but they also don't enjoy the freshest, most nutritious grasses, or any of the other perks of being spunky, and this is why all wildebeest aren't lingerers—because on average these gnus are likely to have poorer nutrition and in lean times may die of hunger or thirst more often than those at the spearhead. Notably, most of the wildebeest herd is somewhere in the middle.

What I hope to explain with this picture is how the environment shapes psychological traits and how those traits fall along what is known as the bell (or, *natural*) curve—in this case the most intrepid and the most hesitant wildebeest making up the tails of the curve. Now, population genetics among the wildebeest are obviously far more complex than what I have just described, and this explanation is more illustrative than scientific. However, there is a growing body of science to show that humans, like other creatures of the natural world, share similar basic predispositions to approach or avoid. It is not possible to fully understand human politics without understanding the ancient dangers of the natural world that shaped these modern-day inclinations. Before we explore what those dangers were for humans, we will first come to understand their outcome—our personality traits.

OPENNESS TO EXPERIENCE

Human personality traits represent distinctive patterns of thought, emotion, and behavior that characterize each individual's adaptation to life circumstances. Personalities are detectable in early childhood and to a certain degree remain stable across one's life span. They are also heritable— estimates based on twin research indicate that 40–60 percent of the variance in personality styles can be attributed to genetic inheritance.[1]

Social scientists have developed various models for understanding human personality, the most widely researched of which is known as the "Big Five." These dimensions include openness to experience, conscientiousness, extroversion, agreeableness, and neuroticism (or *OCEAN*). Cross-cultural research has consistently found evidence of the Big Five dimensions around the globe—one study, for example, found the Big Five in fifty societies and across six continents worldwide.[2] The ubiquity of these findings strongly suggests that the Big Five patterns of interfacing with the world are genetically based universals. Not surprising, then, personality dimensions tend to fall along the natural curve. This means that there is a great deal of variation *within* societies (and similar curves *across* societies). While we will explore other personality dimensions throughout this book, openness to experience merits some special attention here.

If there were a human analogue to our first river-crossing wildebeest, it would probably be people high on openness to experience. This personality construct includes a general appreciation for novelty and adventure, things like world travel, trying new foods, listening to different kinds of music. Those with high "openness" are also described as abstract thinkers, creative, curious, imaginative, independent, and as being more sensitive to emotions. While the Big Five factors are generally considered distinct, there is a moderately high correlation between openness to experience and another dimension in the model, *extroversion*—the tendency to be talkative, to be assertive, to seek social interaction, and to have high social ability.[3] Openness is also related to *sensation-seeking*, or a drive to experience sensations that are "varied, novel, complex and intense," and by the readiness to "take physical, social, legal, and financial risks for the sake of such experiences."[4] While risk-taking is not a central feature of openness, the construct does correlate with measures assessing risk-taking tendencies.[5]

Those scoring low on openness, on the other hand, are described as being *closed to experience*. Closed individuals tend to choose routine over new experiences, prefer predictability, and tend to be more traditional in their thinking. Think of the person who would rather stay at home, watching his or her favorite shows over the weekend, or dine at the same café that he or she always does, versus someone who would rather try a new ethnic food restaurant, or even kayak the Grand Canyon. If we could test the personalities of the wildebeest lingerers, they would probably score *low* on openness to experience.

As it turns out, human personality traits, in particular openness to experience, reliably correlate with political orientation. In one revealing longitudinal study, researchers started by conducting personality assessments on nursery school children.[6] Some children were described with adjectives such as "initializing," "impulsive," "curious," "talkative," "confident," "openness in expressing negative feelings," and "autonomous," among other descriptors. Other children were described as "anxious when confronted by uncertainties," "distrustful of others," "indecisive and vacillating," "ruminative," "self-unrevealing," "shy," "fearful," "neat," "compliant," and "adult-seeking." Before we get hung up on how negative the adjectives describing the latter group of children sound, consider that, as in the case of the wildebeest lingerers, these personality traits arise directly from their survival utility. In any case, the traits described in these preschoolers were observable long before they developed what we could call political identities.

Twenty years later, these same individuals were rated on their political orientation. The ratings were fairly thorough—they included self-identification on a liberal-conservative continuum, political participation, along with a variety of psychometric instruments measuring agreement on attitudes about things like socialized medicine, racial and gender equality, affirmative action, welfare, and military spending.

What the researchers found was that preschoolers who were rated as curious, impulsive, talkative, and so on reliably grew up to be liberals, whereas those who were described as shy, distrustful of others, compliant, and adult-seeking grew up to be conservatives. The ability of childhood personality traits to predict politics across such an impressive time span shows that genetic predispositions can influence our political orientations. Indeed, a large volume of research has found that openness is associated with tendencies like self-identifying as liberal,[7] voting liberal, and supporting liberal policies.[8]

One large study of over twelve thousand Americans examined the Big Five personality traits as predictors of core political values, such as economic attitudes (e.g., increasing taxes on the wealthy, government involvement in healthcare), social attitudes (e.g., on abortion and supporting civil unions), as well as on self-reported ideology (a five-point scale ranging from very liberal to very conservative).[9] The authors found that higher openness was associated with greater liberalism across all three of these means of measuring orientation. The authors explain that "political issues and ideological labels are 'stimuli' to which the Big Five traits shape responses," and "it follows that this attraction to novelty and tolerance for complexity encourage not only overall liberalism, but also support for liberal social and economic policies, which typically involve new programs or interventions that overturn existing practices." Crucially, this personality dimension reflects openness not only to things like new policies or programs but also to *other people*.

Consider another study in which researchers rated how liberals and conservatives interacted with confederates (researchers posing as non-researchers).[10] The researchers found that while conservatives tended to be reserved, socially distracted, and withdrawn, liberals smiled more and oriented their seats in the direction of the confederate more. In the same study the researchers examined offices and bedrooms of liberals and conservative for what they called "behavioral residue" of openness. They found that the personal spaces of conservatives were, on average, more likely to have group-oriented paraphernalia like American flags and sports teams memorabilia, which suggests an orientation toward people comprising one's in-group—known people, rather than those in the out-group. Conservatives' rooms were also neater, better organized, more conventional, and less stylish.

Personal spaces of more liberal subjects were more likely to contain books on travel, travel documents, international maps, cultural memorabilia, CDs that include world music and a wide variety of music, and an overall greater number and variety of books. Their spaces also were rated as more colorful and stylish. Again, a prominent thread in the tapestry of openness is an attraction to new people, new cultures, and traveling to distant lands (where you find new people). The attraction to and interest in outsiders, which we see so strongly among liberals, has been termed *xenophilia*.

Conversely, a strong current in the literature points to conservatives being more xenophobic, far beyond the shy, mistrustful preschooler or the socially distracted research subject, as I elaborate below. Before we explore this literature, it is worth emphasizing that conservative xenophobia should not be reduced to simple racism, a dislike of an outside people who have different skin, hair, or body features than one's own; it often extends to differences in language, custom, dress, sexual orientation, religion, nationality, political party, or even sports team. And xenophobia also results not only in a dislike of outsiders but also a corresponding preference for in-group members and values. This preference often manifests as a sense of patriotism and loyalty, of which the sports memorabilia and national flags that conservatives collect are small examples.

FEAR OF OUTSIDERS

In 2016, Donald Trump won the American presidency on the Republican ticket in part by stirring up a wave of racial tension and riding the rising swell into the seat of the most powerful man on Earth. One promise that he made to his followers was to build a massive wall to keep Mexican immigrants on the other side of the US-Mexico border. He stoked fear in a huge swath of the American electorate by claiming that Mexican immigrants are "bringing drugs. They're bringing crime. They're rapists."[11] He railed against federal judge Gonzalo Curiel, who oversaw a lawsuit against Trump University, calling him Mexican (he's from Indiana) and suggesting Curiel could not be impartial, because his Mexican ancestry tainted him to Trump's own xenophobic rhetoric about Mexicans.[12] Trump said that the United States should impose a "total and complete shutdown of Muslims entering the United States"[13] and suggested that Muslim Americans be entered into a national registry, like the Jews of Hitler's Germany.[14]

If Trump's rhetoric was an act put on to win the election, he certainly had completed a decades-long character study. John R. O'Donnell, former Trump Plaza Hotel and Casino president, wrote in his 1991 book *Trumped* that Trump said, "Laziness is a trait in blacks. It really is, I believe that. ... It's not something they can control," and "Black guys counting my money! I hate it."[15] Nor has Trump taken trouble to distance himself from such remarks. In a 1997 interview for *Playboy* magazine, Trump said of O'Donnell's remarks, "The stuff O'Donnell wrote about me is probably true."[16]

But equally noteworthy as Trump's rhetoric was the insurgent xenophobia and bigotry that subsequently echoed across the United States. Not only did Trump's blatant racism earn him the eager endorsement of the Ku Klux Klan and neo-Nazi groups, but it also set off a wave of hate-related propaganda. "Heil Trump," "Trump Nation: Whites Only," and Trump's campaign slogan "Make America Great Again" with the modification "Make America *White* Again" were spray-painted along with swastikas on buildings, walls, and black churches all across the country.[17] Emboldened by Trump's rise, physical attacks on Muslims and other ethnic minority groups surged, as did outbreaks of racial harassment that seemed to drag the United States back to the pre–civil rights 1960s.

The anti-out-group firestorm Trump created, along with his brash, strongman persona, did not go unnoticed by world leaders, particularly those in Europe, whose homelands bear the not too distant memory of charismatic Fascist leaders who exterminated millions of souls during World War II, using similar rhetoric. Former British prime minister David Cameron labeled Trump's discourse as "divisive, stupid, and wrong."[18] French prime minister Manuel Valls said, "Mr. Trump, like others, stokes hatred." German foreign minister Frank-Walter Steinmeier called Trump a "preacher of hate." Italian parliament member Sandro Gozi said, "Trump solutions for me are false solutions, but they're not original. They're things that we have heard in Europe from extremist sections." Mexican president Enrique Peña Nieto made a more direct comparison when he placed Trump's propaganda in context, saying, "In the past, some leaders address their societies in those terms," and "Hitler and Mussolini did that and the outcome, it's clear to everyone."[19]

By speaking openly and negatively against groups perceived as outsiders by his core base of conservative white Republicans, Trump was able to win their vote and ultimately the 2016 US presidential election.

This momentous political event illustrates a highly consistent empirical finding—namely that conservative political ideology predicts prejudice against the outside group. As an example, there are a multitude of studies examining racial stereotypes of African Americans in the United States, asking questions like whether blacks are intelligent or unintelligent, or more or less prone to violence. In study after study, conservatives report more negative attitudes and racial stereotypes than liberals.[20]

As we might expect, if our political stances were based on our shared, evolved psychology as humans, such correlations are found in other countries, with different out-group targets. As one example, researchers found that conservatives in Spain hold more anti-Arab prejudice than liberals.[21] A much larger study, called the Eurobarometer survey, assessed predictors of out-group prejudice in four thousand respondents across four European countries: the French were asked about North Africans, Vietnamese, and Cambodians; the Dutch about Surinamers and Turks; the Brits about West Indians, Indians, and Pakistani; and the Germans (West Germany at the time) were asked about Turks. Among a large number of predictors *political conservatism* was the major predictor of out-group prejudice.[22]

For some readers, this connection between conservatism and suspicion of outsiders, or liberalism and attraction to outsiders, may seem intuitive. What may not be as intuitive is the *reason* for these connections. As it turns out, the pressures of deadly infectious and genetic diseases in our ancestral history drove both liberal and conservative psychologies and, as a means to survive those diseases, distinctive liberal and conservative mating strategies.

INBREEDING AND OUTBREEDING

Xenophobia and xenophilia among humans may be related to inbreeding and outbreeding. Much of what I share on this specific topic comes from evolutionary anthropologist Avi Tuschman's book *Our Political Nature*.[23]

Here Tuschman operationalizes inbreeding as "when kin mate with one another more than would be expected by chance" and outbreeding as "mating between individuals that have a greater genetic distance between them than one would expect at random, given the size of the population." For humans, outbreeding could mean mating with members of a different tribe or race, or, even at one time in our distant past, mating with Neanderthals; recent genetic research has revealed that most non-Africans have up to 4 percent Neanderthal genes,[24] which means when our modern human ancestors left Africa and found Neanderthals living in Europe, they mated with these fairly distant hominids.

The Benefits of Outbreeding

Outbreeding can help avert what biologists call *inbreeding depression*. Too much inbreeding increases risk of *genetic* disorders while also causing other problems, such as birth defects and higher infant mortality rates related to congenital diseases.[25] Cystic fibrosis—a disorder that mostly damages the lungs but also the kidneys, liver, pancreas, and intestines—is one condition that can arise from inbreeding and one that for most of our species' history killed young children before they reached reproductive maturity. Like other genetic diseases, this condition occurs when two copies of a problematic, recessive gene are transmitted to offspring.

Given the disastrous consequences of cystic fibrosis, why hasn't natural selection weeded out this gene eons ago? As Tuschman points out, this gene has positive as well as negative potential outcomes, as is the case for other often fatal genetic conditions like sickle cell anemia, which, in addition to causing health problems, provides resistance to malaria. Likewise, having one recessive copy of the cystic fibrosis allele is thought to help us resist a host of deadly diseases, such as cholera, typhoid, tuberculosis, and diarrhea.[26] Thus a degree of outbreeding can reduce the risk of offspring with two copies of the allele.

Inbreeding can also create overspecialization for a certain environment, making populations more vulnerable during periods of environmental change. Weather can produce drastic environmental change, such as ice ages, periods of global warming, drought, or flooding, all of which can impact the availability of critical resources like water or edible plant life. Imagine the fate of an animal that is highly specialized to eat a certain fruit should weather eradicate that species of fruit tree. Similar risk can come from things like blights or pests, which often target specific plant species. The right amount of outbreeding, then, brings the genetic diversity needed to roll with the punches of environmental change.

Much of the environmental change in the lives of early humans came from migrations. Having first emerged in Africa, humans have migrated across the whole planet and continue to do so today. But migration for our early human ancestors was a far more dangerous affair than simply boarding an airplane, train, or bus. Migrations often brought violent conflict with outside groups, moving through dangerous environments like deserts or jungles, and encounters with predators, severe weather, famine, or disease, all of which culled populations and created bottlenecks where the genetic diversity of populations became constrained. Notably, bottlenecks often reduce genetic resistance to *infectious* disease.[27] However, mating with local populations, who had had many generations to adapt to their environment, including time to develop resistance to local pathogens, would have produced better adapted offspring and restored needed genetic diversity to a population.

In making this point, Tuschman cites genetic research that has uncovered some fascinating facts about a family of genes related to the human immune system, called human leucocyte antigens (HLAs). HLAs play a key role in helping the body to determine self from nonself, allowing it to identify harmful invaders, an essential survival task in the world of microorganisms. Recent genetic research has found that a high percentage of variations in one kind of HLA in modern humans came from outbreeding with Neanderthals and *Denisovians*, another extinct early human who ranged from Siberia to Southeast Asia, as we migrated from

Africa into Europe and Asia.[28] Here we can see how inbreeding depression can be a selective pressure shaping xenophilia, the draw toward other people that allows us to outbreed.

Much of what makes people xenophilic, open to experience, and liberal, then, is evolutionarily pragmatic. Openness to new experiences, particularly to things like travel, puts us in contact with new people. Openness to new people allows us to interact with those we encounter in our travels and to exchange knowledge, goods, and technology. There is even research showing that liberals possess adaptations that allow them to be more open to eating a greater variety of foods,[29] which would be valuable in novel environments or cultures. Moreover, *sexual openness*, a hallmark of being liberal, would allow us to exchange useful genes. Essentially, being liberal has its survival advantages.

The Benefits of Inbreeding

On the other hand, being xenophobic and closed to experience (i.e., conservative) also would have had its survival advantages. For one, a tendency to prefer the company of the in-group would have made inbreeding more likely, which can increase altruism in a population by increasing the amount of shared genes (something we will discuss in greater detail in the next chapter). *Outbreeding depression* has shaped these tendencies as well. All of the migration-related dangers that cull populations, cause genetic bottlenecks, and make outbreeding necessary can be avoided by simply not migrating. Thus those who are closed to new experiences, travel, or outsiders gain a certain fitness advantage by simply staying put.

Tuschman also reminds us that too much outbreeding can also cause obstetric problems. Preeclampsia is a condition that can lead to a host of health problems in the pregnant mother, such as kidney and liver failure, and even death. One large study examining 23,358 pregnancies in Turkey found that women who were married to first or second cousins (which is common in the Muslim world) were far less likely to suffer from preeclampsia, whereas outbreeding women were 60 percent more likely to experience it.[30] While the causes of the condition are debated, some believe it is related to immunological incompatibility; for women, reproduction involves taking in foreign DNA into their bodies, and sometimes women's bodies will reject the fetus.

Other problems of outbreeding relate to immunology. Through natural selection, populations develop genetic immunities to local pathogens. But when humans begin breeding with outsiders whose immune systems were not adapted for their locality, the resulting offspring have less genetic resistance to those local diseases. Further, mating with "foreigners" by definition involves exchanging bodily fluids, which can carry foreign diseases that could kill outbreeders. And here is where it gets interesting. If xenophobia among conservatives reflects an adaptation that helped our ancestors avoid contagious diseases from outsiders, we would also expect to see conservatives exhibiting more fear of contagion.

THE DANGERS OF GERMS

A deeper look into the microbiological world inside us reveals that xenophobia among humans—which ultimately results in things like separate water fountains, race riots, or even genocide—may at least in part be related to germs. Complex organisms like human beings are actually immense networks of individual life-forms (in us, roughly 37.2 trillion),[31] cells that over many millions of years of evolution have joined with other cells to form symbiotic relationships. This joining allowed single-celled organisms to merge with others to build more complex cooperative units of life that were better at surviving the microscopic biome.

It is worth noting that survival in this universe inside our bodies is a savage field of combat organized with a stunning degree of militaristic complexity. Here I provide a favorite citation from a scholar who enumerates the sophistication of both attacks and defense of the wars raging inside us and how in many ways the respective strategies have analogues in the wars fought by humans:

> Military alliances (could apply to synergistic pathologies, where more than one pathogen act in concert) ... suicide mission (cells that self-destruct to kill the intruder) ... camouflage (coating on gram negative bacteria that inhibits recognition as foreign body by failing to provide earmarks of enemy) ... wolf in sheep's clothing (could be applied to viruses which have envelope made from host cell membrane) ... distress signals (chemicals released by injured and dying cells) ... sabotage of communications (microbes commonly bind to cell signaling receptors on surface distorting or blocking communication...). The key to a host's defense is being able to recognize its own cells and molecules from those of the pathogen (i.e. SELF from NON-SELF). In the military context, such recognition is accomplished by wearing different uniforms.[32]

What is important to grasp here is that human survival is contingent not only on macro-level phenomena like mating, finding food, or not getting eaten but also on the epic microscopic wars within us. The impact of these wars on the human mind can be profound. In a way, the mind (and even our political behavior) is designed to serve the microorganisms that comprise our bodies.

The emotion of disgust, for example, is an adaptation that allows thinking, acting humans to help our cellular networks avoid pathogens. For instance, imagine what the consequences would be for a human who was unable to experience disgust when presented with feces, or rancid meat, or fruit infected with maggots. If she ate any one of those, or perhaps even handled them, she would insert battalions of hostile enemies into her biome, causing the breakdown of her biological machinery.

Here it is important to understand that much of the diseases that threaten humans are transmitted by other humans. Could fear of disease translate into fear of outsiders or even political conservatism? A large volume of research would suggest so. For instance, researchers using measures to assess perceived vulnerability to disease with questions such as "I prefer to wash my hands soon after shaking someone's hand" and "I have a history of susceptibility to infectious diseases" have found that those with higher perceived disease threat show more ethnocentrism,[33] greater xenophobic attitudes toward foreigners,[34] and increased willingness to stigmatize socially marginalized groups, for example obese people,[35] or gays and lesbians.[36]

Likewise, research consistently finds that higher disgust sensitivity is related to self-placement on the Left-Right spectrum.[37] One study of 31,045 men and women from 121 countries around the globe found that those who self-rated as conservative showed significantly higher disgust sensitivity than those who self-rated as liberal.[38] The researchers in this study also found that among Americans disgust sensitivity predicted the intent to vote conservative—in this case for John McCain over Barack Obama in the 2008 US presidential election.

Another study measured disgust sensitivity by having subjects rate how grossed out they were by statements such as, "I might be willing to try eating monkey meat, under some circumstances," "You see a bowel movement left unflushed in a public toilet," and "You sit down on a public bus, and feel that the seat is still warm from the last person who sat there." The researchers found that those with higher disgust sensitivity were more likely to see immigrants and foreign ethnic groups as less than human, as well as to score higher on measures strongly associated with political conservatism, such as social dominance orientation and right-wing authoritarianism (measures we will unpack in later chapters).[39]

Tellingly, much research in this area links fear of pathogens to disapproval of nonnormative sexual behaviors,[40] which suggests that our sexual morality is rooted in adaptations designed to help us survive reproduction in a world filled with pathogens. The intensity of this protective disgust also appears to vary in relation to the potential risks versus benefits of sexual openness in a given environment. Canadian psychologists Mark Schaller and Daimian Murray examined epidemiological maps around the globe to determine the prevalence of diseases such as leishmania, schistosoma, trypanosoma, malaria, filaria, leprosy, dengue, typhus, and tuberculosis.[41] Not only did they find that openness to experience was greater where there was less disease but also that where disease was more prevalent, women in particular showed more sexual restraint. Men's sexual openness, on the other hand, was not affected by local disease prevalence, which makes sense when you consider that women, typically on the receiving end of bodily fluids in sexual intercourse, may be at greater risk than men of contracting disease from an infectious partner. Conversely, Schaller and Murray found that in places with less infectious disease, women showed more interest in new sexual partners and more comfort with casual sex, showing a liberal-leaning openness to experience. In the same vein, another study found that the farther away people are from the equator, where the climate is hotter and home to more pathogens, the higher they are in extraversion, a trait associated with liberal voting.[42] Microbiological threats, and our evolved strategies for managing them, then, have impacted our political orientations.

While research suggests that germs were a principal danger in our past, the natural world teems with dangers of many varieties, and conservatives may be more sensitive to all of them. In addition to conservatives being more closed to experience, and more sensitive to disgust, research finds that conservatives tend to be generally *more fearful*. When subjects are shown threatening pictures in the research lab—for instance, a spider on the face of someone showing intense fear—those with more conservative attitudes have more fearful reactions.[43] These differences may be reflected in our neurology; at least one neuroimaging study has found that conservatives have larger amygdalae—an ancient region of the brain that generates defensive emotions such as fear and anger.[44]

Still, research continues to find that fear of other humans is strong among conservatives. One study, for example, found that when shown photos of people making ambiguous facial expressions, Republicans, far more than Democrats, will project threatening emotions like anger.[45]

Such findings underscore the centrality of humans as a primordial danger and point to something beyond them being carriers of communicable diseases.

THE DANGERS OF MEN

Compared to most animals, we seem inconceivably vulnerable. We're not particularly strong or fast, nor do we have protective armor or jabbing appendages to deter predators. Imagine walking unarmed through the natural environments of the world, which swarm with fearsome animals with the power to eviscerate us with claws or fangs, trample and crush us, or inject us with a pharmacopeia of deadly poisons. Many of these beasts are predators that would probably enjoy a naked ape as a meal.

That said, with our outsized brains, we have mastered the ability to use tools, make fire and weapons, coordinate complex actions, and devise strategies, and in doing so we have taken over the world. For these reasons, although humans were not always the apex predators of their day, it is also true that for a large span of our evolutionary history other animals were not the biggest threat to humans. Rather, *other humans were*—not only as vectors of disease but also as *murderers*. Archaeological research has brought to light the stories embedded in broken bones, cranial injuries, and embedded spearpoints, showing whole populations of people rubbed out in the massacres of our species' past, and these findings are startlingly consistent. Thus, danger from the lethal hands of humans may have been among the biggest selective pressures driving our personality differences and their associated political ideologies.

But this is only half the story; specifically *men* are the most dangerous humans. Even today men account for an astronomically higher percentage of all kinds of violence than women, and recent psychological research suggests that men have been so dangerous across evolutionary history that our brains are primed to fear them.

Scientists have come up with ingenious ways of unearthing the threats of our evolutionary past. By pairing a mild electric shock with certain stimuli, like pictures, researchers can examine how quickly we acquire a fear response to those pictures, or how slowly fear is extinguished once the shock is removed. Fast acquisition and slow fear extinction (i.e., a slow decline in fear responses) indicate that a threat was prevalent in our species' history. For example, researchers in one study showed subjects pictures of snakes and spiders, as well as pictures of birds and butterflies, while giving them a mild electric shock.[46] The researchers measured fear, using *skin conductance*—when fear is present, we sweat more, sweat being a survival mechanism designed to cool the body down as we're fighting or fleeing for our lives. The resulting moisture gives our skin higher conductance. When the pictures were later presented without the shock, the subjects quickly habituated to the pictures of the bird and butterflies (they stopped sweating with fear), but they did not fully habituate to the snakes or spiders. This makes sense enough—butterflies and birds were never the killers of humans as were snakes or spiders, and so our brains easily relinquish fear of these creatures. The psychological stamp left by these evolutionary dangers can be seen in the fact that phobias of spiders and snakes are far more common than fears of things like cars, even though in the modern day motor vehicle accidents (MVAs) account for an exponentially higher death rate than snake or spider bites.[47] This is because in our modern lives the dangers of MVAs have had little time to influence the design of our brains.

What is interesting is that the researchers repeated the experiment with black and white subjects, but instead of showing them animal pictures, the researchers showed them photos of unfamiliar black and white people. Perhaps predictably, given the findings about xenophobia presented above, black subjects habituated fully to the black faces in the absence of shock but not the white faces, while white subjects habituated to the white faces but not the black faces. This does not necessarily mean that we have genes coding for fearing outside races. Race is a superficial category that does not always accurately reflect genetics—for instance, there is more genetic diversity among native Africans than in all the rest of the world. However, our brains may use race as a heuristic for *outsider*, and we seem to be pre-primed to fear outside people.

The results of another similar study, however, were even more telling. Researchers took the prior procedure one step further and examined the impact of *sex* on fear extinction.[48] In this study, black and white subjects were shown pictures of black and white *men* or *women*. During the non-shock phase, fear toward women extinguished irrespective of whether the women were from the in-group race or the out-group race. The only photos to which fear did not extinguish were those of out-group men. What this tells us is that our brains are prepared to fear not simply outsiders but outside *men*. Men from the outside tribe were a prominent threat to our survival across the history of our species, and our brains "know" this. And as we will come to understand, male mate competition has been an essential source of male violence, with profound implications for our political selves.

SHOULD WE OUTSMART OUR GENES?

Throughout this chapter we have explored how natural selection has left us with political preferences that originally took hold because they afforded our ancestors certain survival advantages. However, there are times at which a particular adaptation becomes a *disadvantage* when it no longer matches the current environment—known as an *evolutionary mismatch*. Mismatches typically occur as a function of temporal change (e.g., environmental change over time) or spatial change (e.g., an organism migrates to a new environment). Humans are unique in that our success with technology has created drastic, rapid environmental changes, far faster than we could adapt genetically. This progression has created a number of evolutionary mismatches.

One example comes from what and how we eat. Following animal migrations, relying on seasonal rains and the plant life, our hunter-gatherer ancestors lived far more at the mercy of nature. Notably, this way of living was marked by high physical activity and punctuated by periods of scarcity. In such an environment, it paid to binge when food was available, to crave high-calorie foods (such as fat and sugar), and to efficiently convert food to fat stores. Such adaptations allowed our ancestors to draw upon stored energy in times of hunger. But as technology advanced, we became much better at bending the natural world to our will. The advent of agriculture made food sources continuously available. Our ability to modify food has made salt, sugar, and fat available in higher concentrations and easier to obtain than in our evolutionary history. Finally, mechanization, specialization, and the domestication of animals have eliminated the need for most of us to chase down game or to toil in the fields in order to eat. In sum, our sedentary lifestyles combined with unfettered access to food sources that were scarce in our evolutionary past have resulted in epidemics of morbid obesity, high blood pressure, heart disease, type 2 diabetes, and numerous other "mismatch diseases." Indeed, in industrialized societies, we are more likely to die from noninfectious, mismatch diseases than any other cause of death.[49]

The concept of the evolutionary mismatch can help to illuminate the political challenges of our modern age. We evolved in small bands of competing tribes, in wild, uncertain environments where the competition between clans for scarce resources was often a zero-sum game (where one competitor's gain/loss equals the other's loss/gain). Across our history competition of this kind has led to staggering levels of human bloodshed. Yet today we literally have the capacity to feed the world in overabundance. Despite these gains, in many ways we remain closed, suspicious, tribalistic people straining to form a globalist union while using our Stone Age minds. Thus one important question is, How xenophobic do we really need to be in the face of our unprecedented ability to sustain ourselves?

Once again, evolutionary science suggests that another force behind our enduring political tribalism is an adaptation designed to help us avoid deadly pathogens. This adaptation was useful for more than 99 percent of our evolution when there was no such thing as sterilization, antibiotics, or vaccines. Thus our ancestors died from simple afflictions, such as the common cold, the flu, or diarrhea, with crushing regularity. Under those conditions, developing a prejudicial psychology to help us avoid human vectors of disease was evolutionarily practical. But we have made profound strides in the field of immunology. Many pathogens that wiped out entire populations of humans have since been eradicated, and many that remain can be deflected with cheap, widely available vaccines. Despite that today we are exponentially safer from pathogens, our mastery over germs has existed over a mere eye blink of our history as a species, far too recently to erase germ-driven prejudice from our psychology. The question, then, is how much an adaption designed to protect us from germs serves us in the face of these advancements in medicine, particularly since xenophobia has created so much bloody conflict over our species' history. The reasons why humans could not openly cooperate on a global scale, freely sharing resources, information, and technology to advance humankind seem to lie less on the practical than the emotional. This is where evolutionary science can serve us. By examining the *ultimate* reasons for our fears, we have already achieved a critical degree of emotional distance. It is only with distance that we may judge which of our fears continue to serve us and which should be left on the savannas of our ancestors.

CHAPTER 3

IS CONSERVATISM AN EXTREME FORM OF THE MALE BRAIN?

Arnold Schwarzenegger is an (Austrian-born) American icon who exudes an aura of testosterone from his very persona. Not only did Schwarzenegger win the Mr. Universe bodybuilding contest seven times, but he and his rippling physique also defined the role of the macho, Hollywood, male action star in films like *Commando*, *Last Action Hero*, *Terminator*, and *Conan the Barbarian*. His roles have typified masculine stereotypes such as strength, decisiveness, protectiveness, and conquering. As the sword-wielding Conan, Schwarzenegger paraphrased the words of Genghis Khan, words that epitomize the primary, driving (if not frightening) evolutionary imperatives of men—mate competition, territorial control, resource gain, and sexual rewards: "Happiness lies in conquering your enemies, in driving them in front of you, in taking their property, in savoring their despair, in raping their wives and daughters."[1]

From the worlds of muscle contests and male action hero movies, Schwarzenegger zip-lined into American politics and became the Republican governor of California. With maleness so central to his previous career choices, one may wonder whether his choice of political party had anything to do with his hyper-masculinity. There is research on this question. Interestingly, while liberals are far overrepresented in Hollywood, one study found that right-wing orientation was far more prevalent among Hollywood stars who play male action heroes.[2] These men of brawn included Schwarzenegger as well as Bruce Willis, Clint Eastwood, Sylvester Stallone, Chuck Norris, Dwayne "the Rock" Johnson, and five-term National Rifle Association president Charlton Heston, among others. In this study, right-wing orientation—as measured by things like political donations, party support, and support for military actions—was exorbitantly more prominent among action stars (56.3 percent) than among dramatic actors (4.2 percent), and the researchers also found that actors who leaned Right were actually more *physically formidable* than those who leaned Left.

Perhaps more telling, during Schwarzenegger's tenure as California governor, he repeatedly referred to Democrats as "girlie men." While the phrase was originally a joke from a *Saturday Night Live* skit (poking fun at Schwarzenegger himself), it had such resonance that Schwarzenegger used it, for example, while campaigning for George H. W. Bush in 1988 and 1992, during the 2004 Republican National Convention, and in 2004 as governor during budget fights with the California legislature.[3]

The stereotype that political liberalism reflects a feminine orientation, and conservatism a masculine one, has been around for some time, and research on gender stereotypes has revealed interesting findings. Political scientist Nicolas Winter, for instance, looked at US survey data from the American National Election Study from 1972 to 2004.[4] The researcher and his team examined the types of responses people gave in describing the Democratic and Republican parties and coded the responses into stereotypically positive masculine traits (e.g., "A military man; a good military/war record. . . . [The research participant] speaks of party/candidate as good protector(s); will know what to do"), and negative masculine traits (e.g., "Not humble enough; too cocky/self-confident. . . . Unsafe/unstable; dictatorial; craves power; ruthless"). The researchers also developed codes for stereotypically positive female traits (e.g., "Generous, compassionate, believe in helping others. . . . Listens [more] to people; takes [more] into consideration the needs and wants of people"), and negative stereotypes (e.g., "Speaks of party/candidate as bad protector[s]; won't know what to do. . . . Doesn't believe in work ethic; believes in people being handed things / in government handouts"). Overwhelmingly, the researchers found that voters used more masculine stereotypes to describe GOP candidates and more feminine stereotypes to describe Democrats.

One study systematically assessed the connection between gender and partisanship. Political scientist Monika McDermott collected the Bem Sex Role Inventory (BSRI) from 780 Americans, along with a series of questions about their political beliefs and behaviors. The BSRI is one of the most widely used instruments to assess gendered psychology. For feminine traits the BSRI asks participants to rate how much the following descriptors apply to him or her: "understanding, sympathetic, warm, loves children, compassionate, gentle, eager to soothe hurt feelings, affectionate, sensitive to needs of others, tender." Masculine traits are captured by the following descriptors: "willingness to take risks, forceful, strong personality, assertive, independent, leadership ability, aggressive, dominant, willing to take a stand, defends own beliefs."[5]

What McDermott found was that men and women who scored high on femininity were significantly more likely to identify as Democrat, and that men and women who scored high on masculinity were more likely to identify as Republican.[6] Among those studied, vote choices in the 2008 US presidential and 2010 congressional elections were similar—"masculine" men and women voted Republican; "feminine" men and women voted Democrat. In this study there were sex differences too, along the same lines, but not as strong as the gender differences. While McDermott's study seems to corroborate the observations made by so many pundits in the popular media, far less has been proffered about *why* gender-based partisan differences exist.

As I elaborate in later chapters, these differences go far deeper than stereotypes, or societal gender role expectations, tying directly into reproductive strategies. Conservatism, I argue, is a male-centric strategy shaped significantly by the struggle for dominance in within-and-between group mate competitions, while liberalism is a female-centric strategy derived from the protracted demands of rearing human offspring, among other selective pressures. These aren't fixed or unitary strategies—that is, they can be adopted, or rejected, or even adapted tactically, depending on social and environmental circumstances, and both men and women can employ more or less male- or female-typical approaches. I explore this adaptability further in chapter 7 and explain conditions in which different pathways are taken. For now, let's take a moment to consider one evolutionary mechanism by which reproductive strategies can diverge *within* either of the sexes.

Frequency-dependent selection is an evolutionary process by which the fitness of some phenotypes depends on their frequency relative to the frequency of other phenotypes within a population. Take for example *Uta stansburiana*, a small reptile native to the western regions of Mexico and the United States, and more commonly called the *side-blotched lizard*. In a population of these lizards, there are different throat color polymorphisms among males, corresponding to different mate competition strategies. Males with orange throats have higher testosterone, are highly aggressive, and defend expansive territories with large harems of females. Males with blue throats are less aggressive and control smaller territories. Males with yellow throat stripes, which mimic receptive females, do not control territory. Instead, disguised as female lizards to avoid attack, they infiltrate other males' territories and mate with their females.[7] The fitness of all three morphs is dependent on the fitness of the others. The aggressive orange males are more energetic, and good at stealing mates from the blues, but are more susceptible to cuckoldry by the yellow-striped males and have lower survival rates overall. The blues defend a smaller harem and are usually better at defending against the yellow-striped, but they're prone to having their females stolen by oranges. Moreover, in response to the death of a nearby blue, the yellow-striped sometimes morph into blue and take over his behavior patterns.[8] These dynamic interactions, which keep the three polymorphs in existence, reflect what biologists have called the *rock-paper-scissors* game of male mating strategy.[9] And so, it is fair to say that being aggressive, amassing territory, and mating with as many females as possible is a male-oriented strategy among these lizards. But not all lizards take this tack. Similarly, not all females are inclined to mate with the orange guy and may use different tactics as well.

The same holds true for politics. Not all men enact a conservative strategy, nor do all women enact a liberal strategy. But we do see sex-based leanings. Imagine two bell curves, one tilting toward the (political) Right for men, and another to the Left for women, with significant overlap between the curves. And so frequency-dependent selection may be one force behind sex *and* gender differences in both mating strategies and politics. Among humans, there are profound societal or cultural processes that impact gender, mating, and politics, but they are not divorced from biology. Indeed, the tendency toward psychological differences between men and women, as well as between conservatives and liberals, are represented by distinct differences in brain structure and function.

Before we explore the evolved purposes for these differences, let us consider prior research that has attempted to understand the typical "male brain." British developmental psychologist Simon Baron-Cohen has developed an intriguing theory about autism spectrum disorders. He argues, convincingly, that autism, which is far overrepresented in males by a ratio of ten to one, is an extreme variant of the "male brain."[10] Here, I use many of the cognitive, emotional, and social differences between males and females that Baron-Cohen draws upon to prove his point about autism as a means to understand the very same kinds of differences between liberals and conservatives. I use his framework for several reasons. First, the differences examined by Baron-Cohen are specific, measurable, and supported by empirical research. Second, to understand individual differences, looking at extreme examples of a particular trait can make those differences emerge from the intuitive and often reflexive social backdrops against which they are so often camouflaged from everyday view. Third, I build on Baron-Cohen's existing framework because it has established that there even can be such a thing as an "extreme form of the male brain."

Now, before we go any further, let me just acknowledge that evoking a heuristic used to understand psychopathology in order to explain political psychology risks giving the impression that I am pathologizing certain political ideologies. To the contrary, the range of diversity among the world's population of humans, including the personality traits that underlie our political diversity, has endowed us with great adaptability, allowing us to survive the incredibly harsh environments of our ancestral past. In fact, like other kinds of genetic diversity, it is fair to say that such diversity is one of the reasons why we, the naked apes, didn't dissolve away into extinction.

Here too, lest we also worry about the social implications of using the term *male brain* as a heuristic, it is also important to understand that men and women's brain morphology and function exhibit vastly more similarities than differences. Even so, existing differences have meaningful implications for our political psychology. Studying those differences in no way makes a rational case for gender inequality—something those making the moralistic fallacy may fear, and those making the naturalistic fallacy may seek to force upon others.

With all this being said, let's examine Baron-Cohen's argument. First, he clarifies that not all females have the female-typical brain and not all males have the male-typical brain, but that there are certain quantifiable, male-typical extremes evidenced in those with autism spectrum disorders. As it turns out, the numerous and important differences between females and males that Baron-Cohen uses to explain autism sequelae are glaringly present between liberals and conservatives on nearly every difference. Here I briefly pair together those differences for comparison and use some that have not been explicitly listed by Baron-Cohen.

THEORY OF MIND

One rather extraordinary talent of the human brain is imputing mental states to others, to have *theory of mind* (other minds), or to *mindread*—to understand that others have thoughts, intentions, emotion states, and so on. Compared to other animals, humans are the undisputed world champions at this remarkable skill. We are able to perform feats of mindreading acrobatics, such as "he knows that I know that she knows (something)," so easily that we take the skill for granted, with the notable exception of those suffering from autism. The inability to "read minds," what Baron-Cohen has described as *mindblindess*,[11] is one of the hallmarks of autism.

Theory of Mind: Differences between Women and Men

There is ample research demonstrating that women outperform men on theory of mind (ToM) tasks and that these differences are evidenced early in life. Studies have found, for example, that preschool-age girls perform better at understanding others' false beliefs (the understanding that another person can hold an erroneous belief about something, a skill requiring ToM)[12] and at understanding others' emotions.[13] Other research found that girls in grades 4–12 score higher than boys on social understanding tasks.[14] Yet other research has found sex differences in secondary-school students (age twelve), with girls performing better on ToM tasks,[15] and there is evidence that this difference is visible by three years of age.[16] Moreover, some research suggests that the female advantage in ToM tasks may continue into adulthood.[17] In sum, the evidence shows that women are typically much better at understanding the minds of others.

Theory of Mind: Differences between Liberals and Conservatives

While to date few studies directly measuring differences in this ability between liberals and conservatives have been conducted, two neuroimaging studies offer a preliminary look literally inside the political brain. One study measured gray-matter volume and found that those who self-identified as liberal exhibited greater volume in the anterior cingulate cortex while conservatives exhibited greater brain volume in the amyg-

SEX, POWER, AND PARTISANSHIP

dala.[18] The anterior cingulate cortex is a brain region considered to be an integrative hub for social interactions, implicated in both theory of mind and feeling the pain of others. The amygdala, as previously noted, is the fear center of the brain. Another study examined fMRIs of Republicans and Democrats while performing a risk-taking game. As in the previous study, researchers found that Republicans showed greater activation in the amygdala, and Democrats in the anterior cingulate insula, a brain region also activated during ToM tasks.[19] The authors point out that this region of the anterior cingulate insula is adjacent to a central hub for ToM, the temporal parietal junction.[20] And so mindreading differences between liberals and conservatives may ultimately be a function of differences in brain structure.

EMPATHY DIFFERENCES BETWEEN FEMALES AND MALES

One corollary of mindreading is the capacity for empathy, to feel what another person is feeling. While women leading men in this capacity is an intuitive assumption, it is one with the backing of empirical research. Research finds that women show more comforting behaviors than men, even to strangers; share emotional distress with their friends more than men; and that girls from one years of age show more empathy to others' suffering than boys—through sad looks, comforting gestures, and making more sympathetic vocalizations.[21] More directly, women score higher than men on questionnaires specifically designed to measure empathy.[22] In people with autism, the ability to experience empathy is usually impaired.[23]

EMPATHY DIFFERENCES BETWEEN LIBERALS AND CONSERVATIVES

The liberal penchant for empathy is seen in the tendency to do things like join Greenpeace to save baby seals, or to feel sadness and moral outrage when loggers saw down the forests of Amazonian Natives, basically all the stuff that makes conservatives roll their eyes and think, *Run along and hug a tree or something.* Or perhaps more illustrative—during the 2016 US presidential race, campaign buttons, T-shirts, and other paraphernalia were circulating among the Right, saying, "Trump for President: Fuck Your Feelings." Research confirms these stereotypes. Studies find that liberals show more signs of distress about violence and suffering than conservatives, and tend to score higher on empathy measures with statements such as, "Other people's misfortunes do not usually disturb me a great deal," or "When I see someone being treated unfairly, I sometimes don't feel very much pity for them" (both reverse-scored).[24] By default, conservatives show relatively less distress about suffering and score lower on empathy measures.

DIFFERENCES IN FACIAL EXPRESSIONS BETWEEN FEMALES AND MALES

Humans have far more facial muscles than any other animal (a whopping forty-three in total), which, through a nuanced and nearly infinite array of facial expressions, allows us to send and receive a stunning volume of social information. Research finds that women are far more skilled than men at decoding facial expressions, as well as other nonverbal forms of expression, such as tone of voice.[25] This reflects a higher level of theory of mind, where more incoming information is being processed to infer intention, meaning, emotion states, and so on, which facial expressions convey brilliantly. This female skill of using faces as communication channels can be detected early; for example, from birth girls look longer at faces than boys, whereas boys look longer at inanimate objects.[26] Women are also more accurate and faster than men at identifying emotional facial expressions.[27] Further, women are even better than men at basic facial detection skills, such as detecting pictures of faces embedded in drawings with other objects, and identifying faces they had previously seen.[28] Research also finds that women show greater facial *expressivity* than men.[29] Thus the ability to send and receive information through the human visage is more pronounced in females. People in the autism spectrum, which, again, favors males by a ten-to-one ratio, have a difficult time decoding and making meaningful facial expressions.

DIFFERENCES IN FACIAL EXPRESSIONS BETWEEN LIBERALS AND CONSERVATIVES

While to date there is a dearth of research examining possible links between partisanship and *decoding* facial expressions, some research finds that conservatives are less facially expressive than liberals. For example, when people make facial expressions, their facial muscles contract and emit electrical current. Researchers have been able to quantify facial expressivity by attaching muscle sensors to subjects' faces and measuring facial electrical activity, a technique known as electromyography (EMG). In one study, researchers gathered data on subjects' political orientations, hooked up their faces to EMG sensors, presented them with a series of negative and positive images, and then measured their facial responses. Facial expressivity was high in women, regardless of political orientation, and overall women were more emotionally expressive than men. Liberal men, the researchers found, were as facially expressive as women. What stood out in this study was that the faces of male conservatives, on the other hand, were essentially nonreactive.[30] In another study, researchers measured expressivity, using the "Berkeley Expressivity Questionnaire," which includes items such as, "Whenever I am feeling positive emotions people can see exactly what I am feeling" and "What I'm feeling is written all over my face." Similar to the EMG studies, the researchers found that Democrats scored higher than Republicans.[31]

LANGUAGE DIFFERENCES BETWEEN FEMALES AND MALES

Adding to findings that women tend to be better at nonverbal communication, a significant body of research shows that women tend to have better language skills. Girls develop vocabularies faster than boys,[32] and tend to master bilingualism more than boys.[33] Research has also found that girls exhibit greater activation in linguistic areas of the brain while performing language tasks.[34] Some research finds that girls retain their advantage in language skills well into their primary and secondary school years,[35] and even into later adulthood, for instance in verbal memory skills,[36] and word fluency.[37] In keeping with Baron-Cohen's theory, both expressive and receptive language skills are commonly impaired in those with autism.

LANGUAGE DIFFERENCES BETWEEN LIBERALS AND CONSERVATIVES

Language differences are also seen in the direction we have been observing, according to political ideology. A 2001 Gallup poll indicated that those who identified as being liberal are more likely to be bilingual than moderates or conservatives.[38] Other studies have found that liberals score higher than conservatives on verbal ability tests,[39] and on vocabulary tests.[40] Lower verbal ability has also been associated with right-wing authoritarianism and social dominance orientation,[41] two constructs highly related to conservative ideology that we will discuss later.

EYE GAZE DIFFERENCES BETWEEN FEMALES AND MALES

An important and highly developed ability in humans is joint attention— the ability to follow another person's eye movement, which allows us to infer things like intention and interest, and to perform other kinds of mindreading. This ability can be observed in the research lab by showing subjects cartoon pictures of faces with averted eyes, and it can be measured by examining how strongly the subjects' eyes are drawn to the direction of the picture's gaze—known as *gaze cuing*. Across different kinds of cuing tasks, research finds that men process eye gaze less efficiently than women and do not orient toward gaze as strongly.[42] Research has also found stronger joint attention skills in twelve-month-old female infants as compared to twelve-month-old male infants,[43] and that overall male infants make less eye contact than female infants.[44] Accordingly, those in the autism spectrum, who Baron-Cohen says possess extreme variants of the "male brain," do poorly at gaze cuing.[45]

EYE GAZE DIFFERENCES BETWEEN LIBERALS AND CONSERVATIVES

Research has found that, like the differences between women and men on eye-gaze direction tasks, liberals show a greater response to gaze cuing than conservatives.[46] One study examined directional cuing using not only illustrations of eyes but also arrows pointing in a particular direction—a common research tool used to study the impact of nonsocial direction cues.[47] The researchers found that conservatives showed lower cuing effects in response to eye gaze, but not to arrows, suggesting that conservatives are less responsive specifically to *social* directional cuing.

EGALITARIANISM VERSUS COMPETITIVENESS BETWEEN FEMALES AND MALES

A large volume of research shows that females are generally more concerned with fairness, and males more concerned with dominance hierarchies. These tendencies are observable early. Young girls, for example, tend to share and take turns far more than boys, whereas boys tend to be more competitive. One study found that girls exhibited turn-taking twenty times more than boys, and boys exhibited competitive behaviors *fifty* times more than girls.[48] Further, when put together, boys often quickly form dominance hierarchies, and this pre-primed social dynamic is measurable in early childhood.[49] Summarizing this dynamic captured by studies on language use between boys and girls,[50] Joyce Benenson writes, "When speaking to one another, young boys issue directives, command others, insult them, tell jokes at others' expense, ignore what someone else just said, disagree with another's point, call one another names, brag, tell stories highlighting their own accomplishments, curse, threaten others, use direct statements, and generally behave in a domineering fashion toward one another."[51] Researchers find that young girls, on the other hand, generally spend more energy trying to solve differences with using politeness, tact, and diplomacy.[52]

Boys are also more inclined toward intergroup dominance. Research finds, for example, that young boys playing in sports teams tend to never let the losing team forget the outcome of the game, whereas girls more often try to make the players feel equal and deemphasize who won or lost.[53] Intergroup dominance among males continues into adulthood and is seen everywhere from professional sports teams to street gangs to militaries.

EGALITARIANISM VERSUS COMPETITION BETWEEN LIBERALS AND CONSERVATIVES

It is no secret that liberals in the United States more strongly back policies like equal pay for women, affirmative action, and antidiscrimination laws, policies supported by the worldview that all people have equal worth, equal potential, and the fundamental right to equal opportunities. Nor is it shocking to learn that liberals demonstrate against things like corporate abuses of power, unfair banking practices, and colonialist exploitations in third-world countries. One well-known example was the Occupy Wall Street protests of 2011, which grew as a resistance to economic inequality, corruption, and greed emerging from the financial sector. The rallying cry for this movement was "We are the 99 percent," referring to unequal wealth distribution in the United States between the wealthiest 1 percent and the rest of the population. One small but illustrative survey found that 80 percent of protesters self-identified as slightly to extremely liberal, 15 percent identified as moderate / middle of the road, whereas 6 percent rated from slightly to extremely conservative.[54] Other research more definitively confirms the primacy of fairness concerns in liberals. Using a scale measuring agreement on unambiguous statements like, "When the government makes laws, the number one principle should be ensuring that everyone is treated fairly," one large international study (34,476 subjects) found that while across the political spectrum people care about moral fairness, fairness concerns are reliably higher among those identifying as liberal.[55]

Conservatives, on the other hand, are more comfortable with social hierarchies, tend to oppose policies such as affirmative action, and participate little (as we saw above) in efforts to redirect social wealth. Researchers have found that conservatives tend to score higher on the social dominance orientation scale,[56] which was designed to measure exactly what the name suggests; the measure includes statements like, "It's probably a good thing that certain groups are at the top and other groups are at the bottom," and, "If certain groups of people stayed in their place, we would have fewer problems."

COGNITIVE DIFFERENCES: PREFERENCE FOR CLOSED, RULE-BASED SYSTEMS BETWEEN FEMALES AND MALES

In addition to overall differences in the preference for social hierarchy, men and women generally process information differently, with men showing a tendency to prefer what Baron-Cohen describes as "closed systems"—

systems that are predictable, factual, rule-based, knowable, and to some extent controllable, such as computers. For this reason, men generally tend to perform better at math, physics, and engineering, and are far over-represented in those fields. Here let us again avoid the pitfall of confusing increased likelihood with determinism, or some preposterous conclusion that such research means (or even intends to argue) that women *can't* excel in these fields—they can, and often do. Indeed, studies find that sex differences in these areas are small, and more visible primarily on the extreme ends of ability and achievement.[57] But differences remain, and we continue to look into the gaps for the wealth of understanding they provide. It is striking that while sociocultural factors may explain some of these sex variances, a fairly substantial body of research has found higher autism traits among those in science, technology, engineering, and math (STEM) fields than those in non-STEM fields.[58]

People with "extreme male brains" may be especially gifted at things like engineering, writing coding language, or doing physics; however they tend to get confused and overwhelmed by ambiguity. Human beings are "open systems" with highly variable (and therefore less predictable) patterns than, say, math or computers. For this reason human interaction often causes distress in those with autism. As Baron-Cohen explains it, in social interactions (higher-functioning) individuals with autism attempt to "work out a huge set of rules of how to behave in each and every situation, attempting to develop a mental 'manual' for social interaction of 'if-then' rules. It is as though they are trying to systemise social behaviour when the natural approach to socialising should be via empathizing."[59] As a result, those in the autism spectrum tend to prefer solitude, along with clear rules in the home, at school, or in their mental activities, such as writing coding language or doing physics.

A corollary is that people with autism tend to prefer neatness and order. They will arrange their personal effects in a line or meticulously categorize them according to color, purpose, size, or some other rule-based category. Often those with autism can immediately detect if something has been misarranged, which tends to cause immensely more stress than it would those without the disorder.

COGNITIVE DIFFERENCES: PREFERENCE FOR CLOSED, RULE-BASED SYSTEMS BETWEEN LIBERALS AND CONSERVATIVES

One measure of preference for open versus closed systems may be the field of academic study or vocation. English, the social sciences, and the humanities have been found to correlate with both professors' and students' liberal orientations—perhaps not surprising since these fields are highly person-focused (focused on open systems)—whereas conservatives are more represented in vocational studies and the applied sciences.[60]

Conscientiousness, another Big Five personality trait has been consistently associated with political conservatism.[61] Among other things, the factor tends to involve concern about orderliness, control of one's environment, and a preference for planned (rather than spontaneous) behavior. Some sample conscientiousness items from the Big Five personality index: "I am always prepared; I pay attention to details; I like order; I follow a schedule; I leave my belongings around (*reverse scored*); I often forget to put things back in their proper place (*reverse scored*)." As mentioned in the prior chapter, one study found that conservatives also tend to keep their living spaces neater and more organized than liberals.[62]

Related to a preference for closed systems is cognitive rigidity, or lower cognitive complexity. A highly robust research finding is that conservatism is related to less tolerance for ambiguity and lower aptitude for integrative complexity—the ability to grasp alternative perspectives or dimensions, and to synthesize those varying perspectives into a cohesive framework.[63] As one hypothetical, simplified for the sake of clarity: *All immigrants are criminals*, instead of reasoning, "Some immigrants may commit crimes. But many do not, and there are a variety of factors that may lead to such behaviors."

DIFFERENCES IN SOCIAL RULES BETWEEN FEMALES AND MALES

Developmental research finds that compared to girls, boys seem to be obsessed with rules. For instance, research has found that boys choose to engage in rules-oriented play more than girls, and when disputes arise they spend a great deal of time trying to renegotiate the rules and enlist the counsel of respected peers on rulemaking. On the other hand, girls usually spend more time playing turn-taking games that rely little on formal rules, and if those rules are broken, they often stop playing. Further, research finds that when boys and girls play together, boys stick to rules far more than girls, and while they quarrel more than girls, they appear to enjoy the quarrelling, especially when the point of contention concerns making, breaking, or following rules.[64] Even when boys seem to be disregarding a particular set of rules, they are often following another set. One study found that while girls tend to respond to rules set by teachers, boys tend to ignore rules set by both teachers and girls but naturally form their own complex set of rules and follow them with intense focus.[65] Joyce Benenson notes that not only have sports competitions involved complex rules for thousands of years (which are still predominantly the realm of men) but that even when men break the broader rules of society, they often follow a strict set of rules established by the criminal element or by militias.[66] As I will discuss in chapter 5, this focus on rules is a by-product of the evolutionary pressure to form male coalitions.

DIFFERENCES IN SOCIAL RULES BETWEEN LIBERALS AND CONSERVATIVES

Compared to liberals, conservatives are far more rules oriented. One study of political views among Europeans, for example, asked subjects to rate how much the views of a hypothetical person reflect their own, on statements like, "He believes that people should do what they're told. He thinks people should follow rules at all times, even when no one is watching." Conservative ideology predicted rule following.[67] This is a fairly robust research finding across the literature. In the United States, for example, conservatives score higher than liberals on measures of conscientiousness, which includes indices of rule following.[68] In many ways, the conservative tendency to be rule oriented links with several other predictors of conservatism. For example, conservatives tend to value *traditionalism*, a dedication to existing ways of doing things, including following established rules, and conservatives are inclined to resist social change more than liberals.[69] A fairly emphatic example of rules orientation among conservatives is the greater tendency to favor harsher punishment for rule breakers, such as the death penalty or longer prison sentences.[70]

In summary, our examination of the cognitive, affective, language, social, and even brain morphology differences found between women and men vividly mirror the same differences between liberals and conservatives. Once again, the use of Baron-Cohen's framework is to establish a base of empirical support to our gendered political psychology hypothesis, rather than to pathologize conservatism. In fact, the differences we see across gender, sex, and partisanship exist today because of the adaptive functions they once served the lives of our ancestors.

EVOLVED UTILITY

The value of evolutionary science is not only in the understanding that differences exist but also in the evolved purposes that those differences serve. Such insights illuminate the origins of our political divisions and hopefully also expand our capacity to bridge them. In the previous chapter we considered how natural forces, such as germs and genetic diseases, were selective pressures shaping the personality differences that undergird our orientations. Throughout this book, we will also examine the pressures shaping the sex and gender differences that in turn give us "masculine conservatism" and "feminine liberalism." To start, and to make better sense of the science above, let us consider the pressures that gave us differences in ToM.

Most evolved traits have multiple influences. One common explanation for greater ToM in women is that women have generally been tasked with interpreting the needs of offspring, who as infants are incapable of expressing their needs through language, and who remain in dependency for a far greater stretch than the young of other species. As one example of this ability put to use, women are more likely to hold infants in the face-to-face position than men,[71] and as we saw above, women's brains appear to be far better at reading facial expressions. We have also seen that another output of ToM, the ability to experience empathy—to understand and share another's emotional experience—is also found between men and women (and between conservatives and liberals). That the marathon of provisioning and care required for human offspring should demand empathy is intuitive, as is that women would command a comparatively greater capacity to empathize. Indeed, in keeping with our gendered political brain hypothesis, empathic men (who, as noted, also tend to be liberal) tend to have lower testosterone and make better fathers than high-testosterone men, as we will explore in greater detail in chapter 7.

Conversely, there is evidence to suggest that *less* empathy among men has fitness benefits, aiding in male mate competition (which is often violent) and in facilitating killing in warfare.[72] Once again, it is important to remember here that natural selection doesn't particularly care what traits get passed on to the next generation. It is a mindless algorithmic process in which traits that provide an advantage get passed on. Sometimes the advantage can involve experiencing empathy, at other times suppressing it. It is not difficult to see how empathy might be a liability in the heat of battle, or how burying empathy would help men to kill their competitors and live to pass on male genes coding for staving empathy, particularly for men of the outside tribe.

In a similar vein, intolerance for ambiguity would also be useful in dangerous environments, such as combat. For instance, seeing a rival group as possibly dangerous, depending on the circumstances, would potentially get men killed more often than those thinking in strictly categorical terms. In other words, when the stakes are life and death, it makes more sense to think in black-and-white terms. Indeed, when combat veterans' thought patterns get stuck on the parameters of the war zone, such as in the case of post-traumatic stress disorder, a common psychotherapeutic technique systematically recalibrates black-and-white thinking in favor of greater integrative complexity.[73]

Even men's overrepresentation in STEM fields may reflect the pressures of a violent ancestral environment. Across the globe, males show an advantage on spatial tasks as compared to women,[74] and research finds that spatial abilities are critical for STEM fields, for example, architecture, engineering, robotics, or other domains that require the ability to mentally rotate objects in three-dimensional space.[75] This ability has long been hypothesized to be an offshoot of adaptations for hunting and defense, both of which make use of projectile weapons, which require spatial abilities for effective use.[76] Indeed, research finds a relationship between spatial tests and throwing accuracy, with men being consistently better at hitting their target than women.[77] These sex differences are seen early; by three years old, boys outperform girls on throwing speed, accuracy, and distance, and there is no other motor performance skill in which boys excel so much in the early years.[78] And as we discussed, there is a significant relationship between conservatism, masculinity, and spatial abilities, along with so many other adaptations geared for using violence to survive a harsh, ancestral environment. We will continue to explore these connections.

In all, the stereotypes about liberalism having a feminine quality and conservatism a masculine one have empirical backing and are rooted in our neuropsychology, which was shaped by selective pressures of the natural and social environments of our ancestors. In turn, our evolved

political orientations reflect those pressures. While there have been boun-
teous explanations for what drives our political stances, few have as much
explanatory power as the strategies we employ to survive and reproduce.
In the next chapter we will come to understand how these strategies
underlie the often contentious divide between liberals and conservatives
on social equality versus hierarchy in human affairs.

CHAPTER 4
EQUALITY VERSUS HIERARCHY

Every year since 1945, there has been a white-tie fundraising dinner for Catholic Charities held at the lavish Waldorf-Astoria hotel in New York City. This is an elite event where the rich, the powerful, and the famous gather to donate and be seen. In an election year, it is usually the last event during which the two presidential candidates will share a platform before the election. The candidates typically use this forum to deliver humorous speeches and gently roast their competitors and his or her respective party.

In 2000, Al Gore and George W. Bush shared the stage. Gore's joke took a feathery jab at conservative tax policies favoring the rich: "One of my favorite shows is *Who Wants to be a Millionaire?* Well, it should really be called *Who Wants to Be after Taxes a $651,437.70 Person?* Of course, that's under my plan. Under Governor Bush's plan it would be *Who Wants to Be after Taxes a $701,587.80 Person?*"[1]

The crowd erupted with laughter. George W. Bush followed with a now infamous quote that seemed to flaunt Gore's satirical accusation, which also drew laughs: "This is an impressive crowd—the haves and the have-mores. Some people call you the elite; I call you my base."

The exchange between Gore and Bush exemplifies the tamest, most playful example that one may ever see of disagreement on the issue of how best to divide resources. Bush was no doubt also taking a poke at himself and his party, however wrapped in truth it may have been. But the remarks touched upon an ancient struggle over resources, one linked to powerful emotion centers in the brain. Perhaps not surprisingly then, Bush's words left many liberals incensed, and the joke was repeated to portray Republicans as greedy, unempathic crony capitalists, including in Michael Moore's 2004 documentary *Fahrenheit 9/11*. In John Kerry's 2004 run for president, he even used "Haves and Have Mores" as a slogan for the Republican opposition, which he opposed with slogans such as "John Kerry: Leaving Billionaires Behind since 1945."

Still, these were just words. Concern over the control of resources has historically played out in arenas far more contentious and far more dangerous. Poignant examples include the Communist and Socialist revolutions that have arisen around the world, far more globally than most of us know—in Europe (e.g., France, Russia, Finland, Hungary, Spain, Yugoslavia), Asia (e.g., China, Mongolia, Vietnam, Laos, Malaya, Afghanistan, India), South America (e.g., Cuba, Peru, Nicaragua, El Salvador), Africa (e.g., Ethiopia, Congo), and in many other nations. At their core, all of these leftist revolutions arose in an effort to equalize unequal wealth, and their opposition countered to prevent redistribution. These revolutions have resulted not just in good-natured ribbings but also in mass destruction and rivers of blood.

Political scientists have had no difficulty placing ideological differences on how to distribute wealth along the liberal-conservative continuum. A highly consistent empirical finding is that political liberals tend to favor wealth equalization, whereas conservatives tend to favor the economic status quo. But political ideologies and the economic policy preferences associated with them are only recent expressions of ancient evolutionary imperatives. Thus, our ideology-based economic disputes are usually driven, often unconsciously, by the timeless competition over resources necessary to survive and reproduce. Among humans, as among all social animals, a higher position on the dominance hierarchy affords preferential access to territory, food, and mates. And so, while political science rarely describes socioeconomic stances in evolutionary terms, the struggle to *maintain dominance hierarchies*, or to *equalize them*, reflects our long history vying for position in rank-stratified primate social groups. Moreover, if conservatism reflects an "extreme" form of the male brain, and liberalism its inverse, then we would expect to find evidence that conservative economic policy is embedded in male reproductive strategy, and liberal economic policy in female reproductive strategy. Indeed this is exactly what we find.

RANK AND RESOURCE REDISTRIBUTION: THE LIBERAL ENDEAVOR

In evolutionary terms, we can operationalize the liberal position as an effort to restrain dominant men from monopolizing resources, which can impinge on the evolutionary fitness of those with less power. Note my use of gendered language here, for the struggle for dominance and the privileged access to resources that dominance confers are disproportionately a human *male* concern. This is not to say that women are not or should not be competitive. Women also benefit from higher rank and access to resources, and female-female competition is a widely observed phenomenon across the animal world. But for our entire history as a species, male competition has been far more extreme, more violent, more oppressive, and has resulted in greater power distances than competition between women. Though rarely discussed, these differences are rooted in male reproductive psychology. Liberal egalitarianism, therefore, can be seen as a political strategy to impose limits on male ambitions.

One might imagine this reining in of males is a development of the post-feminist world, but on the contrary, it reflects an enduring prehistoric undertaking. In his study of foraging peoples around the world, anthropologist Christopher Boehm reveals how tribal societies, which are thought to mirror the social environments in which humans evolved, strive to maintain an egalitarian order.[2] In small-scale tribal groups, order is achieved largely through cultural taboos designed to keep men from rising up to violently monopolize resources, power, and women.

For example, anthropologist Richard Lee has documented how among the !Kung foragers of the Kalahari desert there is a practice in which men returning to camp after a successful hunt denigrate their own quarry. Writes Lee,

> Say that a man has been hunting. He must not come home and announce like a braggart, "I have killed a big one in the bush!" He must first sit down in silence until I or someone else comes up to his fire and asks, "What did you see today?" He replies quietly, "I'm no good at hunting. I saw nothing at all . . . maybe just a tiny one."[3]

The clan follows. When they go in to retrieve the kill they respond, "You mean you have dragged us all the way out here to make us cart home this pile of bones? Oh, if I had known it was this thin, I wouldn't have come. To think I gave up a nice day in the shade for this."

This practice is an intentional strategy to prevent boastful young males from amassing too much power, according to one tribal member:

> When a young man kills much meat, he comes to think of himself as a chief or big man, and he thinks of the rest of us as his servants or inferiors. We can't accept this. We refuse one who boasts, for someday his pride will make him kill somebody. So we always speak of his meat as worthless. In this way we cool his heart and make him gentle.

When cultural taboos among the !Kung fail to prevent an ambitious young man from becoming violent, the group may agree to execute him. Thus while some social scientists will argue the relative egalitarianism among hunter-gatherers reflects our true nature, before humans became corrupted by wealth or Western civilization, the existence of such strident efforts to tamp down male upstarts suggests a different story about who we are. Writes Boehm,

> When the subordinates take charge to firmly suppress competition that leads to domination, it takes some effort to keep the political tables turned. For the most part, the mere threat of sanctions (including

ostracism and execution) keeps such power seekers in their places. When upstartism does become active, so does the moral community: it unites against those who would usurp the egalitarian order, and usually does so preemptively and assertively.[4]

Keeping upstart men in check, then, takes vigilance and is not a fool-proof effort. Research on hunter-gatherers and horticulturalists—tribes that supplement hunting and gathering with simple gardening—has found strikingly high murder rates and suggests that unequal resource distribution and women-hoarding can arise despite the best efforts of the moral community. For example, some Amazonian *Yanomamö* men (mostly those who have killed other men in raids[5]) tend to have more wives and more children, whom they support with food given in tribute by lower-ranking tribesmen.[6]

Yet, compared to our modern nations of millions, tribe-sized groups are easier to regulate from within. Because hunter-gatherers can't store vast amounts of food to leverage their power base, there are limits to how much wealth and influence they can acquire. When humans began to master agriculture, things changed, drastically. The increased ability to produce and store grains led to a corresponding growth in man's ability to amass power.[7] Men used this power to achieve reproductive success in a zero-sum game, and zero-sum games are the root of inequality.

This historical fact about males and fitness inequity has recently been verified by a rather stunning genomic study, which found that humans exhibit far less diversity in Y chromosomes than in X chromosomes. This finding suggests that some ancestral males disproportionately won the struggle to reproduce while others lost out entirely. By analyzing our genome, researchers were able to calculate that for a period after the introduction of agriculture, *one man reproduced for every seventeen women*.[8]

It was not unusual for dominant men to code such drastic carnal inequities into law. For example, among the Inca, sexual privilege was carefully allotted according to rank (with high rank typically being synonymous with high material wealth), as described by Felipe Guaman Poma de Ayala:

Caciques or principal persons were given fifty women "for their service and multiplying people in the kingdom." Huno curaca (leaders of the vassal nations) were given thirty women; guamaninapo (heads of provinces of a hundred thousand) were allotted twenty women; waranga curaca (leaders of a thousand) got fifteen women; piscachuanga camachicoc (over ten) got five; pichicamachicac (over five) got three; and the poor Indian took whatever was left![9]

Thus, anthropological, genomic, and historical evidence reveals that male dominance has propelled human inequality since the age of hunter-gatherers, which involves disproportionate access to women, and wealth sometimes measured as simply as greater access to food. Large-scale democracy is only a fairly recent attempt to equalize the vast power differences that so often characterize human social life. America's Founding Fathers expressed this intention plainly in the Declaration of Independence with the seminal words, "We hold these truths to be self-evident, that all men are created equal." This timeless sentiment occurs throughout the letters and documents of America's first statesmen. Thomas Jefferson went so far as to write, "The foundation on which all [constitutions] are built is the natural equality of man, the denial of every preeminence but that annexed to legal office, and particularly the denial of a preeminence by birth."[10]

Other Founding Fathers expressed similar ideas, such as James Madison who wrote, "Equal laws protecting equal rights . . . the best guarantee of loyalty and love of country."[11] The struggle to redress inequities of power formed the basis of democratic governance, which, having fallen from prominence with ancient Greece, was reintroduced to the world in 1776 in the United States. Here America's Founding Fathers were the moral community, and their efforts to frame the Constitution were a direct response to the monarchic dominance hierarchies that had ruled Europe for centuries, not uncommonly by hoarding wealth and by butchering those who voiced dissent.

But even this historic move was stepwise. The Founding Fathers espoused democracy as a means to achieve equality, yet still enforced rank status by allowing slavery and excluding men of color and (all) women from the political process. Even the Framers, in tendering their radically egalitarian American experiment, could not fully disengage from the primordial *male* pull to subjugate the rival tribe and oppress women. In light of the competitive reproductive psychology of primate males, this failing makes sense.

Nevertheless, the Founding Fathers' political descendants have carried their work forward—slavery has been outlawed, women vote and serve in office, and today liberals more strongly support a vast number of social and economic policies all rooted in social egalitarianism: affirmative action; equal pay for women; increasing the minimum wage; increasing taxes for the rich or reducing them for the poor; increased spending on social welfare programs, like welfare, food stamps, unemployment benefits, and Medicaid; socialized medicine; free college education; and equal marriage rights for gays and lesbians (which equalize the economic benefits of being married).

Moreover, liberals have generally favored a government role in enforcing an equal playing field. In 1963, Democratic president Lyndon B. Johnson famously declared to a joint session of Congress, "We have talked long enough in this country about equal rights. . . . It is time now to write the next chapter, and to *write it in the books of law*."[12] The next year Johnson indeed signed the Civil Rights Act into law, outlawing racial segregation in schools and discrimination on the basis of race, color, religion, sex, or national origin. Once again, while both sexes engage in discrimination, men historically waged war on outside groups on the basis of race, color, religion, or national origin, or enslaved them, and we all know that laws prohibiting discrimination by sex is meant to protect women from male dominance, rather than the other way around. But the takeaway message here is that the liberal position is an old one, and its egalitarian and feminist flavor reflects the goal of keeping alpha male ambitions in check.

Conservatives, on the other hand, tend to exhibit less support for egalitarian policies and generally oppose legislation granting the government the authority to regulate power and resource differences. This political stance reflects male reproductive psychology, for in terms of fitness men have much more to gain from unequal resource distribution than do women, who have more to gain by resource sharing. This is not to say that all egalitarians are women or that those who prefer dominance hierarchies are only men—they are not. But there is a monumental tilt among males toward inequity, and this tilt is rooted in evolution.

COMPETITION FOR FOOD AND SEX AMONG APES

By considering the behaviors of our closest relatives, chimpanzees, we gain greater insight into how male mate competition formed our own political orientations, into their emphases on hierarchy or equality, as well as their underlying gendered psychologies. In the *robust* chimpanzee (*Pan troglodytes*), male alliances are central to survival, particularly in competition with outside troops. It is remarkable how much competition between chimpanzee groups resembles human warfare. Using a cadence reserved exclusively for raids, all-male squads will set off on patrol, moving silently and in single file toward the edges of their territory, scanning the trees and looking out across valleys in search of the enemy.[13] When these chimps on patrol find a lone male, or a smaller squad from the rival troop, they will gang up, strike, stomp on, and rip their opponents to death, sometimes biting off genitalia, at other times going so far as to drink the blood of their victims.

Through raiding, male coalitions will expand their existing territory and absorb females of the conquered troop into their own.[14] In doing so they not only expand their mating opportunities but also their access to fruit trees and colobus monkeys, a favorite chimpanzee prey species.[15] In the world of chimpanzees, there is no egalitarian order between groups—

that is, there is no sharing between groups of male chimpanzees; competition for sex and food is normative and brutal, and one group's loss is the other group's gain.

Chimpanzees exhibit in-group competition as well, fueled by a competition for rank and the privileged access to resources that rank provides. Higher-ranking males steal meat more often and are given meat more often by lower-ranking males.[16] Dominant males also feed higher in the canopy of trees, where fruit is more plentiful and its sugar content higher. When conflict arises, lower-ranking chimpanzees are pushed down to less bountiful parts of the tree, or off the tree altogether.[17] Further, dominant males will monopolize in-group mating whenever they can by attacking rival males or punishing females that stray. In short, there is little egalitarian order *within* the male-dominated chimpanzee in-group as well. It is worth noting that the "moral community" among robust chimpanzees may also unite to contain male despots—both male and female chimps have been observed forming alliances to overthrow overly aggressive alphas. Sometimes despotic alphas will be killed and even cannibalized.[18]

Patterns among robust chimpanzees suggest a common root with political conservatism among humans. Their societies are male dominated, highly stratified, xenophobic, and warlike. They compete with outside troops and seek to monopolize food and mating. By contrast, our other chimpanzee cousins, bonobos (*Pan paniscus*), differ from robust chimpanzees in ways that resemble political liberalism. Bonobo societies are female-led, egalitarian, open to outside groups, and largely peaceable. There is little competition between bonobo groups, and groups often eat and mate relatively freely with one another.

How do we understand such radical differences between our respective cousins? *Competition for resources.* Unlike that of the robust chimpanzees, bonobo territory does not interweave with that of gorillas. Separated from gorillas by the Zaïre River, bonobos have more access to foods normally consumed by their colossal cousins. Thus one critical reason that male bonobos don't wage war on one another, why they can afford to be female oriented, egalitarian, and "liberal," appears to be that their opulent food supply doesn't force violent competition. Or as primatologists Richard Wrangham and Dale Peterson put it, "Bonobos have evolved in a forest that is kindlier in its food supply, and that allows them to be kindly, too."[19] Conversely, robust chimpanzees were pressured to adapt to the overall less available plant life. They did so by becoming male dominated and militaristic, and by conducting raids on rivaling troops to secure greater resources for the in-group. This male orientation pushed male reproductive imperatives to the foreground, and chimpanzees evolved to be more sexually controlling and competitive than bonobos. And so, among our closest primate relatives, both "liberal" egalitarianism and "conservative" allegiance to male social hierarchies appear to have been driven by male competition (or the relative lack of male competition) for natural resources.

COMPETITION FOR FOOD AND SEX AMONG MEN

It should come as no surprise, then, to find that competition has shaped human political psychology in similar ways. It is only recently that humans have mastered food production such that billions can survive with little fear of starvation. But feeding ourselves was not always so easy in our ancestral past. Archaeological evidence suggests that periods of scarcity caused by environmental change or population explosions were not uncommon and compelled intergroup conflict and warfare among our prehistoric ancestors.[20] And so, even though many of us now live in societies that produce staggering surpluses of food—not to mention epidemics of morbid obesity—our brains evolved amid the very real threat of starvation. This may be why conservatives living in obscenely overfed nations can still experience intense emotion over policies related to the distribution of food, such as welfare subsidies or food stamps, which in the United States are often utilized more by racial minority groups.[21] It is probably no coincidence, then, that negative attitudes about outside races robustly predict opposition to welfare programs.[22] Moreover, as with chimpanzees, warring with outside groups to control food sources has always been the enterprise of male humans. Thus the xenophobic, male tenor of conservative economic policies reflects a history of fighting with outsiders for the privilege to eat.

Evolutionary fitness, however, is not achieved by bread alone. Like other male primates, men also compete for mates, and the dynamics of male mate competition are equally relevant in understanding political orientation. To make sense of how mate competition forms the conservative stance, it is necessary to understand that men and women employ markedly different mating strategies.

MEN AND THEIR NUMBERS STRATEGY

Sex-based reproductive strategy differences are based in part on differences in potential reproductive output. Like the male chimpanzees, and males of many other species, men can exponentially increase their genetic fitness (i.e., their number of offspring) by mating with as many women as possible. This is not the only available strategy—some men will pair bond with their wives, devote virtually all their time, energy, and resources to rearing their offspring, and swear off sex with other women. Other men are terminal philanderers. Innumerable men lie somewhere in between. But the algorithmic advantage to male genes coding for a preference for sexual numbers is without question, whereas the reverse is largely not true for women. For this reason, men *generally* tend to prefer a variety of casual sexual partners. Women, on the other hand, *generally* tend to prefer stable, committed relationships with partners willing and able to contribute resources to childrearing, which requires extended provisioning.

Parental investment also drives these differences. Biologically, men invest about a teaspoon of semen and theoretically can walk away after that. But women spend nine months in pregnancy, endure risky child-births, and generally continue to provide the majority of parental care-giving across the globe. Further, sperm is cheap and produced by the millions, whereas ova are scarce, released only during the period from adolescence to menopause (about five hundred total across a woman's life span). This scarcity drives female selectivity, as does the need for quality, committed mates who can provide resources.

Evolutionary psychologist David Buss has conducted surveys among tens of thousands of people, drawn from across cultures, religions, race, socioeconomic status, and every continent on the globe, and found repeatedly that men prefer casual sex and more sexual partners more than women (endorsing a *quantity* strategy), and that women prefer resource investment about twice as much as men (reflecting a *quality* strategy).[23] In one study, Buss found that out of sixty-seven potentially desirable traits in the partner of a casual affair, men had lower standards than women on forty-one of them. Buss writes that men "require lower levels of such assets as charm, athleticism, education, generosity, honesty, independence, kindness, intellectuality, loyalty, sense of humor, sociability, wealth, responsibility, spontaneity, cooperativeness, and emotional stability."

When asked about undesirable traits, men had fewer problems with "mental abuse, violence, bisexuality, dislike by others, excessive drinking, ignorance, lack of education, possessiveness, promiscuity, selfishness, lack of humor, and lack of sensuality." In fact, men rated only four characteristics as less desirable than did women: "low sex drive, physical unattractiveness, need for commitment, and hairiness," all of which speak to potential problems in fertility, or, as in the case of the need for commitment, an impediment to the quantity strategy.[24]

Other researchers have set up scenarios where attractive confederates approach the opposite sex and promptly offer casual sex. Seventy-five percent of men accepted the offer, compared with *none* of the women.[25] Research has also found that men fantasize more than women about group sex,[26] and that men are four times more likely than women to fantasize about having sex with over one thousand different partners throughout their lives.[27] Men, on the whole, appear hardwired to prefer a shotgun-blast approach to reproduction.

The problem with all this male readiness, however, is that in any given population, there are fewer sexually receptive females than there are males. The sex ratio, the number of men to women, is roughly one to one worldwide (slightly favoring men). But the *operational sex ratio* (OSR), or the number of *reproductively viable males* competing to reproduce as compared to the number of *reproductively viable* competing females, tends to skew much higher on the male end. There are a variety of reasons for this difference, including men's longer span of reproductive viability and the fact that many women are already reproductively committed (e.g., pregnant or nursing) at any given time. Add the fact that, when possible, powerful men will engage in polygyny and the reproductive future for low-ranking men looks increasingly bleak. For men, these factors create scarcity and the risk of total reproductive failure. Like chimpanzees, and males of many species, men will use violence as a strategy to secure scarce resources, including access to mates.

HOW NUMBERS STRATEGIES DRIVE INEQUALITY

While political discourse usually measures inequality in terms of economic wealth rather than access to women, reproductive resources are competed for just the same. Moreover, wealth for men has traditionally been a vehicle for attracting mates. Indeed, a highly robust research finding is that men with more resources have better mating prospects.[28] Female selectivity and the need for resources, in turn, accelerate male competition—for women and for the resources required to attract them. But economic resources are also finite, meaning some men end up with more than others. And since men have more to gain from wealth in terms of reproductive fitness than women, *men have a greater evolutionary incen-*

tive to prefer economic inequality. Thus the male-dominated, economically competitive orientation of political conservatism reflects a male reproductive strategy.

We have seen how male chimpanzees use violence to outcompete rival troops for access to mates. Is there evidence that mate competition could possibly drive *human* violence and inequality? The archaeological and historical records leave no doubt. For example, archaeologists excavated a seven-thousand-year-old massacre site in Austria from the Neolithic Age, and found that the remains of reproductive-aged women were notably absent amid the bashed-up skulls and bones, suggesting that young women were not killed but taken captive.[29] Fast-forward to the Dark Ages, and the great historian William Durant has described how during the Crusades Christian men were lured to fight Muslims with the promise of great riches and "dark beauties" as their prize of war.[30]

A historical exemplar of wealth and reproductive inequality is Moulay Ismail ibn Sharif, a warrior king who ruled Morocco from 1672 thru 1727 with such brutality that he was nicknamed "Ismail the Bloodthirsty." History books assure us that he earned his moniker; Ismael is reputed to have ordered that the heads of ten thousand enemy (male) combatants adorn the walls of his city.[31] Moreover, by attacking neighboring territories, killing or enslaving the men, and appropriating their riches, he managed to acquire five hundred concubines and sire 888 children.[32] The wealth he wrenched from neighboring peoples not only supported his expansive harem, and mind-boggling number of children, but also fed his armies, fortified his cities, and built his empire, all of which served to ensure his reproductive dominance over other men.

One could fill an entire book with examples. Laura Betzig did just that in her book *Despotism and Differential Reproduction.*[33] Betzig studied 104 societies, across every continent on the globe, and found that when men amass power and wealth, they have predictably created despotic laws that support continued success in the male numbers strategy—most directly by making rules to funnel women their way and to ensure the wealth required to support and contain their sexual prizes. Betzig identifies how strategies such as these have resulted in harems ranging from two to literally thousands of women. Like male chimpanzees attacking genitalia, history's despots have often made laws allowing them to castrate lower-ranking males—surgically eliminating them as sexual competitors.

In the modern day, another example is provided by the Islamic State of Iraq and Syria (ISIS), by all accounts an extreme conservative political movement. Although making claims to religious ideology, ISIS competes for both economic and sexual resources. Here *Newsweek* provides a summary of their economic exploits:

> The ISIS economy and its fighters predominantly rely on the production and sale of seized energy assets—Iraq has the fifth-largest proven crude oil reserves in the world. ISIS also depends on the steady income it extracts from private donors, the heavy taxation and extortion it levies on its captive population, the seizure of bank accounts and private assets in the lands it occupies, ransoms from kidnappings and the plundering of antiquities excavated from ancient palaces and archaeological sites.[34]

Clearly, pilfering in war is not a gesture of between-group egalitarianism. But when ISIS rampaged across northern Iraq, slaughtered all the men, and took Yazidi tribeswomen as sexual slaves, they revealed the desire for a far more ancient resource than money. These attacks, like so many others, were the epitome of male mate competition. One journalist reported how the men of ISIS systematically targeted not only grown men but also any young boys who showed secondary sex characteristics. In evolutionary terms, these boys had made the transition from children to *male sexual competitors*. Having achieved this developmental milestone was a death sentence:

> Adolescent boys were told to lift up their shirts, and if they had armpit hair they were directed to join their older brothers and fathers. In

village after village the men and older boys were driven and marched to nearby fields, where they were forced to lie down in the dirt and sprayed with automatic fire.[35]

Tellingly, ISIS also hired gynecologists to determine whether their Yazidi sex slaves were pregnant at the time of their capture and forced those who were to have abortions, thus eradicating the genes of rival males.[36] Horrifying as they are, these are the exact patterns we would expect to see among a group of warring male primates.

Such patterns can be elicited among men living peaceful civilian lives. In one study, young men attending a Chinese university were shown full body images of women rated as attractive or unattractive.[37] After this, they were given a series of questions about making war with other countries. Men who viewed the attractive female photos "showed more militant attitudes," according to the researchers. This effect was not seen among women. In another experiment in the same study, the researchers showed men a photo of either a woman's legs or a Chinese flag. Subjects then were measured on how quickly they responded to either words related to war or words about innocuous stimuli such as "farms." Seeing women's legs made men respond more quickly to war-related words than seeing a flag, suggesting that even civilian men during peacetime are primed for violent competition for mates.

With an understanding of the male mate competition, we can begin to illuminate the ultimate roots of political inequality and male-oriented conservatism. Unequal economic wealth and power continues to result in reproductive bonanzas for men. The same is not true for women—women could not achieve the same reproductive windfalls by tearing into rival villages, killing rival women, taking their goods, and having sex with as many men as possible. The evolutionary incentive for men, however, is abundantly clear.

Men will fight for greater resources, be they wealth or women, and striking research is beginning to bring the links between inequality, male mate competition, and political conservatism into even sharper focus.

One study found that higher upper body muscularity in men was associated with a greater sense of entitlement, as measured by agreement on responses to statements such as, "I deserve more than the average person."[38] Greater muscularity in this study was also associated with less egalitarian attitudes, less likelihood to share resources in a laboratory game, higher competitiveness, and higher *social dominance orientation*, which, once again, is a preference for social inequality strongly associated with political conservatism. These relationships were not found in women, and women were less likely to endorse these attitudes than men across all of the measures. Other research has found that men with higher endogenous testosterone,[39] as well as men who were administered testosterone,[40] are less likely to share money in laboratory games. Notably, the same hormone associated with resource hoarding wealth also increases muscle mass and underlies both aggression and sex drives. Thus the staunch conservative opposition to policy that levels the playing field—such as social welfare programs, affirmative action, or taxing the rich—emits a distinctive male musk that links back to a time when our hirsute male ancestors were *physically* competing for scarce resources on the savage savannas in which we evolved.

It is not difficult to see male mate competition expressed more vocally among conservatives, and with our evolutionary insights, we can see how such mate competition underlays conservative xenophobia. Male KKK members, who have notoriously engaged in the most bestial means of mate competition—threatening to castrate black men,[41] or actually perpetrating the crime[42]—strongly endorsed Republican candidate Donald Trump in the 2016 US presidential election. Part of Trump's appeal to xenophobic men was that he made promises that tap into the ancient primate male concern over reproductive rivalry, particularly with outside men, like when he vowed to build a wall to keep out Mexican "rapists."

During the same period, Maine Republican governor Paul LePage (a white man) described the heroin trade in his home state: "The traffickers ... these are guys by the name D-Money, Smoothie, Shifty [stereotyped names for black men]. These types of guys that come from Connecticut and New York. They come up here, they sell their heroin, and they go back home … incidentally, half the time they *impregnate a young white girl* before they leave."[43] Here there is no question that LePage saw black men as part of the outside tribe, and that his impulse was to block them from sex with women from his in-group.

But the key insight is that our male ancestors have competed for food, territory, and ultimately females in zero-sum competitions since before we were even fully human. Today, conservatism's male and inegalitarian tenor embodies our male primate ancestry's competitive struggles. While those struggles reflect competition for rank within groups, they prominently reflect group-based dominance struggles. Interestingly, central constructs in political science research have unwittingly tapped into these ancient competitions. Here I explain social dominance orientation and its deep roots in male coalitionary violence.

SOCIAL DOMINANCE ORIENTATION

Men like Trump and LePage have managed to epitomize primate out-group competition, and political scientists have developed a scale to measure it called *social dominance orientation* (SDO). Essentially, SDO reflects the extent to which an individual wishes his or her group to be dominant over another (versus the extent to which he or she prefers intergroup relations to be equal). The authors of the SDO scale explain that "people who are more social dominance oriented will tend to favor hierarchy-enhancing ideologies and policies, whereas those lower on SDO will tend to favor hierarchy-attenuating ideologies and policies."[44] SDO has been consistently found to predict political conservatism and its corollaries, including economic conservatism and racial prejudice.[45]

Important for our gendered political brain hypothesis is a robust finding that men score higher on SDO than women. This difference holds across age, culture, nationality, religion, income level, educational attainment, and political ideology.[46] Researchers have attempted to determine whether higher SDO among men can be accounted for by their higher status, which is the norm in most human societies. However, sex differences in SDO remain stable across cultures that vary greatly in terms of women's social standing—across the highly divergent cultures of Palestine and Southern California, for example.[47] With its male concentration, it is perhaps not surprising that those with high SDO are more likely to support war,[48] the most profound and violent means of establishing male dominance over other male groups, or preventing domination by them. Because primate male dominance struggles occur *within* groups as well, SDO also has implications for domestic policy, particularly around issues concerning access to resources and sexual control of women. For example, SDO correlates negatively with affirmative action, social welfare programs,[49] and support for women's rights,[50] which often concern women's sexual freedom.

It may seem strange that SDO, which measures in-group preference, predicts bias even against those with a shared national identity—why seek to keep resources from other Americans? However, competition between subgroups *within* a nation's borders reflects ancient adaptations for *out-group* competition. The human brain evolved in small, close-knit, competing bands of people, and evidence suggests that it remains calibrated to process social information within tribe-sized alliances topping out at around 150 individuals.[51] Fighting units in modern militaries, for example, mirror the group sizes of early hominids,[52] as do farming communities, business organizations, and many other social groups. When groups exceed those sizes, social cohesion and organization tend to break down.[53]

What this means is that even though citizens technically share a national identity, our brains may have difficulty recognizing an in-group that is millions of times larger than the small band sizes in which we evolved. Instead, our Stone Age brains—already sensitive to signals of out-group difference—often encourage us to form smaller, competing groups within our national boundaries. Thus the ease with which nations can become divided between blacks and whites, Arians and Jews, Hutus and Tutsis, Sunni and Shia, Southerners and Yankees, Republicans and Democrats, rich and poor, and so on.

It may also seem strange that people of marginalized groups can become conservatives, given that conservatives tend to be higher on SDO, more xenophobic, and opposed to policies that would level the playing field for those very same groups on the margins. Here there are two important points to understand. Political orientation and its corollaries, such as SDO, are not set like eye color or some other static trait—rather, like many other adaptations they are malleable but with a predilection toward one strategy over another. This malleability allows humans to adapt to changing social, hierarchical, and environmental circumstances. Most psychological traits exhibit this kind of (limited) flexibility.

Accordingly, we also find differences in SDO according to position in the hierarchy. Meta-analytic research has found that people belonging to lower-ranking gender and ethnic or racial groups tend to reject group-based social dominance, whereas those in higher-ranking groups tend to favor social dominance.[54] Low SDO would allow someone in a subordinated position to reject the dominance hierarchy or to level the playing field by constraining dominance hierarchies altogether.

But an alternate strategy one may choose to join the prevailing dominance hierarchy even in a subordinated position (people of color, women voting for Trump, for example). Even at a cost to fitness, doing so can be a better choice than standing with a weaker (albeit more egalitarian) alliance that is more vulnerable to total annihilation by outsiders. Research finds, for example, that those near the World Trade Center during the 9/11 attacks reported growing more politically conservative, rather than more liberal, after the attacks.[55] This shift occurred across party lines and was associated with both greater patriotism and militarism. Thus, SDO, like our political orientations, is neither completely pliant nor completely rigid—it has the capacity to flex.

Another crucial point to remember is that social dominance is not only about disfavoring the out-group but also *favoring the in-group*. Accordingly, SDO is associated with greater patriotism,[56] which, not surprisingly, is more strongly expressed by Republicans.[57] Beyond the national flags, the parades, and the anthems, patriotism is essentially a commitment to the tribe, particularly in competition with outsiders. The ubiquity of SDO across the world underscores the fact that we navigate through our increasingly globally interfaced world, using the narrow parameters of our tribalistic brains. This mismatch poses certain challenges.

One challenge is that SDO is associated with the belief that one's group is inherently better than others, and also predicts support for inter-group aggression.[58] Humans share this pattern of in-group altruism and out-group enmity with robust chimpanzees. Jane Goodall observed that "as a result of a unique combination of strong affiliative bonds between adult males on the one hand and an unusually hostile and violently aggressive attitude toward nongroup individuals on the other," the chimpanzee "has clearly reached a stage where he stands at the very threshold of human achievement in destruction, cruelty, and planned intergroup conflict."[59] Among humans, tribalism is also at the root of societies being torn apart from the inside, along sectarian, racial, ethnic, or partisan lines. But once again, we typically find male competition at the center of human divisions, whether between nations or tribesmen, and in turn, we find genetic processes at the center of male competition.

SHARED GENES, SDO, AND MALE VIOLENCE

As Ismael the Bloodthirsty's five hundred concubines and 888 children evince, men are driven by personal reproductive ambitions. However, amassing power requires alliances. Moreover, because men in more violent times stood the risk of being annihilated by rival male groups, they had great incentive to form warring coalitions. Men unable to do so would be ground into dust. This dynamic, which makes the maxim *join or die* a rather literal evolutionary imperative, forged a powerful selective pressure. And so today we see group-level violence between men across many levels of human social organization, from intertribal conflicts to gang fights to world wars.[60]

While rarely discussed, shared genes have a role in male intergroup conflict. British biologist Richard Dawkins popularized the idea of a gene-centric view of evolution in his book *The Selfish Gene*.[61] Dawkins explained how genes design organisms in ways that maximize their own reproduction, and went so far as to say that organisms are the "survival machines" of genes. One common means of understanding this relationship is by considering the impact of genes in acts of altruism—acts that may endanger the life of one individual in the service of helping another. The willingness to perform such acts is generally highly correlated with the amount of shared genetic material. Hypothetically, if I were going to save someone from a burning building, I would save my child first, my cousin next, an unrelated stranger after that, and I might just leave my pet goldfish to boil—or, as British geneticist J. B. S. Haldane famously said, "I would lay down my life for two brothers or eight cousins."[62] Thus genes code brains to engage in behaviors that ensure more copies of themselves get passed on across time, even if those genes reside in others. That said, when I burst into a burning building, I'm not consciously thinking of my genes. But my genes make my brain experience an intense sense of emotional, cognitive, and moral urgency to save my child first.

Patterns of migration appear to have intensified moral commitments between men. Historically, humans have been mostly patrilocal, meaning women have left their natal group far more often than men, whereas men stayed put along with their male relatives. Research has found that up to 70 percent of all human societies follow this pattern of emigration.[63] The resulting concentration of male blood relatives encouraged naturally strong, trusting, and cooperative male bonds based on shared genes.

Accordingly, across human history, men have had stronger kinship ties than women.[64] The love and trust that related men have for one another has had profound implications for the human condition across time.

For one, higher relatedness gives men greater confidence in risky cooperative enterprises, such as war, with closer kinship providing genetic incentive to take risks in defending one another. As a corollary, research has found that patrilocality in human groups is associated with more frequent warfare.[65] This too is a pattern that human males share with our chimpanzee cousins. Renowned primatologists Richard Wrangham and Dale Peterson write that among four thousand mammals, and over ten million other animal species, *only* chimpanzees and humans follow this pattern of patrilocality accompanied by "a system of intense, male initiated territorial aggression, including lethal raiding into neighboring communities in search of vulnerable enemies to attack and kill."[66]

Further, the hostility created by patrilocality locks us into patrilocality. Chimpanzee males, for example, are so extremely hostile toward outside males that males rarely if ever transfer between groups; any male attempting to transfer would be summarily killed by the males of the out-group. By contrast, 50–90 percent of female chimpanzees transfer to other groups to breed once they reach sexual maturity.[67] Whereas male transfers are seen as sexual competitors carrying foreign genes, females are welcomed as potential mating partners.

Male transfer is more common among humans than chimpanzees but still not the predominant pattern—like male chimps, men are hostile to strange men. Thus xenophobia is concentrated among men, and it has reflected real dangers for men. Most of the world's perpetrators of violence are men, but most of its victims are as well (the United Nations, for example, recently found that globally 80 percent of homicide victims are men[68]), and this pattern of killing is very old. Male-on-male violence persists particularly among humans living in groups similar to those of our ancestors. Archaeologist Lawrence Keeley examined contemporary foragers across the world, such as the Jivaro, Yanomamö, Mae Enga, Dugum

Dani, Murngin, Huli, and Gubs, and found that male-on-male violence accounted for a whopping 30 percent of all male deaths.[69] If this population of men were all five boroughs of New York City, roughly the population of Brooklyn would be annihilated. The resulting fear of out-group males perpetuates the cycle of violence, for, as we learned in chapter 2, xenophobia promotes inbreeding. Inbreeding increases the degree of shared genes in a population, which in turn increases xenophobia, further locking humans into patrilocal, xenophobic, patriotic groups of violently competing male primates.

The cycle of xenophobia has held strong even with our shared genes thinning out as populations swell. Military men exaggerate genetic relatedness by calling themselves "brothers-in-arms" fighting for their "fatherland" or "motherland." And fighting men have reported feeling closer to their fellow soldiers than to their own wives,[70] which suggests that our long history of patrilocality may have greased the way for contemporary male tribalism. Even modern-day men living as civilians in peaceable societies have the tendency to fall back into these patterns, which have proven easy to elicit in the research lab. When experimenters posit an outside threat, men close ranks, identify with their group, and start cooperating more, whereas this response is generally not found among women.[71]

An important point in all this is that if ancestral human men couldn't leave their groups for fear of death, then turning inward to their band of brothers, remaining xenophobic toward outsiders, and favoring dominance over other groups was *evolutionarily sensible*. The overrepresentation of men among conservatives and the preponderance of male interests embedded in conservative ideologies, then, reflect these ancient selection pressures on men.

Certainly, in a dangerous world, with groups of men amassed on the border, waiting to annihilate my tribe, I would want to be surrounded by a close-knit, aggressive, xenophobic tribe of men. Similarly, if my children and I risked starving to death without access to a contested resource, I would want my tribe to win control. Once again, the question remains, however, how much utility this psychology retains as we move from small tribes competing for scarce resources to an interconnected community of nations, bound by a global economy, and with the technological capacity to erase starvation from the human experience.

Moreover, evolutionary science teaches us that inequality is often driven by the *personal* reproductive ambitions of men. Man's exorbitant reproductive capacity has given him incentive to disproportionately hoard power, wealth, and women, and, when allowed, to use despotic violence as a means to this end. So the impulse to extract wealth from the rival tribe is about not only survival but also feeding insatiable male reproductive greed. When we understand these roots of inequality, we may begin to question how far we allow them to influence our economic policy. But merely posing this question can be challenging. Across our history, powerful men have achieved godlike status in their roles as protectors, or as *oppressors*, which has made questioning their methods both risky and emotionally complex. The next chapter will explore why.

CHAPTER 5

ON BIG APES AND PRESIDENTS

T he 2016 US presidential election stunned the world. After a mete-
oric rise through the Republican primaries, a reality TV show host,
professional wrestling dabbler, and political novice with zero experience
in public office upset former Democratic senator and secretary of state
Hillary Clinton to win the most politically muscular office in the world.
Donald J. Trump's xenophobic and warmongering rhetoric on the road
to the White House, and his subsequent election, strongly divided American society, set off a wave of protests in the United States and abroad, and
drew searing international criticism.

Regardless of how Trump is viewed by history, his election serves as
an illuminating case study of our political psychology. Clearly, a presidential election involves a large, convoluted flow of influences, like so many
tributaries pouring into a twisted, torrential, and sometimes dirty river.
A large swath of the Democratic electorate lost trust in Hillary Clinton
during the primaries when leaked emails from top officials at the Democratic National Committee suggested that it may have colluded against
Clinton's opponent, Senator Bernie Sanders.[1] Similarly, credible evidence
emerged that Russian hackers tried to influence the election in favor of
Trump. There was the role of third-party candidates, such as Jill Stein,
who shunted votes away from major party candidates, as well as the
rural-leaning influence of the Electoral College, which went against the
popular vote in 2016. But the most potent factor in Trump's victory was
something far more primal. Human political psychology operates on a
set of adaptations designed for ancestral environments in which powerful
men protected the clan against outsiders, predators, and starvation. This

ancient history continues to have a tremendous, largely subconscious influence over our present-day political stances. To be sure, it played a central role in 2016.

Before we explore how this history influenced Trump's win, let us consider the criticisms that have been raised of his qualifications for leader of the free world. Intellectuals, world leaders, and civilian spectators have offered an unusually candid litany of reproaches, far more extensive than the standard political commentary. To begin, many have criticized his level of sophistication. Gavin Newlands, a British member of Parliament (MP) with the Scottish National Party, said plainly, "Let's be clear, Donald Trump is an idiot. I have tried to find different, perhaps more parliamentary adjectives to describe him but none was clear enough. He is an idiot." Similarly, former British prime minister David Cameron labeled Trump's rhetoric as "divisive, stupid, and wrong." Ecuadorian president Rafael Correa said, "His discourse is so dumb, so basic," while Gavin Robinson, British MP from Northern Ireland, said, "The person you are dealing with may be a successful businessman, but he's also a buffoon." And we have Paris mayor Anne Hidalgo's blunt and exasperated exhortation: "Mr. Trump is so stupid, my God!"[2]

Others have opined on Trump's psychological stability. Former Mexican president Vicente Fox said, "This nation [the United States] is going to fail if it goes into the hands of a crazy guy." Australian opposition leader Bill Shorten followed, "I think Donald Trump's views are just barking mad on some issues."[3] Many suggested Trump suffers from narcissistic personality disorder, citing the fact that he often talks about himself in the third person, that he actually bragged about his penis size during the presidential debates, and that he has a tendency to frame himself as the best at things: "There is nobody who has done so much for equality as I have," "There is nobody more conservative than me," "Nobody has ever had crowds like Trump has had," "Nobody is better to people with disabilities than me," "Nobody builds walls better than me," "Nobody loves the Bible more than I do," "Nobody would be tougher on ISIS than Donald

Trump," or "There's nobody that understands the horror of nuclear [*sic*] better than me."[4]

Trump's behavior inspired Democratic representative Ted Liu from California to introduce legislation that would require a psychiatrist at the White House. This sentiment is not restricted to the Left. Charles Krauthammer, a conservative columnist who was a frequent panelist on Fox News, cited Trump's "pathological narcissism" as one reason for his disqualification as president.[5] Notably, Krauthammer was not just a conservative mouthpiece but also a psychiatrist who contributed to the *Diagnostics and Statistical Manual of Mental Disorders*, the manual used to diagnose psychiatric conditions.

Compounding concerns over Trump's mental fitness were his foreign policy approaches, which to many came across as not only warlike but also wincingly simplistic. While campaigning, he outlined his solution to ISIS: "I would bomb the shit out of them. I would just bomb those suckers, and, that's right, I'd blow up the pipes, I'd blow up the refineries, I'd blow up every single inch, there would be nothing left. . . . It will be beautiful, and I'll take the oil."[6] He also promised that he would happily bring back torture ("I'd bring back a hell of a lot worse than waterboarding") and that he would kill the families of suspected terrorists, defying the Geneva conventions.[7]

Trump's style of propaganda stoked fears across the globe, particularly among those who have studied the history of fascism, or come from a land that suffered under it. Mexican president Enrique Peña Nieto warned, "That's the way Mussolini arrived and the way Hitler arrived." Former minister of Sweden Carl Bilt cautioned, "If Donald Trump was to end up as president of the United States, I think we better head for the bunkers." Elmar Brok, German member of the European Parliament and chair of the European Parliament's foreign affairs committee, said, "He is not predictable and this unpredictability is a danger."[8] During Trump's inauguration, Pope Francis chimed in to observe, "Hitler didn't steal the power, his people voted for him, and then he destroyed his people."[9]

Moreover, Trump's behavior seems directly at odds with the ethical positions of many of the Christian conservatives who voted for him. Trump has changed stances on abortion and fumbled with Bible passages, as when during his convocation address to Liberty University he called *Second Corinthians* "Two Corinthians."[10] Further, he has been married three times and was caught on audio, boasting that he tried to have sex with a married woman ("I tried to fuck her, and she was married") and that because of his fame he could do anything to the women he meets, including "grab them by the pussy."[11] He has thus violated cherished values held by the conservative Right in America, particularly among Evangelicals, such as sexual restraint, devotion to marriage, and religion.

The point of all this is that Trump seems a monumentally unlikely conservative presidential candidate. Yet he was elected by slightly under half of the US voting population (he narrowly lost the popular vote, but won the Electoral College). Despite everything covered above, which is the condensed version, Donald Trump exuded a mesmerizing, magnetic pull that drew in a stunningly large swath of the American electorate, including Evangelical Christians who should by all reason have been appalled by his personal life and shaky grasp of their religion. Trump's election has dumbfounded rational minds on both sides of the political spectrum. His appeal, however, does not reside on the plane of the rational; it resides on the primordial plains of Africa, where human leadership preferences were formed by the brutalities of daily living.

OF LARGE APES AND BIG MEN

In *The Republic*, Plato asks, "Imagine . . . a ship in which there is a captain who is taller and stronger than the crew, but he is a little deaf and has a similar infirmity in sight, and his knowledge of navigation is not much better."[12] In keeping with the ancient Greeks' savvy grasp of political psychology, Plato argues that the crew will be biased by the large, physical stature of the man with little to recommend him even as a sailor, and that this bias will hamper their ability to rationally select a competent captain. Size, as the ancient Greeks appear to have understood, can be an emotionally appealing criterion for leadership ability, even when seemingly irrelevant.

The truth is that size matters in a violent world where survival is won by raw physicality. Across social animals, powerful, larger, aggressive males play a critical role in the group's survival—dispatching predators, providing protection against outsiders, securing and defending territory, and winning contested resources. Perhaps not surprising then, primatological research finds that larger size is related to higher social rank in nonhuman primates, including baboons, gorillas, and chimpanzees.[13] The same is true for humans.

Because lethal intergroup violence was terrifyingly common among our ancestors, today we tend to prefer larger leaders, even though our presidents will never physically represent us in a fight. The empirical evidence on this preference is robust. For instance, subjects in the research lab show preference for taller leaders,[14] reflecting real-world political choices: between 1789 and 2008 the taller of the US presidential candidates won the race the majority of the time, and all pairs of major-party US presidential candidates have been taller than the average US male citizen.[15] Greater height also predicts higher status in labor markets, whether someone holds a blue- or white-collar job.[16] On a more primal level, height among men is associated with greater physical strength,[17] fighting ability,[18] or even reproductive success.[19] The latter makes sense when we consider that sexual dimorphism among animals originates as a result of mate competition; the bigger, stronger male usually wins fights over females and passes on his genes coding for size and strength.

But could our choice of political leaders be reduced to something as primitive as how we size them up in a fight? Male leaders across the political spectrum seem to think so, often going out of their way to demonstrate their fighting prowess. For example, Canadian prime minister

Justin Trudeau has arranged to be filmed working out in a boxing gym,[20] as has Russian president Vladimir Putin. Putin has also been filmed lifting weights or riding shirtless on horseback—slightly more sublimated displays of his fighting toughness.

But in the 2016 race for US president, displays of fighting prowess became unusually raw and literal. During a Democratic debate, candidate Jim Webb boasted with an eerie smile about having killed an enemy soldier in Vietnam.[21] Republican candidate Ben Carson bragged that in his youth he tried to stab someone, that he attacked a schoolmate with a combination lock, and that "I would go after people with rocks, bricks, baseball bats, and hammers" (claims none of his contemporaries seem to recall).[22] When an audience member raised protest at a campaign rally in Nevada, Trump yelled, "I'd like to punch him in the face, I tell ya!" *to roaring applause.*[23] The history or desire for violence was not hidden from view, but intentionally trumpeted and to a primate crowd who alighted.

But again, Trump's actual fighting prowess has little relevance for his competence as US president. In fact, playing out a thought experiment in which our world leaders actually fight, war correspondent and author Sebastian Junger has suggested that Trump's life of comfort and privilege would equate to him getting flattened in a real brawl against other heads of state, such as Putin.[24] Putin studied judo and sambo from the age of twelve and trained among the brutal ranks of the KGB, whereas Trump dodged the draft because of heel spurs. However, in our current world, appearances are everything.

Accordingly, Trump also highlighted his relative size and strength by derogating his rivals—plainly when he continually called former Florida governor Jeb Bush "weak," when he repeatedly referred to Florida senator Marco Rubio as "*Little* Marco," and when he called Texas senator Ted Cruz a "pussy" at a rally.[25] Further, when Trump announced his run for president on *The O'Reilly Factor*, he boasted, "There's nobody *bigger* or better at the military than I am."[26] Trump's choice of words could not have been more evolutionarily apropos. Nor could those of his running mate, Mike Pence.

Researchers have linked the sexually dimorphic male trait of broad shoulders to fighting ability, and in particular to the effective use of deadly handheld weapons, a specialty of male humans.[27] Perhaps not surprisingly, then, the standard of dress among politicians, the business suit, enhances shoulder width, and female politicians often wear business suits with exaggerated shoulder pads. In evolutionary terms, women's shoulder pads give the illusion of a male adaptation designed for fighting to an audience evolutionarily programmed to find it meaningful. (Interestingly, the fashion of shoulder pads in women's professional attire hit their most exaggerated breadth during the 1980s when women began entering the world of politics and business in large numbers.)

Fittingly, while on campaign for Trump, Pence referred to Trump as "broad shouldered" on at least seventeen different occasions. On CNN, he said plainly, "Look, Donald Trump's got broad shoulders." At other venues he emphasized the importance of Trump's shoulder width in interactions with other nations. On ABC's *This Week*, for example, he claimed, "He's going to be out there advancing America's interests first with that broad-shouldered leadership," and on NBC News' *Meet the Press* that Trump is "a strong leader with a clear vision, with broad shoulders who's going to advance America's interest." On Fox News he directly tied Trump's shoulder width to our national safety: "Donald Trump is going to provide the kind of broad-shouldered American leadership on the world stage that I think will make the world a more stable place."[28]

To many (Jane Goodall included),[29] Trump's behavior on the campaign trail effused a certain male chimpanzee aroma as he vied to make more noise than his political rivals. But his tactics resonated. During the campaign, T-shirts, buttons, and other campaign paraphernalia surfaced, reading, "Trump: Finally a Candidate with Balls." Interestingly, while testicles (or penis size) would also seem irrelevant to political elections, balls produce testosterone, the hormone that generates sexual and aggressive drives, and muscularity, which is used for mate competition. Testosterone also produces masculine facial features, such as wide jaws, square faces, and pronounced eyebrows.[30] More masculine facial features are associated with dominance,[31] and research finds that dominant faces have an impact on human rank status. In one study, subjects were shown photos of West Point cadets and instructed to rate their faces on perceived dominance. Cadets rated with higher facial dominance attained higher military rank later in their careers.[32] Likewise, facial dominance has also predicted success in elections across the world.[33]

What is perhaps even more telling is the fact that this preference for big men appears to be context-dependent. Research finds that people prefer taller leaders with more masculine facial features in times of war, and more feminized faces in times of peace.[34] Similarly, in lab studies, people choose more masculine faces during competition with an outside group, and feminine faces in contexts where in-group cooperation is needed.[35] In general, women are seen as more competent at resolving conflicts than men and are preferred in times of in-group tension.[36] Still, our impulse to turn to big, powerful males for protection is nearly ubiquitous, found not only in the ranks of government but also in the halls of religion.

ALPHA GODS AND THE MEN WHO REPRESENT THEM

The prehistoric role of the "strong man," as protector and conqueror, is a continuous theme in the Judeo-Christian Bible and may even be how Trump won fully 80 percent of the white Evangelical vote.[37] Evangelicals tend to be staunchly conservative, and we have now demonstrated that conservatives are wired to be threat-sensitive, to be wary of outsiders, and to seek comfort from dominant males with fighting abilities. Nearly all of biblical patriarchs were warrior-kings or fighters, as was the Judeo-Christian god, per the Bible: "The Lord is a man of war."[38]

In my book *Alpha God*, I detail how the god of the Abrahamic faiths (Judaism, Christianity, and Islam) is based on the dominant, territorial, protective males of our evolutionary past.[39] Like male primates, that male god protects against outsiders and acquires territory for his in-group (e.g., "I will drive out nations before you and enlarge your territory"[40]); provides resources necessary for survival (e.g., "Behold, I will rain bread from heaven"[41] and "He hath given meat unto them that fear him"[42]); and even protects against predators (e.g., "But you, LORD, do not be far from me. You are my strength; come quickly to help me. Deliver me from the sword, my precious life from the power of the dogs. Rescue me from the mouth of the lions; save me from the horns of the wild oxen"[43]).

In many ways, men like Trump offer the same protections. By claiming Mexico is sending America its rapists, and promising that Mexicans would finance a wall to keep themselves out, Trump simultaneously addressed the tribe's primal need to protect women (as we have discussed, warring tribes often stole and raped each other's women), and defined territorial boundaries (in plainest terms by literally erecting a border wall) and competed-for resources (by making Mexico pay for said wall). Other world leaders have promised to address our evolutionary fears in more sublimated ways. Trump's tactic was simply to be incredibly concrete about it all.

For the religious, whose devotion is spent striving to draw closer to the protective embrace of their omnipotent male god, powerful men have always been ready to serve as proxies. History is filled with examples of dominant men possessing divine authority, considered walking gods on Earth, or having a special war alliance with God. For example, Trump's closest religious advisor, Evangelical pastor Robert Jeffress, claimed, "In the case of North Korea, God has given Trump authority to take out Kim Jong-Un."[44] For believers, being aligned with the most powerful male in the universe is sure to relieve fear, particularly in bloody conflict with outsiders. US general William Boykin, a man central to the "war on terror," once claimed of George W. Bush, "Why is this man in the White House? The majority of Americans did not vote for him. He's in the White House because God put him there for a time such as this."[45] When Somali warlord Osman Otto was captured, Boykin pitted the Christian god's size against the god of Islam: "He [Otto] went on CNN and he laughed at us, and he said, 'They'll never get me because Allah will protect me. Allah will protect me.' Well, you know what? I knew that my God was bigger than his."[46]

Never mind the fact that size should be irrelevant to an omnipotent being without physical form, as the god of Christianity is described. Size is not psychologically irrelevant to us humans. Larger size even has influence on the ranks of men in church hierarchy; research has found that height can predict whether one is a bishop or a priest.[47]

But recall again that size connotes strength, and strength has been used in violent (and by definition inegalitarian) male mate competition far before we humans developed anything that could be described as political ideology. Bearing this legacy in mind, it should be no surprise that our political efforts to create egalitarian societies so often strain against the evolved ambitions of men.

BIG MEN ON THE LEFT

In considering the connection between conservatism and masculinity, the presence of leftist strongmen across history may seem paradoxical. Let us briefly consider whether alpha leftist and alpha right-wing leaders are really the same animal. French philosopher Jean-Pierre Faye was the first to describe the *horseshoe theory*, the concept that political orientation forms more of a horseshoe than a continuum, with the extreme Right and extreme Left nearly touching in the middle. On the extreme Right you have authoritarianism (where the dominant male has total power) and on the extreme Left totalitarianism (where the state has total power), both of which bear striking resemblance to one another. Avi Tuschman explains the theory:

The two ends of the horseshoe spectrum do not actually touch. . . . The extreme right's ideology takes ethnocentrism and hierarchy to an extreme. In practice the extreme right's policies are more likely to result in genocide. The ideology of the extreme left takes anti-ethnocentrism and egalitarianism to an extreme. In practice, these governments are more prone to ethnocidal assimilations and politicidal purges (such as Stalinist Russia, or Cambodia under Pol Pot).[48]

Ideologically this model has merit, and conceptually it brings the ruling fists of men like Stalin and Hitler even closer together. When we distill ideology down to its evolutionary base, the two "sides" become even less distinguishable. The behavior of prominent male leaders of the extreme Right and extreme Left suggests both are equally driven by evolutionary competition for power, wealth, and females, which, as we have been discussing, are all zero-sum (i.e., inegalitarian) enterprises.

For example, leftist totalitarians also strive to project bigger size and strength, which among primates is essential to male dominance. Kim Jong Il, for example, wore platform shoes and a bouffant hairstyle purposefully to make himself appear taller and more imposing.[49] Joseph Stalin wore shoe lifts also, stood on wooden platforms during parades, and changed his given name Iosif Vissarionovich Dzhugashvili to Stalin, which translates in Russian to "man of steel"—not exactly a moniker conveying disinterest in power.[50] China's Communist leader Mao Tse-Tung also understood the need to project power, as well as the populace's need for dominant leaders. Mao argued that the personality cult was necessary to "stimulate the masses." It was difficult, said Mao, to "overcome the habits of 3,000 years of emperor-worshipping tradition."[51] While Mao may have underestimated the span of time humans have been engaged in leader worship, he and his cabinet were sure to emphasize power difference, promoting even Mao's ideas to take a greater status than those of other men. In one speech, his defense minister Lin Bao said, "Every sentence said or written [by Mao] is truth," and that "one sentence is equal to ten thousand sentences by us."[52]

Nor have leftist dictators been soft on outside tribes. Mao called for violence against the enemy, said to include "all those in league with imperialism—the warlords, the bureaucrats, the comprador class, the big Landlord class and the reactionary section of the intelligentsia attached to them," and he too preached xenophobia: "After the enemies with guns have been wiped out, there will still be enemies without guns; they are bound to struggle desperately against us, and we must never regard these enemies lightly. If we do not now raise and understand the problem in this way, we shall commit the gravest mistakes."[53] Like other alphas, Mao exterminated his political enemies. Under his Communist, social, and economic campaign, the Great Leap Forward, up to forty-five million people were starved, beaten, or worked to death[54] (by comparison, fifty-five million died in the entirety of World War II[55]). Stalin, the man of steel, was responsible for the deaths of some nine million.[56]

Among leftist dictators, xenophobic aggression also comes with sexual conquest, as we would expect from male primates. Despite being the leader of the largest left-wing political movement in the world, championing an ethos of equality (that included sexual equality), Mao was a notorious womanizer who was reported to have indulged in sex parties and who kept a constant flow of young women on rotation in his quarters.[57] Needless to say the male proletariats of Mao's China weren't invited to share in his sexual spoils. Similarly, despite Fidel Castro's carefully crafted public image as a modest, fatigue-wearing comrade, his ex-bodyguard reported that the Cuban dictator kept some twenty lavish properties, a yacht, a private island, and a battalion of mistresses.[58] When asked in an interview how many children he had, he boasted, "Almost a tribe."[59] Kim Jong Il and his successor, Kim Jong Un, have also used their power and wealth to keep "pleasure squads," hundreds of teenage girls used to service them and elite government officials, while they gorged on Black Sea caviar and French cognac.[60] This while the North Korean populace starved.

Moreover, when liberal dictators ascend the primate hierarchy, the public deifies them, sometimes with great encouragement by the leaders themselves. The Vietnamese Communist revolutionary Ho Chi Minh achieved godlike status, and like the pious lining up for a glimpse of Christ's reliquaries, hundreds of devotees still queue daily to see Ho's embalmed corpse in Hanoi. Lenin's body is treated similarly in its Moscow shrine, and while alive his atheistic propaganda machine coopted deist concepts; in a play on words and concepts, one maxim transformed the idea that God (or Jesus) is always with us, with "Lenin is always with us." But for an unabashed case of a contemporary walking god on Earth, we look to North Korea. Mandatory images of the Kim dynasty alpha gods are worshipped everywhere. Rare footage inside the insulated nation shows citizens prostrating themselves in front of Kim Jong Il's photo, wailing, and praising his greatness and omnipotence. North Koreans are literally instructed to worship the Kims as their gods.[61] Needless to say, appointing oneself a god is not an egalitarian gesture.

In trying to understand the clear contradiction between egalitarian word and hierarchical deed among these leaders, it's worth noting that many of them didn't start out as dictators; they often began living closer to their egalitarian ideals, only to turn as they gained power. As philosopher Peter Singer poignantly asks, "What egalitarian revolution has not been betrayed by its leaders? And why do we dream the next revolution will be any different?"[62] As we have previously discussed, male primates lower on the hierarchy have a fitness incentive to adopt political philosophies that seek to right power imbalances. The problem, however, is that those same primates also have a fitness incentive to revert to a hierarchical order once they assume power, increasing their influence, expanding their territory, and maximizing their access to women. In this sense, the leaders of leftist movements have an incentive to shift "right," moving from their emphasis on equality, toward hierarchical control, and ultimately taking on the role of dictator. But the crucial point is that male mate competition is a unifying theme between both the extreme Left and right-wing leaders of the world. This commonality helps to explain the ideological inconsistencies we notice when so-called egalitarian leaders behave as despots.

SEX, POWER, AND PARTISANSHIP

In fact, research on the general populace, examining psychological traits such as aggression, the desire to force conformity, and obeisance to leaders, has largely failed to find "true" left-wing authoritarians. Canadian psychologist Robert Altemeyer, for example, developed a scale to measure left-wing authoritarianism (LWA) with statements such as, "Socialist revolutions require great leadership. When a strong, determined rebel leads the attack on the Establishment, that person deserves our complete faith and support," and "A leftist revolutionary movement is quite justified in attacking the Establishment and demanding obedience and conformity from its members." Analyses failed to find strong left-wing authoritarians but instead found that those who scored high on LWA also scored high on right-wing authoritarianism (RWA) and displayed the highest hostility and dogmatism.[63] American psychologist Sam McFarland examined political psychology in the Soviet Union and found that high RWA predicted hostility toward and mistrust of America, bias against women, prejudice against outside groups such as capitalists, and that those high on RWA were typically members of the Communist Party.[64] Altemeyer explains these results:

> The most cock-sure belligerents in the populations on each side of the Cold War, the ones who hated and blamed each other the most, were in fact the same people, psychologically. If they had grown up on the other side of the Iron Curtain, they probably would have believed the leaders they presently despised, and despised the leaders they now trusted.[65]

In other words, the male-oriented, tribalistic psychology that we find on the right wing runs deeper than political parties, or even political systems. In this sense, the extreme *politically* Left citizen can be better understood as the *gendered psychological* Right in the manner we have been exploring, just like the brash cults of personality that they tend to follow.

RIGHT-WING AUTHORITARIANISM DENUDED

In cults of personality, the personality is often a dominant male primate. History is riddled with powerful men—Ismael the Bloodthirsty, Mao Zedong, Kim Jong Il and Kim Jong Un, and Stalin, to name a few—who have used fear to draw in followers and command mass murder on their behalf, ultimately to serve their own evolutionary interests. While some men have murdered more, none stand out in the memory of Westerners quite like Adolf Hitler, such that today when men of power start making demagogic postures, Hitler's name and image are evoked as a warning. The rise of Hitler offers a poignant historical case study in the dangers of demagoguery.

In 1933, German president Paul von Hindenburg appointed Hitler as chancellor. When Hindenburg died the next year, Hitler quickly consolidated power to become absolute dictator of Germany. Hitler's rise coincided with a swell of fear and uncertainty brought about by the aftermath of World War I, when Germany was left in complete economic ruin. Hitler relieved Germany's woes in part by building a massive military-industrial complex and greatly expanding public works, which included the construction of the autobahn. Led by its strongman, the Nazi Party gained wide popular support for soothing the existential fears brought upon by Germany's Great Depression.[66]

In the alpha role, Hitler quickly began exerting totalitarian control over all aspects of German life. His word became law and his power godlike. Joseph Goebbels, the Reich's minister of propaganda, declared in a 1936 broadcast that "Germany has been transformed into a great house of the Lord where the Fuhrer as our mediator stands before the throne of God."[67] Hitler's subordinates pledged unconditional loyalty to him, personally, both above any political ideal and even above the state of Germany. Any challenge to his supremacy was summarily crushed— political dissenters were jailed, publications uncomplimentary to the Nazi regime were suppressed, and civil liberties were tightly constricted in order to cripple any potential for opposition.[68] From this seat of absolute power, Hitler behaved as we might expect of a dominant primate male, with the added advantage of enormous manpower, modern weaponry, and purported alliance with God: he began seizing territory. Starting with Austria, and then Czechoslovakia, he continued his expansionist pursuits across Europe. With the help of Joseph Stalin, Hitler attacked Poland, and so began the start of World War II in Europe.

Germany's economic depression was a result of reparations that the Allied forces required under the Treaty of Versailles in the wake of World War I—in a way, the reparations could be considered pressure from an outside tribe that resulted in resource shortages. Following the classic pattern, Hitler responded by demonizing outsiders, and, mesmerized by this evolutionary terror, his loyalists rallied behind him with an emotional fervor. The Nazi Party soon became deeply rooted in racism—anti-Semitism in particular, though all so-called "outside races" were deemed inferior. To secure the ascendancy (social dominance) of the Aryan race above all others, Hitler's men exterminated millions. Some were killed with bullets, others were burnt in ovens, others were starved to death, and others died as subjects of macabre scientific experiments. In total, WWII brought the death of some fifty-five million human beings (to date the deadliest conflict in human history), and much of Europe was bombed into ruin. The volume of human suffering set in motion by one man's personal ambition stupefied the world. Perhaps equally stunning was the fact that Hitler's subordinates followed him with such unquestioning obeisance.

Since WWII, an army of social scientists has set itself the task of understanding the psychology that gave the world Hitler. Refining the work of Berkeley researchers—including Theodor Adorno, Else Frenkel-Brunswik, Daniel Levinson, and Nevitt Sanford—psychologist Robert Altemeyer devised a concept called right-wing authoritarianism (RWA). By pairing down the Berkeley scientists' original notions of *authoritarian personality*, three discrete factors emerged, explains Altemeyer:

RWA is characterized by (a) "a high degree of submission to the author-ities who are perceived to be established and legitimate"; (b) "a general aggressiveness, directed against various persons, which is perceived to be sanctioned by established authorities"; and (c) "a high degree of adherence to the social conventions which are perceived to be endorsed by society."[69]

RWA shares some similarities with social dominance orientation (SDO), which we talked about in chapter 4. Like SDO, RWA is associ-ated with xenophobia,[70] being closed to experience,[71] and, strongly, with political conservatism.[72] There are theoretically meaningful differences, however. In discussing those differences, Altemeyer argued that RWA best captures passive deference to authoritarian leaders, the tendency to "trust unworthy people who tell them what they want to hear," whereas SDO best captures the tendency to target out-group members for domination.[73]

As it turns out, RWA and SDO are only modestly correlated.[74] Citing Altemeyer,[75] political scientists John Jost and his colleagues explain that while SDO and RWA reflect different concerns,

> Together, they account for both halves of the "dominance-submissive authoritarian embrace" and they predict more than half of the statis-tical variance in prejudice and ethnocentrism. One can therefore infer that the most inexorable right-wingers are those who are motivated simultaneously by fear and aggression.[76]

From an evolutionary standpoint, these two constructs reflect the survival strategies underlying the conservative political stance—on the one hand seeking to identify, villainize, and target outside competitors (SDO), and on the other hand deferentially following authorities who protect against the external threat (RWA), particularly large, aggres-sive male leaders. Ultimately these strategies are rooted in reproductive strategy. Tellingly, RWA and SDO do not develop until adolescence when humans reach reproductive capacity.[77]

WAR AS THE SOURCE OF RWA

What has never been fully explored is how RWA, like SDO and political conservatism more generally, reflects a long and violent history of mate competition among men. Some illustration of its value can be seen in how neatly the three constructs of RWA—aggressiveness, submission to authority, and adherence to social convention—map onto military social organization. First, deference to authority forms the very basis of military hierarchy. In the combat theater, unquestioning obeisance down the chain of command is essential. Military actions require quick, coordinated, and decisive action, which is facilitated by adhering to a strict hierarchy with centralized decision-making capacity. Imagine how slowly a military force would act (and how quickly it would be defeated) if decision-making was democratic and all men were not particularly obliged to obey commands. Second, aggression against outsiders "sanctioned by established authorities" (as Altemeyer describes RWA) is the very purpose of militaries. Third, high conformity to military convention is not only evident in military jargon, dress, haircuts, and formations but also in conformity to rules and procedures, which is necessary both for maintaining order among testosterone-filled men and for coordinating their actions. Perhaps understandably, then, military cadets score higher on authoritarianism than do those in the civilian world.[78]

Further "submitting to authority" and "adherence to the social conventions" are often one and the same, for it is often the male authorities who dictate social convention. In other words, conforming to the social order can also mean accepting the dominance hierarchy, which includes the authority and rules of the alpha male at its apex. This dynamic is ubiquitous and captured neatly in the phrase "for king and country," a maxim that originated in Britain and was meant to connote in-group loyalty. Practically speaking then, for men, observing convention means *not* competing for dominance with the in-group leaders or "jumping rank," as the behavior is known in the military.

The takeaway message is that RWA reflects a group-level survival strategy among humans in a dangerous and highly competitive natural world. Among Earth's life-forms, the ability to engage in organized, cooperative enterprises provides a powerful survival advantage. This ability to coordinate not only explains intergroup competition but also why the small, relatively weak naked apes of our ancestral past were not wiped from existence on the predator-laden plains of Africa where they arose. Without organized alliances we would not exist today.

SUPPRESSING COMPETITION AND IN-GROUP ORDER

Achieving stable alliances, however, requires overcoming certain challenges, most particularly the male drive to ascend the hierarchy; thus alliances require suppressing competition within the ranks. In the struggle for survival, the most effective maneuvers come from groups able to suppress in-group competition to serve joint goals such as defense. Ants and other social insects offer a vivid example. By suppressing competition within the colony, ants have been able to achieve complete dominion over individualistic insect species by displacing them or turning them into food. If there is any species that rivals humans for its coordinated, militaristic dominion, it is ants. As renowned myrmecologists (ant scientists) E. O. Wilson and Burt Hölldobler describe, "The foreign policy aims of ants can be summed up as follows: relentless aggression, territorial conquest, and genocidal annihilation of neighboring colonies whenever possible."[79]

Through self-sacrificing alliances (which have been studied by the US military[80]), ants rule the insect world, and every macrocosmic life-form in their vicinity is either chopped to pieces, stabbed, or sprayed with acid, and dragged back to the nest and consumed. So successful has this strategy been that collectively these miniature warriors equal the total biomass of humans on Earth, and no family of ultra-social insects (such as ants, wasps, bees, etc.) has ever become extinct.[81]

But, as mentioned before, for cooperation at this level to work, ants have to suppress competition. Ants are able to achieve this in part by sharing 75 percent of their genes (human siblings share 50 percent) and through sterility in their soldier class.[82] Sterility removes mate competition from the alliance and creates genetic incentive to defend the queen, as their only means of passing on genes, with complete, self-sacrificial loyalty.

Alliances among men are also cemented through shared genes and restricted competition. Through our history of patrilocality, male alliances emerged from bands of highly interrelated male kin. Among men in groups, the risk of annihilation by outside men creates genetic incentive to defend one another as brothers and to sequester the rival tribe's territory and females. And while shared genes have thinned out as the human population exploded around the globe, today's male collectives use cultural means to suppress competition by exaggerating similarity—through group identity, common language and dress, and psychological adaptations such as RWA.

But men have a tendency to violently compete for mates, which destabilizes alliances. Rather than developing an entire sterile class, as with ants, the solution for men has been to enforce strict adherence to sexual boundaries. Perhaps not surprisingly, then, the concern over sexual boundaries is a prominent feature of the RWA scale, as seen in statements such as the following (all reverse scored):

- There is nothing wrong with premarital sexual intercourse.
- A lot of our rules regarding sexual behavior are just customs which are not necessarily any better or holier than those which other people follow.
- There is absolutely nothing wrong with nudist camps.[83]

Those with high RWA tend to take umbrage with the kinds of sexual behaviors listed here and tend to emphasize sexual rules and customs. But framing these tendencies as mere conservative prudishness, which is not uncommon among liberal critics, misses their utilitarian value.

In military settings, where coordinated male action is most critical, sexual boundaries are legislated far more strictly than in civilian law; US military penal codes harshly punish adultery with confinement, fines, and risk of dishonorable discharge. In 2016, two-star general David Haight was stripped of his stars, demoted to lieutenant colonel, and run out of the military for having an extramarital sexual affair.[84] In contemporary morality, adultery is seen as a regrettable but not mortal error, so this response might seem extreme. But in evolutionary terms, extramarital affairs remove females from the mating pool, which creates mate shortages and can result in male-on-male conflict. And when the affairs involve other men's mates, male fury is roused. In the military context, both of these factors have the potential to erode group cohesion. In fact, evolutionary scientists have surmised that marriage may have arisen as an in-group rule designed to help men respect each other's mating claims, which makes alliance-making possible in a sex with programming designed to aid in violent competition for women.[85]

As it turns out, suppressing male mate competition is powerfully wired into our endocrine systems. Research has found that olfactory sensitivity to androstenone, a chemical related to testosterone, is related to a preference for social order and social hierarchies. This preference, moreover, is concentrated in those with conservative political ideologies.[86] In other words, we can (literally, if unconsciously) smell this chemical, and those who are better attuned to its smell are more likely to prefer a clear, stable hierarchy. Testosterone itself appears to be regulated in part by male alliances. Research on rural villagers in the Caribbean island of Dominica finds that when male teams compete in games against men from outside villages, their testosterone levels rise. But in competitions with men from their own villages, testosterone levels stay *low*, providing a biological means to keep coalitionary peace.[87] Strikingly, research has even found that men show elevated testosterone in the presence of attractive women but not in the presence of women who are pair-bonded with men from their own coalition.[88] Thus, the sexual restrictiveness that so often characterizes the conservative Right has some basis in maintaining male coalitions.

Given the concentration of religiosity on the Right, it is perhaps not surprising that religion, too, codifies the rules of male coalitions. The Judeo-Christian religion emerged during a shockingly violent era in the Fertile Crescent, where tribes of men regularly raided the neighboring tribe, hacked their male rivals to pieces with dull bronze weapons, and captured their women. In this era, suppressing in-group male competition was urgently necessary to ensure coalitionary defense. Thus, we have the seminal commandment from Moses: "Thou shall not covet thy neighbor's wife."

Raping the wives of the out-group was fair game for Moses's men, however, and the Bible is replete with wartime rape references. Here, rape is commanded against foreign nations but suppressed within nearby nations, which were very likely tied through kinship:

> When the LORD your God delivers it into your hand, put to the sword all the men in it. As for the women, the children, the livestock and everything else in the city, you may take these as plunder for yourselves. And you may use the plunder the LORD your God gives you from your enemies. This is how you are to treat all the cities that are at a distance from you and do not belong to the nations nearby.[89]

There are other evolutionary reasons for sexual control among conservatives, which we will explore in the next chapter, but maintaining warring male coalitions is central among them. Another means to maintain coalitions, also captured by RWA, is the conservative emphasis on social conformity.

CONFORMITY AND ORDER

Competition within human groups is inevitable because each individual is programmed by selfish genes. And so countrymen and countrywomen will compete with each other for resources such as mates, status, and wealth. However, the value of suppressing in-group competition in order to ensure successful competition with outsiders is fundamental. This imperative is captured in a famous American pre–Revolutionary War song, written by Founding Father John Dickerson, which rings, "Then join hand in hand, brave Americans all! By uniting we stand, by dividing we fall!" The Bible too presages the dangers of division: "Every kingdom divided against itself will be ruined, and every city or household divided against itself will not stand."[90] Such maxims derive from an ancient human instinct to drop in-group differences in the presence of an outside threat.

Psychological research can measure this impulse in action. After the terrorist attacks of 9/11, for example, crime rates dropped precipitously across the United States as Americans banded together. Murder rates in New York City dropped 40 percent in the six months following the attack, and we find the same drop in antisocial behaviors in many other societies in the midst of war or environmental crises.[91] Research has also found that witnessing death or injury during the 9/11 attacks predicted a higher RWA score.[92] These results underscore the idea that political conservatism is an evolved strategy that switches on in response to male coalitionary violence; a glaring yet rarely mentioned fact is that every one of the 9/11 hijackers was male.

The drop in antisocial behavior (violence, stealing, and rape against the in-group) and the increase in RWA after 9/11 help to illustrate that conforming to group norms to promote collective defense is an important component of the conservative strategy. This purpose becomes clearer when we consider the extent to which conservatives view breaches in the social order as dangerous. Concerns tapped by items drawn from the RWA scale are also illustrative here (note, too, the role of dominant leaders in enforcing norms; italics are mine):

- The facts on crime, sexual immorality and the recent public disorders all show we have to crack down harder on *deviant groups* and troublemakers, if we are going to save our moral standards and preserve law and order.

- The situation in our country is getting so serious, the strongest methods would be justified if they eliminated the troublemakers and got us back to our true path.
- The only way our country can get through the crisis ahead is to get back to our traditional values, put some *tough leader in power*, and silence the troublemakers spreading bad ideas.
- What our country needs most is disciplined citizens, *following national leaders in unity*.[93]

Thus, from the RWA perspective, social order has practical value as a means to facilitate defense (or even conquest). Perhaps not surprisingly, both maintaining order and providing defense are enterprises championed by powerful men.

Whether in war or peacetime, functioning societies require order, and dominant males have an ancient role in enforcing order among their male subordinates. Strong alpha chimpanzees, for example, maintain order in the troop with violence and threat displays, which makes male upstartism a costly proposition.[94] Yet when we grant men too much power, we invite abuse. Granting power to the largest, loudest, most aggressive males may at times protect the in-group, but authoritarianism is a poor strategy for improving the human condition overall, particularly as we engage in ever more cooperation across national boundaries. Authoritarians may temporarily keep the peace at home, and their projections of strength may occasionally dissuade attack from the outside, but they also start wars and oppress their subordinates. Moreover, not all means of establishing order require a powerful male. In fact, there is a good case to be made that social order is best established by placing a ceiling on the amount of power that men can acquire and by transferring greater power to women. The following chapters will explore this dynamic, as well as the reasons why men have historically resisted giving women control.

CHAPTER 6

THE POLITICS OF SEXUAL CONTROL

We humans sometimes think of our morals as reflecting a higher order of being, something that sets us apart from the other animals of the earth. But our most consecrated moral convictions are often the ones most leavened with primal instinct. Accordingly, sexual behavior, among the most ancient instinctual endeavors, is often a cardinal focus of what we regard as morally right or wrong. And it's fair to say that across cultures, religions, and political systems, women's sexuality commands a greater share of our moral scrutiny. But why women's sexuality, and men's only to a lesser degree? Females hold a crucial resource—their precious half of the genetic coupling required for reproduction. The scarcity of women's reproductive output triggers male mate competition, and men in power have made managing that scarcity a focal point of our politics, broadly manifesting as sexual control. A deeper look into the politics of sexual control uncovers specific primate male reproductive imperatives—avoiding cuckoldry, and competing with rival male groups for greater representation in the gene pool. This chapter will explain why these efforts are concentrated in political conservatism and how they can create societal instability and violence.

THE DEFENSIVE GAME OF MALE MATE COMPETITION

There is a group of birds from the family *Cuculidae* that engage in a notorious evolutionary reproductive strategy called *brood parasitism*. Three New World and fifty-six Old World species of bird engage in this strategy, which involves laying their eggs in other birds' nests—often birds from different species. By doing so, the *cuckoo* birds, as they are commonly known, offset all the energy expenditure and risk associated with rearing offspring onto another animal. Worse yet, the cuckoo nestling kills its forced adoptees' offspring by ejecting their eggs. Unaware of the switch, the host species instinctively feeds the cuckoo chick into adulthood. Sometimes the costs incurred by the *cuckolded* birds, which are often much smaller species, are painfully clear, with an outsized cuckoo chick greedily demanding food from tiny stepparents who practically kill themselves trying to keep up with the voracious imposter's caloric needs. Critically, this herculean feeding effort is done to support a chick with foreign DNA, which makes it not only evolutionarily profitless but also dangerous; in an uncertain natural world filled with hazards, spending an entire breeding season on an imposter chick could mean complete failure to reproduce, an evolutionary dead end.

The risks of *cuckoldry* are not limited to birds, however, and in fact turn out to form the basis for an enormous share of male human reproductive psychology. Despite the fact that men tend to seek casual sex, they also take risks and invest time and resources in caring for their offspring. Because provisioning human offspring can take decades, the concern over being cuckolded is an important adaptation that prevented our male ancestors from being duped into nurturing foreign DNA. Even today, a large body of evidence shows that, when compared with women, men worldwide are more jealous of sexual infidelity, which places them at risk of cuckoldry.[1] Women, on the other hand, tend to be more jealous of emotional intimacy, which might lead to resources being diverted to another woman's children.[2] This is not to say that women don't get sexually jealous (or that they shouldn't). But a woman always knows whether a child is hers, which makes sexual jealousy (relatively) less critical for her reproductive success.

Cuckoldry, moreover, is a concern shared with other nonhuman male primates, including chimpanzees, baboons, and gorillas, all of whom use a variety of strategies to prevent it. They may attack potential rivals or straying females. Male monkeys and apes have been seen chasing, biting, and dragging females as punishment for flirting with or grooming other males, or simply being within a rival male's vicinity. They may also engage in mate guarding, constantly monitoring the female during her fertility phase to ensure sexual primacy.[3]

Men too engage in these ancient behaviors. Unlike ovulation in most other primates that show obvious sexual swellings, ovulation in women is hidden. Yet research has found that men have the unconscious ability to smell fertility. In one study, researchers had women wear cotton underarm pads at different phases of their menstrual cycle. When the researchers asked men to rate the smell of those pads on "pleasantness" and "sexiness," men consistently rated pads worn during the follicular phase (when the egg is ready for fertilization) higher on sexiness.[4] Compelled by this primitive sense, men are inclined to mate guard. One study found that men engaged in more mate guarding during their mate's follicular phase—calling their partners unexpectedly, monopolizing their time, or displaying anger when they talk to other men.[5] As among nonhuman male primates, mate guarding can become aggressive, and men may attack their mates in an effort to dissuade partner defection. Research finds that sexual jealousy is a primary motivation for spousal violence, including spousal homicide, both of which are almost always perpetrated by men.[6]

Once again, because men usually run human societies, male reproductive strategies have a way of working themselves into the political arena, where they are often concretized into law. In Texas, for example, it was legal to murder your wife if you caught her cheating as late as 1974.[7] In Italy, men committing this kind of murder were given special light prison terms (three to seven years) until 1981.[8] In Uruguay, a conservative penal code allowed judges to completely pardon men who committed murder as a result of "passion provoked by adultery" until 2017.[9] There are other examples, but the key message here is that conservative laws enforcing female sexual control are greatly driven by male cuckoldry concerns.

For a deeper understanding of how the ancient, animalistic fear of cuckoldry forms a major pillar of present-day statecraft, we turn our attention to the nations where political conservatism tends to be most concentrated. If our hypothesis about conservative politics as a male reproductive strategy is correct, female sexual control should also be at its peak in those nations.

CASE STUDIES OF CONSERVATISM AS MALE SEXUAL CONTROL

The Islamic World

Political conservatism is measurably most concentrated among Islamic nations. In the most comprehensive study into this phenomenon, American political scientist Ronald Inglehart used an enormous World Values Survey dataset (with a 114,800 average sample size per question) to examine the cultures of citizens from eighty-two countries.[10] Inglehart organized responses into two continuous orientations. He termed the first the *traditional—secular/rational* continuum. Here the traditional orientation reflects an emphasis on "religion, family and child-bearing, national pride and respect for authority, and rejection of abortion and divorce," and the secular/rational orientation largely the opposite values. He termed the second continuum *survival—self-expression*, and writes, "Self-expression values gives high priority to environmental protection, tolerance of diversity, and rising demands for participation in decision making in economic and political life," with survival being largely the opposite. What emerged from Inglehart's study is that countries from Islamic traditions—for example, Morocco, Algeria, Egypt, Jordan, Bangladesh, Pakistan, Indonesia, Iran, Turkey, and Saudi Arabia, among others (along with a smattering of Christian-majority nations like Zimbabwe and Uganda)—were far overrepresented among nations scoring highest on the *traditional* and *survival* continua, signaling national pride, respect for authority, emphasis on religion, low tolerance of diversity, few environmental protections, rejection of abortion and divorce, and other hallmarks of politically conservative ideologies.

With such values at the prow, authoritarian regimes flourish in Muslim-majority countries. Political scientist Steven Fish studied data from 157 countries worldwide to identify factors that predict democracy or authoritarianism.[11] Among those nations, the most robust predictor of authoritarianism was having a predominantly Muslim population. This trend was seen across languages, ethnicities, and geographic regions, in the forty-seven countries worldwide that predominantly follow Islam; only a few could be classified as democracies. Among the Arabic-speaking countries, which make up one-third of all Islamic-tradition nations, *none* were democracies. Authoritarianism was even pervasive among OPEC members, oil-rich countries, and this suggests that the lack of democracies among Islamic nations is not dependent on wealth, as is sometimes argued. Fish surmises that the wealth produced by oil "may enable the state to sustain a large and powerful internal security apparatus capable of repressing challengers." Fish's speculation is consistent with the winner-take-all mentality of male mate competition.

How do we understand this connection? Before anything else, by avoiding logical fallacies. There are those on the Left who may erroneously frame any inquiry into Islamic culture as racism. However, suffice it to say that Islam is not a race. Islam is a religion practiced across every race around the globe. Indeed, Islam's most useful framing here is as a political system, which is true of all religions, particularly those in nations where church and state are not vigilantly kept separate. On the other end of the political spectrum, some on the Right may be tempted to presume moral difference or moral inferiority of Muslims. This too is an error in thinking.

Avoiding either of these fallacies, we can see that authoritarianism is a product of our male-gendered psychology, forged through the pressures of male mate competition. Returning to our initial question, we may ask, "Do societies with the greatest conservatism also show the greatest cuckoldry concerns?" To answer, we may start by considering gender equality. Here we must acknowledge that there is no nation on the planet in which gender inequality means men having less power than women. Seen through the lens of evolutionary science, gender inequality is about controlling female sexuality and thereby protecting male reproductive interests.

The World Economic Forum annually publishes a massive, 144-country survey called the *Global Gender Gap Report*. The report ranks nations on measures of gender equality across four main domains: economic income and opportunity, educational attainment, health factors such as life expectancy, and political empowerment. In 2016, twelve of the fifteen worst-ranked nations on this list were from the Middle East, and all were Islamic-majority countries, with the sole exception of Ivory Coast, where Christians narrowly outnumber Muslims for the majority religion (by 44 percent to 38 percent respectively).[12] The fifteen worst in ascending order were Yemen, Pakistan, Syria, Saudi Arabia, Chad, Iran, Mali, Morocco, Ivory Coast, Lebanon, Jordan, Oman, Egypt, Bahrain, and Turkey. In each of these countries, gender inequality is accompanied by government-endorsed control of female sexuality, enforced by a variety of strategies that serve a clear mate-guarding function, ensuring females are always under the watchful eye of a dominant male, and that their interactions with outside males are highly constricted.

Yemen, worst on the global list for gender inequality, provides some examples. Yemeni women who escape their home to marry the man of their choice may be charged with adultery or "shameful acts," punishable by one hundred lashes. Article 40 in Yemen's constitution mandates that a wife may not leave her residence without her husband's permission (the article also stipulates that she must fulfill his sexual desires). Yemen also has laws designed to dissuade women from straying to the rival tribe. Yemeni women who marry foreign citizens are not allowed to pass on their citizenship to their children, whereas no such restriction exists for men.[13]

The strategies legislated in Yemen are prevalent throughout the Middle East. In Saudi Arabia, for example, it was illegal for women to drive until 2017, and a woman still requires permission from her male guardian to travel, study, or work. Saudis have also managed to harness modern technology to assist that primal endeavor to mate guard; when a woman attempts to travel outside the country, her male guardian is sent a text message.[14] Moreover, voicing dissent from these evolutionary arrangements is often summarily punished. When men have made public calls for an end to male guardianship in Saudi Arabia, they have been arrested and given prison sentences.[15]

Another classic strategy for mate guarding has involved concealing women's sexuality from other men. Historically, in some places, the women of high-status men were hidden behind the fortressed walls of harems. Today women in many Muslim nations remain hidden behind clothing, which can range from the headscarf hijab to the most extreme form of covering, the burka, which conceals every inch of skin and hair, and some even cloaking the eyes. While often framed as a means to protect women, concealing women from competitor males—primed as they are to detect visual signs of sexual fertility—functions as a highly efficient form of mate guarding. And in many Muslim-majority societies, women risk beatings, prosecution, or even being attacked with acid if they are caught without appropriate covering.[16] It would seem that such violent enforcement does little to provide "protection," and that the more basic function of concealment is to deter cuckoldry.

At its most literal, sexual control in many Middle Eastern countries includes men having legal rights over their wives' reproductive organs. Yemeni law, for example, stipulates that women must obtain permission from their husbands for any kind of medical procedure involving the uterus (including a hysterectomy, or a C-section) or for access to contraceptives; this level of control is endemic across the Middle East.[17]

Lastly, in some Islamic nations, conservative interpretations of Sharia law prescribe punishing straying females and form the basis for so-called honor killings, which almost always concern female sexual control. Honor killings most often occur as a result of extramarital affairs, premarital loss of virginity, refusing an arranged marriage, speaking to a male nonrelative, or even *getting* raped.[18]

Notably, in most of the nations in which gender equality is lowest, Islam provides the principal religious, cultural, and political framework. Islamic doctrine and tradition have frequently been used as a rationale for female sexual control. As one example among many, the Koran plainly states,

> Men have authority over women because God has made the one superior to the other, and because they spend their wealth to maintain them. Good women are obedient. They guard their unseen parts because God has guarded them. As for those from whom you fear disobedience, admonish them and send them to beds apart and beat them. Then if they obey you, take no further action against them. Surely God is high, supreme.[19]

These findings raise important questions regarding the relationship between culture, religion, and human reproductive strategy. The stakes become very clear when we observe that male-centric and conservative Islamic-majority societies have unusually high male populations. According to the United Nations, in 2015 twelve of the top twenty largest male-to-female sex ratios occur in Islamic nations, and eight of the top ten are Islamic.[20] In descending order those countries are Qatar (3.066:1), United Arab Emirates (2.722:1), Oman (1.844:1), Bahrain (1.613:1), Kuwait (1.35:1), Saudi Arabia (1.309:1), Maldives (1.302:1), Equatorial Guinea (1.23:1), Bhutan (1.13:1), and Western Sahara (1.105:1). According to the Population Reference Bureau, a nonprofit specializing in world health and environmental data, male-biased sex ratios reflect "various forms of lifelong discrimination against girls and women—particularly inferior nutrition and health care early in life and during childbearing years," as well as "sex-selective abortions or infanticide."[21]

One thing that zoology teaches us is that skewed sex ratios intensify mate competition. Research on a large variety of nonhuman animals finds that when sex ratios are biased, *mate guarding increases* to contend with the surplus of rivals.[22] In other words, cross-species observations predict exactly the correlation we see emerging between male-biased sex ratios and mate guarding, variously expressed by low standards for gender equality and specific practices from veiling to male guardianship to honor killings.

Now, here it is important to acknowledge that Muslim countries are not the only nations with religions or laws that codify male dominance, and that the ultimate cause of male mate competition is not religion or culture or politics—it is the evolved minds of men who express their evolutionary imperatives in the religions, cultures, and political doctrines that they craft. That being said, religions and cultures can codify male privilege to a greater or lesser extent, and there is little question that the doctrines of Islam—coupled with poor separation between church and state in Muslim nations—work in concert with the evolved psychology of men to create the nadirs of sexual control we are exploring here.[23]

Moreover, when we understand male mate competition, the reasons for political stances in Islamic nations become clearer. Research across Middle Eastern nations, for example, finds that most Middle Easterners agree that *democracy is valuable* but disagree with Western approaches to women's rights and women's education. For instance, a World Values Survey study by Ronald Inglehart and Pippa Norris found that Westerners and Middle Easterners consistently agree on statements assessing how well democracies perform as forms of government, and on the value of democratic ideals, e.g., "Democracy may have problems, but it's better than any other form of government."[24] However, the two groups diverged markedly on a scale assessing the value of gender equality, e.g., "A woman has to have children in order to be fulfilled," and "A university education is more important for a boy than a girl." The findings led the researchers to conclude that "the values separating the two cultures have much more to do with eros than demos."

To summarize, nations that are the most politically conservative and authoritarian score lowest on gender quality and are most likely to legislate male mate competition strategies, such as mate-guarding, to include physical punishment or execution for straying females. This is accomplished by intermeshing secular and religious laws that reflect the dictates of dominant male figures, variously represented in the patriarchal family, in a political hierarchy, and in religious structures, including an authoritarian male god.

America

While the more ardent American tribalists see themselves as the religious or moral antithesis of their counterparts in the Middle East, and despite the fact that to many the United States is considered the pinnacle of the free world, the great nation is not first on the 144-country *Global Gender Gap Report* list. Nor is it the twentieth or the thirtieth. Compared to other countries on measures of things like wage equality, literacy rate, women's labor force participation, or the ratio of women in ministerial positions, the United States scores lower than forty-four other nations.[25] With men in charge, it is perhaps not surprising that we find female sexual control to be a focal concern of conservative politics in America as well. Nor is it surprising that such control is tied to fears of cuckoldry.

There are many ways men work female sexual control into law, such as by allowing the murder of unfaithful wives, as we saw above. Another is the historic fight against birth control, which has been spearheaded by conservative men. Tellingly, male worry over birth control has often been framed as a path to women's sexual freedom and the potential for cuckoldry. While it is true that by mitigating the risk of unintended pregnancy, birth control removes a potential disincentive to intercourse, ironically contraception would prevent *actual* cuckoldry in the biological sense, where an extramarital affair results in a man raising another man's child. However, primate males' evolved concern over cuckoldry long predates any form of contraception. Thus male brains remain exquisitely primed for sexual jealousy,[26] which makes even non-procreative adultery emotionally threatening.

During the Victorian age, sexual repression in America hit its historical climax. Anthony Comstock, a US postal inspector on a personal crusade against what he regarded as sexual indecency, was a key figure in setting the cultural and legal standard of sexual control during that period. In 1873, Comstock managed to persuade the US Congress to pass a federal statute (the Comstock Law) that criminalized the distribution or even possession of sexually oriented paraphernalia, everything from sex toys to sexually explicit fiction. These laws extended to medical literature on abortion or contraception, which were regarded as sexually obscene. During this era, those caught selling or even *possessing* contraceptives were fined, given prison terms, or assigned hard labor. Many states followed with "little Comstock laws" that outlawed giving away contraception or even verbally passing on information about birth control. Connecticut even made *using* contraceptives illegal. While men too were targets of these laws of repression, restricting women's sexuality was a central concern, just as we see in Sharia law. American constitutional law scholar Geoffrey Stone explains:

> [The prevailing question was] "If women and men need no longer fear pregnancy as an outcome of sexual intercourse, what would keep wives faithful and daughters chaste?" As women gained control over their own reproductive destinies, the seemingly pernicious thought began to creep into the public consciousness that even for women, sex could be separated from reproduction and that freedom from pregnancy could unleash women's biblical lasciviousness.[27]

During this era, men often voiced the fear that contraceptives would lead to adultery—sex outside the marital contract that gave men ownership of their wives' reproductive capacity, and a potential route to cuckoldry. Comstock argued that contraceptives could reduce venereal disease or unwanted pregnancy, thus removing potential negative consequences preventing premarital or extramarital sex.[28] In 1917, women's reproductive right activist Ethel Byrne (sister of Margaret Sanger, who founded Planned Parenthood) was arrested for distributing birth control to women at her and her sister's Brooklyn clinic. At Byrne's trial her lawyer argued that prohibiting women access to contraception deprived them the pleasures of sex without the fear of pregnancy, and was therefore unconstitutional, violating the clause guaranteeing "free exercise of conscience and the pursuit of happiness." The judge ridiculed the argument, insisting that the fear of pregnancy is an important obstacle to fornication, and gave Byrne thirty days in Blackwell Island Prison.[29]

Comstock laws endured well into the 1960s. Astonishingly, it was not until 1965 that the Supreme Court ruled that it was unconstitutional for the government to prevent married couples from using birth control, and 1972 when the Court extended this protection to non-married couples. Even then there were fears about turning reproductive control over to women. Of the birth control pill, a 1966 headline of a *U.S. News & World Report* cover story asked, "Is the Pill regarded as a license for promiscuity? Can its availability to all women of childbearing age lead to sexual anarchy?"[30]

While attitudes about women's sexual freedom, including access to birth control, have progressed since the Victorian age in recent decades, cuckoldry was an important selective force shaping male jealousy across our ancestral history. That legacy continues to be expressed as resistance to birth control. Given the connection between conservatism and mate competition, it follows that we find anti-contraception attitudes most strongly expressed by modern-day conservatives. In the United States, this resistance takes several forms: insisting on abstinence-only sex education in schools; blocking access to certain contraceptives, such as the "morning-after pill"; fighting the mandate that insurance companies cover birth control; and fighting to shut down reproductive health clinics across the nation. There are other reasons for this resistance, as I discuss below, but sexual control of women is a prominent one.

Republican (male) legislators have taken the trouble to explain this connection. Former Pennsylvania Republican senator Rick Santorum, for example, has lectured on the "dangers of contraception," saying, "Many of the Christian faith have said, well, that's okay, contraception is okay. It's not okay. It's a license to do things in a sexual realm that is counter to how things are supposed to be."[31] Others have blatantly described the availability of contraception as a threat to male dominance. Former Florida Republican congressman Allen West argued that reproductive health clinics castrate men and make them subservient to women: "These Planned Parenthood women, the Code Pink women, and all of these women that have been neutering American men and bringing us to the point of this incredible weakness—[we need] to let them know that we are not going to have our men become subservient."[32] Birth control has in some instances become a symbol of the terrible perils of modern society, as when former Republican House majority leader Tom DeLay linked birth control (and evolutionary science) to the Columbine High School massacre: "Guns have little or nothing to do with juvenile violence. The causes of youth violence are . . . the teaching of evolution in the schools, and working mothers who take birth control pills."[33]

It should be obvious that the pill doesn't cause mass shootings, but that such a link would be proffered betrays (certain) men's reproductive urgency to scare women away from sexual independence. Moreover, conservatives have shown their willingness to legislate punishment for sexual freedom. Reminiscent of the sentiments of Anthony Comstock over a century earlier, in 2009 Colorado Republican state senator Dave Schultheis insisted that he would block a bill requiring HIV tests for pregnant women because the disease "stems from sexual promiscuity" and that the legislature shouldn't "remove the negative consequences of poor behavior, unacceptable behavior."[34]

The divide on contraception is seen between liberals and conservatives in expected ways. For example, a 2012 Pew Research Center surveyed Americans about whether insurance companies should be given a religious exemption to a mandate requiring that they provide birth control. Among those surveyed, 73 percent of Republicans said that

SEX, POWER, AND PARTISANSHIP

insurance companies should be given an exemption, compared to 29 percent of Democrats.[35]

In the religious justifications given for this opposition, we can see the ancient male primate concern over sexual control. For instance, R. Albert Mohler, president of the Southern Baptist Theological Seminary and also a highly influential Evangelical theologian, wrote,

> [The birth control pill] became almost an assured form of contraception, something humans had never encountered before in history. Prior to it, every time a couple had sex, there was a good chance of pregnancy. Once that is removed, the entire horizon of the sexual act changes. I think there could be no question that the pill gave incredible license to everything from adultery and affairs to premarital sex and within marriage to a separation of the sex act and procreation.[36]

As with Islam, in considering religiously motivated opposition to birth control in America, we cannot ignore how loudly man's sexual control of women is prescribed in scripture: "Now the body is not for fornication, but for the Lord, and the Lord for the body."[37] This privilege is handed down to men, who are God's male proxies on Earth, e.g., "He [man] is the image and glory of God: but the woman is the glory of the man. . . . Neither was the man created for the woman; but the woman for the man."[38] Or, more to the point, "Wives, submit yourselves unto your own husbands, as it is fit in the Lord."[39] The emphasis on female sexual control is more subtly, but perhaps most profoundly expressed through the foundational story of the Abrahamic religions, which holds the woman, Eve, responsible for the expulsion from paradise and for bringing suffering and death to all people thereafter. How did Eve sin? By eating the forbidden fruit—an allegory for sexual freedom that hasn't escaped much of anyone.

ABORTION

Research finds that the availability of contraception stems the use of abortion as a means of birth control.[40] Yet political conservatives, far more often than political liberals, tend to oppose both birth control and abortion. The issue of abortion is complicated. One factor making abortion a complex and emotionally charged topic is evolutionary—the profound human empathy for children. Protecting children is central to our survival, especially in the face of human offspring's epic stretch in dependency. Debates as to how many cells constitute a full human aside, when embryos are framed as human offspring—which they often are for political, rather than scientific, reasons—the topic of abortion taps into powerful emotions designed to help us protect our young.

In truth, it is difficult to engage in a scientific debate on the right or wrong of abortion. As Malcolm Potts and Thomas Hayden succinctly put it in their book *Sex and War*, "Religious assertions about when life begins are philosophically parallel to religious beliefs about life after death. They are both strongly held by different groups, but they go beyond the realm of science to prove or disprove."[41] Therefore a foray into the morality of abortion would need to be lengthy but is beyond the scope of this book.

Nevertheless, there is a widely expressed argument on the political Right that access to abortion leads to sexual freedom, the old enemy of males programmed to avoid cuckoldry, which bears some consideration. An excerpt from Conservapedia.com, an "encyclopedic" conservative website (which to date has had over six hundred million views) expresses this connection in plainest terms:

> Abortion and promiscuity refers to the liberal trait of using abortion as a way to deal with unwanted pregnancies caused by promiscuous sexual behavior. Due to immoral public school sex "education" many liberal youths view contraception and abortion as a license to engage in unhealthy premarital sexual relationships.[42]

While religious convictions are often cited for antiabortion stances, the Bible does not comment on when a fetus achieves personhood, nor decree restrictions on abortion. In fact, it may be shocking to learn that in the Old Testament the god of Abraham was described as anything but pro-life. In Numbers (5:11–5:31), for example, God instructs Moses to give women he suspects of having cheated on their husbands poisoned water to make them miscarry—thus eliminating competitor genes. Further, in Hosea, God punishes the Ephraimites for worshipping other gods, which is framed throughout as sexual infidelity: "O Ephraim, thou committest whoredom"[43]; "They are all adulterers."[44] Here God causes the Ephraimite women to miscarry: "Ephraim is smitten, their root is dried up, they shall bear no fruit: yea, though they bring forth, yet will I slay even the beloved fruit of their womb."[45]

Similar disregard for the unborn is seen throughout the Bible, particularly in the context of infidelity. Later in Hosea, Samaria, an ancient city that was considered to be one of God's wives, was also punished for adultery: "Samaria shall become desolate; for she hath rebelled against her God: they shall fall by the sword: their infants shall be dashed in pieces, and their women with child shall be ripped up."[46]

There are several points to be taken from these darkly gory narratives. First, again, is that the god of the Abrahamic religions, who conservatives so often cite for their moral guidance on sexuality, was a jealous male god who did not suffer infidelity. Second is that God is purported to actually cause abortions himself, or command his male representatives to cause them. Third, the preponderance of feticide (and infanticide) in the Bible makes the stated biblical reasons for conservative opposition to abortion greatly suspect.

In fact, before Nixon, Democrats and Republicans were relatively more evenly divided on the topic of abortion. Nixon himself initially took a proabortion stance—for instance, in 1970, he authorized all military hospitals to perform abortions—but quickly changed his position at the influence of political strategists in order to secure the Catholic vote during the 1972 presidential election, framing abortion as an issue of religious morality.[47] A year later, Nixon revealed his true feelings about abortion on tape. Not only did Nixon reiterate the timeworn male stance that abortions lead to sexual promiscuity, or "permissiveness" as he put it, but he also claimed abortion should be allowed to eliminate the genes of outside races—"There are times when an abortion is necessary. I know that. When you have a black and a white."[48] In Nixon's candid words, the importance of controlling women's sexuality in competition with outside races is evident. Whereas the Bible does not explicitly disallow abortions, it certainly emphasizes reproductive competition with the out-group, a sublimated (thus less commonly understood) evolutionary motivation for the Right's pro-life stance.

GROWING A BIGGER CLAN

In all the discussion of contemporary policy on birth control, it is necessary to remember that *natalism* (encouraging reproduction) has been a core tenet of religions throughout the ages and of Christianity in particular. Indeed, across the globe religiosity is associated with higher birthrates,[49] and natalist dicta is often embedded in religious canon. For instance, in the Bible, God kills Onan for spilling his seed—that is, for withdrawing during sex with his brother's widow, Tamar, instead of impregnating her per Levirite law.[50] There are many religious explanations for Onan's execution. But ancient Israel was marred by nearly continuous warfare, and a basic fact of coalitionary violence is that larger coalitions are more powerful.

This rule was painfully evident in the biblical era, during which larger, stronger groups regularly slaughtered smaller, weaker groups with impunity. More specifically, invaders typically slaughtered *men*, whereas, once again, women were often spared and taken as sexual spoils. In violent times, men have a rather obvious incentive to enlarge the warrior class. It is from this incentive that men have created religious dictates that promote an ever-expanding tribe and why political orientations based on male competition favor these dicta. Recall that the Christian god's very first decree to humans is to reproduce, and in it we can see the importance of dominance, not only in competitions between God's "chosen tribe" and other races, as we commonly see, but with all other competitors as well: "Be fruitful and multiply; fill the earth and *subdue* it; have *dominion* over the fish of the sea, over the birds of the heavens and over *every living thing that moves on the earth*."[51]

The Christian formula appears to be winning fitness competitions worldwide. At 2.3 billion as of 2015, Christians make up the largest population of believers on Earth, and fully 31 percent of the world's people.[52] Some of these numbers are a result of evangelizing, but they also greatly reflect high birth rates.[53]

Saint Augustine of Hippo (354–430), whose writings have had a great influence on modern-day conservative Christian sexual morals, saw lust as an abomination, the sin that brought about humankind's fall from God's grace. Despite his convictions, Augustine well understood the need for Christians to reproduce themselves. "The will of God," he insisted, was "not to serve lust" but "to see to the preservation of the race."[54] According to early religious laws, sex could be for procreation only (between husband and wife), and only in the missionary position, which was believed to increase the chance of conception.[55] Following Augustine's enduring authority, the Catholic Church continues to vehemently oppose contraception, and today Catholics make up fully 50 percent of the world's Christians.[56]

And so religion's sustained anti-contraception policy has had the measurable impact of enhancing Christian evolutionary fitness around the globe. Moreover, the value of large groups remains tied to their utility in coalitionary violence. Religious warfare has seared its way across the historical landscape for as far back as we have records. During the conquest of the Americas, for example, fleets of Spanish men set sail across the Atlantic under crosses and banners, thirsting for gold and glory. Stripped down, the conquest was primate males bent on acquiring territory, sequestering resources, killing off the male competition, and breeding with the resident females, all at the explicit command of church and crown, and their natalist agenda. In terms of fitness, these efforts were immensely successful, creating two continents of *mestizo* believers claiming loyalty, surrendering resources to the church and crown, and abiding the command to expand the Catholic population. Today, 40 percent of all Catholics reside in Latin America,[57] and the Catholic Church owns more real estate than any multinational corporation, and, further implicating male competition in all of this, genomic studies find a disproportionate contribution of European *male* genes across Latin American genome.[58] These feats of male mate competition would have been impossible with a doctrine espousing, say, the regular *use* of contraception.

The doctrine of *Manifest Destiny* offers another example of how religious and government powers have used fecundity to swarm the opposition. Manifest Destiny itself highly influenced the US government's expansionist policy during the conquest of America's western territories, which was a violent and protracted competition for territory with the natives already living there. In an 1845 article in the *Democratic Review*, where the term *Manifest Destiny* was first used, westward expansion was equated with "the fulfillment of our manifest destiny to overspread the continent allotted by Providence for the free development of our yearly multiplying millions" (here *Providence*, of course, referring to God's alliance). The "multiplying millions," however, referred specifically to reproduction for European immigrants. To put this bias into perspective, consider that when the US government's extermination of Native Americans ended, it took up the business of sterilizing Native American women by force throughout the reservation system.[59]

A contemporary example of conservative, conflict-based natalism comes from the *Quiverfull movement*, a small but rapidly multiplying anti-contraception conservative Christian group based primarily in America, Australia, and the United Kingdom, which claims its inspiration from an unequivocal Bible passage from Psalms:

Sons are indeed a heritage from the Lord, fruit of the womb a reward. Like arrows in the hand of a warrior are the sons of one's youth. Happy is the man who has his quiver full of them. He shall not be put to shame when he speaks with his enemies in the gate.[60]

Of one of the movement's leaders, Nancy Campbell, offers, "We look across the Islamic world and we see that they are outnumbering us in their family size, and they are in many places and many countries taking over those nations, without a jihad, just by multiplication" and that "the womb is such a powerful weapon; it's a weapon against the enemy."[61] Perhaps not surprisingly, most (if not all) Americans associated with this movement identify with the Republican Party.

Tying all of this back to political psychology, it follows that those with minds calibrated for male-centrism, higher xenophobia, and focusing on competition with the outside tribe for their place in the gene pool would be most opposed to contraception—an effective barrier to winning fitness competitions.

Indeed, this reason for anti-contraception politics was noticed by Margaret Sanger (1879–1966), a community nurse who became the first president of Planned Parenthood. Notes Sanger,

In every nation of militaristic tendencies, we find the reactionaries demanding a higher and still higher birthrate. Their plea is, first, that great armies are need to defend the country; second, that a huge population is required to assure the country its proper place among the powers of the world. . . . As soon as the country becomes overpopulated, these reactionaries proclaim loudly that it is their moral right to expand . . . and to take by force such room as it needs.[62]

Sanger's observations are borne out by history. Joseph Stalin, Adolf Hitler, Nicolae Ceausescu, and Idi Amin, all of whom killed rival groups en masse, also took specific measures to restrict or outlaw access to contraception and abortion, which sent birthrates skyrocketing.[63] Baby booms provide the human fodder that fuels authoritarian ambitions. We can see the purpose of creating population surges (of one's in-group) in the words of ethnocentrists in the modern day. For example, Steve King, a Republican congressman from Iowa, said in a CNN interview, "You cannot rebuild your civilization with somebody else's babies. You've got to keep your birth rate up, and that you need to teach your children your values. In doing so, you can grow your population, you can strengthen your culture, and you can strengthen your way of life."[64]

In short, conservative opposition to birth control is rooted in male mate competition. Not only does birth control stir fears of cuckoldry, but it also keeps populations smaller relative to the rival tribe, which has always been a grave concern of men, who are disproportionately targeted for killing by the invading hordes. However, while growing the tribe may temporarily provide security for one's own kind, there is a large body of research showing that it comes with costs—social instability and male violence.

ON THE BROADER DANGERS OF SEXUAL CONTROL

One of the most common manifestations of sexual control—limiting access to birth control—is increasingly recognized for the manner in which it fuels instability and violence by creating population surges. One major reason population booms are dangerous is that they increase the ratio of young men to women and older men. Malcolm Potts and Thomas Hayden offer an extensive review of how this ratio has been a robust predictor of greater violence, more frequent raiding, greater political instability, more incidence of genocide, and more warfare across history, cultures, and geography—from the conflict among the Mojave tribes in America to the lead-up to World War II in Germany to the enduring conflicts in the Middle East.[65]

This observation has also been put to the test empirically. Researchers Christian Mesquida and Neil Wiener of York University in Toronto quantified the magnitude of conflicts across the globe by tallying the number of fatalities they caused. In their study, the ratio of men aged fifteen to twenty-nine predicted *one-third* of all the variance in the number of total dead.[66] Other research has found similar trends in the United States, where homicide rates increase and decrease along with the relative proportion of men aged fifteen to twenty-nine.[67] Essentially, flooding a population with young men creates a societal powder keg, for reasons ultimately rooted in male mate competition.

Young men often enter the fields of mate competition with fewer resources to offer women, what behavioral ecologists call "embodied capital."[68] They must compete with older, more established higher-ranking men who control more resources, which women generally prefer in light of the costs of child-rearing. In fact, research finds that when male sex ratios are high, women *expect* men to spend more money on them in their mating efforts.[69] With young men facing these demands and the peril of being shut out of the mating game, violent risk-taking among young males has been an evolutionarily sensible strategy.[70] Not desirable, but effective, helping young men in acquiring scarce or monopolized resources, challenging the existing male dominance hierarchy, or raiding the rival clan. Young men in our past who couldn't take risks were more likely to become evolutionary dead ends. Today risk-taking and antisocial behaviors are strongly associated with being young and male across societies worldwide,[71] and men at their reproductive peak tend also to be most inclined to violence, a phenomenon known as *young male syndrome*.[72] In short, more balanced age ratios equal more balanced societies.

Most importantly, outlawing or restricting access to abortions or contraception creates population booms, which cause havoc when male baby boomers grow up to become violent sexual competitors. Conversely, across nations when abortions became legalized, crime rates dropped, including in the United States.[73] Despite the clear links between population swells and social instability, there are many on the right wing who resist the very notion of population control.

On Conservapedia.com, population control is dubiously pitted against one of the most ancient, fundamental survival imperatives—competition with other species: "Population control means reducing the human population of the earth, in favor of other species or to promote political or ideological goals (see eugenics). Population control is based on pseudoscience and ill-founded economic assumptions."[74]

Nonetheless, the danger of population surges is well understood by key sectors on the Right, notably among those with the highest pedigrees in national security. General Michael V. Hayden, former director of the NSA and CIA, identified rapid population growth as among the biggest threats to global security.[75] Similarly, as US ambassador to the United Nations, George H. W. Bush wrote of family planning: "Success in the population field, under United Nations leadership, may, in turn, determine whether we can resolve the great questions of peace, prosperity, and individual rights that face the world."[76] As a Republican congressman (before he too became director of the CIA), George H. W. Bush was nicknamed "Rubbers" for his advocacy of family planning but was forced to disavow these ties when he ran on Ronald Reagan's 1980 presidential campaign ticket as the vice presidential nominee.

In 1985, a string of Islamic terrorist hijackings, bombings, kidnappings, and deadly attacks at the Rome and Vienna airports brought back Rubbers's voice. The next year, as head of a task force on combating terrorism, Bush broke ranks and gave the following warning: "Fully 60 percent of the Third World population is under 20 years of age, half are 15 years or less. These population pressures create a volatile mixture of youthful aspirations that when coupled with economic and political frustrations help form a large pool of potential terrorists."[77]

It is also worth mentioning that Bush's father, Prescott Bush, was once the treasurer of Planned Parenthood (in 1947), an organization frequently in the crosshairs of US conservatives. This tie is believed to have cost him his first US Senate race in 1950, particularly in the heavily Catholic Connecticut where he ran.[78] Family planning is generally considered a signature concern of the Left, and the Left is often portrayed as being naïve about human nature and even soft on security. But Prescott was a Republican, a field artillery captain during World War I, and once wrote a piece in *Readers Digest* that suggested he well understood the power of primate threat displays: "To Preserve Peace Let's Show the Russians How Strong We Are."[79]

George H. W. Bush and Hayden's observations about the dangers of population surges have been strongly corroborated by other US military men; Generals Dwight D. Eisenhower, Al Haig, Colin Powell, and William Draper all voiced the importance of family planning to national security.[80] In addition, after 9/11 a commission was set up under George W. Bush to help us grasp the causes of the World Trade Center attacks. *The 9/11 Commission Report* was unequivocal on the issue of population control: "By the 1990s, high birthrates and declining rates of infant mortality had produced a common problem throughout the Muslim world: a large, steadily increasing population of young men without any reasonable expectation of suitable or steady employment—a sure prescription for social turbulence."[81]

The stabilizing power of contraceptives is further evinced by the fact that the most violent societies are those in which women are kept out of the political process to serve as reproductive machines. Excluding women not only allows male reproductive imperatives to maintain a monopoly on the political process but also tends to reinforce male-centric reproduction policies that are more likely to flood the population with volatile young males. The next chapter will explore female reproductive psychology and will examine what happens when women are allowed into the political arena.

CHAPTER 7

WOMEN, SEX, AND POLITICS

WHY WOMEN ARE MORE LIBERAL

The human brain is comprised of about one hundred billion neurons, with an estimated *one thousand trillion* intercommunicating synapses, leading scientists to posit that this stunning biological marvel may be the most complex entity in the universe. Human brains are unique in the animal world. Ours is the largest brain relative to body weight, and the most densely packed with neurons. Our outsized cortex is considered the seat of complex thought, and the cortex's comparatively mammoth frontal lobe is what allows higher-level functions such as logic, planning, judgment, self-control, and abstract thought—basically all the faculties that make homo sapiens (which means "wise man") uniquely human. Coming into existence with this organ was no small task.

One of the many challenges of growing an enormous brain was that our heads needed to safely pass through the birth canal. When humans began walking upright, the birth canal began narrowing, but at the same time the brain size began expanding. Various adaptations emerged, such as openings in the skull that allowed the head to compress at birth, and folds in brain tissue, which allowed greater surface area to fit within the confines of our skulls.

Another challenge was the time required to build this masterpiece organ. One solution was to start with the brain very early. Babies' head-to-body size ratios are enormous compared to adults, which shows that the size and complexity of the human brain requires developmental priority. But the brain is not nearly done cooking at birth, and this fact has exerted major pressure on the evolved political psychology of women.

Consider the difference between squirming, mute, immobile, utterly helpless human infants and a wildebeest calf that can outrun lions only hours after birth. Our protracted development has inspired researchers to describe human infants as *exterogestate fetuses*[1]—that is, in humans, the unfinished brain continues a stunning rate of development not in the womb but in the real world. In the first year alone, the human brain doubles in size, and it continues to grow and interconnect until we reach our midtwenties. Notably, the "external womb" is a precarious world filled with predators, disease, the threat of starvation, and enemy males prone to infanticide.

In short, human infants and their brains take an epic amount of time to develop, and this period is incredibly costly in terms of attention, nurturance, protection, and cultural input. Women's political psychology reflects strategies for securing these crucial investments. In turn, greater liberalism among women reflects the high demands of bringing the *wise man* into being as a walking, talking, thinking primate.

Liberalism and Long-Term Mating

In the classic 1953 film *Gentlemen Prefer Blondes*, Marilyn Monroe popularized the song "Diamonds Are a Girl's Best Friend." In the scene where she sings it, a cadre of admiring, well-dressed men surrounds her. At first the men swarm the lovely icon with heart-shaped cutouts. She rebukes them with smacks to the head, singing that she'd rather have a man who gives lavish jewelry. The men regroup and then follow her around the stage, competing to present her with collars bespeckled with massive, sparkling diamonds. This scene, among so many others, captures an intuitive, ageless dynamic between men and women, based on our reproductive biology.

A highly robust research finding is that women prefer men with resources. David Buss's international research, for example, has found that "women across all continents, all political systems (including socialism and communism), all racial groups, all religious groups, and all systems of mating (from intense polygyny to presumptive monogamy) place more value than men on good financial prospects. Overall women value financial resources about 100 percent more than men do."[2]

But men with resources are only as good as their willingness to share them. Research shows that women prefer generous (and altruistic) men,[3] and that this preference is ancient—for example, among hunter-gatherers, men who provide more meat to their clan have more sexual partners and younger (more fertile) wives.[4] In one telling study, researchers in the United Kingdom presented women with hypothetical scenarios.[5] In scenario 1, two people sitting by a river see a child being swept downstream and hear a mother screaming, "Help! Save my child." One man jumps into the river to save the child, the other does not. In scenario 2, two people walking through a town find a homeless person sitting near a café. One man goes into the café and then purchases the homeless person a sandwich and a cup of tea. The other man pretends to use his mobile phone and quickly skirts past the homeless person. As you might have guessed, women in this study expressed a preference for the men behaving altruistically—those who showed willingness to share food and to protect children. The preference for these men as *long-term* partners was particularly strong, and it is not difficult to see how the resource demands of our extended development would shape women's desire for kind and giving men.

What may not be as obvious are the underlying traits that potentiate empathy and sharing among men. Strikingly, research implicates male *femininity* and suggests that women may subconsciously "know" this. In one type of study, researchers digitally overlay photographs of men to create a composite image. From there the images are manipulated to appear either more masculine (e.g., wider jaws, more pronounced brow ridge, smaller lips) or more feminine (largely the opposite features). In one such study, women were asked which of the two faces they would prefer for a long-term versus short-term relationship. In the context of long-term relationships, women chose the "feminine" face more often.[6] Other studies using similar techniques have found that women were more likely to rate men with more feminine facial features as having higher "quality as a parent"[7] and as a "good father."[8]

Women's judgments appear to be right on. Testosterone shapes masculine facial features. The same hormone is responsible for aggression and sex drives, which have helped male primates violently compete for sex across our ancestral history. But fighting and womanizing are not particularly conducive to family life. Accordingly, research finds that testosterone levels are relatively high when men are single, but drop significantly when they get married and have children.[9] Another study used various questionnaires to gauge men's interest in babies. The researchers then measured participants' testosterone levels before and after watching a pornographic video. Men who expressed low interest in babies showed a higher testosterone increase after watching porn, whereas men who expressed higher interest in babies showed only slight increases, remained stable, or their testosterone actually dropped after watching porn.[10] These results suggest that high-testosterone men may be geared toward *mating effort*, and lower-testosterone men toward *parenting effort*.

Indeed, research has found that men with larger testicles and higher baseline levels of testosterone score lower on a questionnaire specifically designed to measure parental investment.[11] Having larger testes was also associated with less neural response to pictures of the men's own children while instructed to empathize with them, i.e., "try to share the emotions of the person in the picture." By contrast, fathers with lower testosterone experience *greater* sympathy to sounds of crying babies.[12]

To review, higher-testosterone men are less empathic, make poorer nurturers, share less,[13] and are better at enacting mating strategies that are short term, less invested, and ideally involve numerous sexual partners. Lower-testosterone men are more empathic, make better nurturers, and invest more in children.

The government, which has traditionally been run by men, has always played a role in determining how resources are dispersed. Given this role, it is perhaps not surprising to find that women's preferences for compassionate, sharing men are often mirrored by women's preference for provisioning policies, which are overwhelmingly championed by liberal politics. Research finds that women show greater support for social welfare and organized labor,[14] student loan programs, wage control, and minimum wage laws.[15] In the United States, women consistently prefer greater government spending than men on things like public schools, childcare, social security, welfare, aid to the poor, and food stamps.[16] While some of these preferences may be accounted for by women generally being more empathic than men—which generates greater support for what have been termed *domestic compassion policies*—many of these government programs tie directly into provisioning offspring. All of which underscore our hypothesis that liberal policies are rooted in female reproductive strategies, aimed at ensuring a nurturing environment for vulnerable offspring.

This hypothesis comes into greater focus when we consider research on politics among fathers. One study found that American fathers were more likely to support liberal policies such as pay equity, affirmative action, and subsidized day care *if they had only daughters*.[17] This relationship was not seen among fathers with only sons, which led the researchers to conclude that "when fathers have sons only, their commitment to patriarchy may strengthen to ensure their sons a piece of the patriarchal dividend." A similar pattern was found in the United Kingdom, where having daughters was associated with voting for left-wing parties, whereas having sons was associated with right-wing parties.[18]

The relationship between having daughters and supporting more liberal policies even holds true among lawmakers. One study examining voting records of US congressmen found that the more daughters congressmen had, the more likely they were to vote in support of liberal legislation, and this pattern held among Republicans as well as Democrats.[19] Tellingly, legislation in this study was grouped into seven topic areas: equal rights, safety, economic security, education, lesbian rights and health, and reproductive rights, including access to abortion and contraception. Among other fitness benefits, birth control allows women to choose when and with whom to reproduce. We learned in the preceding chapters how conservative opposition to birth control may benefit male genes. But for men with daughters, *support* of birth control can also benefit male genes—*those residing in their daughters*. Moreover, legislation supporting things like education and economic security benefits daughters in the long-term enterprise of raising human offspring. In other words, because we have a fitness incentive to favor strategies that benefit the fitness of our offspring, men with daughters tend to vote a lot more like women.

To summarize the key message here: (1) women prefer long-term mates and liberal political policies, both of which tend to contribute to the long-term enterprise of raising offspring; (2) liberalism in men is linked to feminine traits such as interest in babies, greater empathy, and lower testosterone, in keeping with our gendered brains hypothesis; and (3) men may shift to supporting more liberal policies when they have female offspring.

Indeed, as I explain below, both sexes may choose from a menu of reproductive strategies, depending on environmental conditions, which allows greater adaptability—an approach that evolutionary scholars have labeled *strategic pluralism*.[20] This adaptability explains why partisanship is not perfectly correlated with biological sex.

Liberalism, Resources, and Short-Term Mating

Access to resources not only helps women raise children but also to engage in short-term mating. Recall that a bountiful natural environment allows our bonobo cousins to be more egalitarian, female-oriented, and to eat and mate relatively freely with one another. Humans are also responsive to local ecology. In more politically liberal societies—where women have greater access to resources via paid maternity leave, paid childcare, and greater participation in the workforce—women also have greater sexual freedom to engage in short-term mating. As David Buss explains, "Where women control their economic fate, do not require so much of men's investment, and hence need to compete less, women are freer to disregard men's preferences. . . . Men everywhere might value chastity if they could get it, but in some cultures they simply cannot demand it from their brides."[21]

The scientific literature confirms this observation. In one US study, researchers analyzed economic factors across all fifty states and found that women's median income levels, and the amount of welfare benefits available to women, were *negatively* associated with both men and women viewing promiscuity as wrong.[22] In other words, where women have greater *direct* access to resources, both men and women were less likely to view women's sexual freedom as immoral. Conversely, the researchers concluded that when economic dependence on men is high, both sexes have an incentive to reinforce monogamy—for men, to avoid cuckoldry, and for women, to assure males of paternal certainty in order to avoid desertion.

In a much larger study, David Schmitt administered a questionnaire called the Sociosexual Orientation Inventory (SOI) to fourteen thousand men and women across forty-eight (developed and developing) nations.[23] The SOI measures *restricted* versus *unrestricted* sexuality, by asking questions like, "How many different partners do you see yourself having sex with in the next five years?" and "I would have to be closely attached to someone (both emotionally and psychologically) before I could feel comfortable and fully enjoy having sex with him or her." The inventory also includes a question on "extra-pair" mating (mating outside a committed relationship): "How often do (did) you fantasize about having sex with someone other than your current (most recent) dating partner?"

Tellingly, the study found that women across these many nations were more sexually open where there was a higher percentage of women in parliament, higher percentage of women-headed households, higher divorce rates, higher gender equality (as measured by the United Nations Gender Empowerment Measure, which assesses economic and political

equality between men and women), and more progressive sex role ideologies. Across the board, greater political, economic, and social freedom was
associated with less restrictive sexuality among women. These correlations
were less strong or were absent among men, who tended to be sexually open
regardless of political circumstance. These data suggest that when women
enjoy more economic and political equality—which translates to, among
other things, *greater access to resources*—they are less bound to male sexual
control, and may then be more likely to engage in short-term mating.

Conversely, Schmitt's study also found that environmental strain
leads women to adopt more sexually *restrictive* strategies. Across nations,
lower gross domestic product, higher child malnutrition, higher infant
mortality rate, lower birth weight, and lower life expectancy—all of
which suggest harsh environments with fewer resources to invest in child-
rearing—were associated with restricted sexuality among women. Overall,
the study showed that women shift toward a monogamous strategy as
environments become more demanding, and toward a less restrictive
strategy when environments are favorable. Here we can see again how
liberal policies like maternity leave, paid childcare, and equality in the
workplace can provide more favorable environments for women, and also
how women tend to trade short-term mating for a greater guarantee of
male support when environmental circumstances are grim.

But why would women want sexual freedom in the first place? While
most women tend to prefer long-term mating strategies, mating with
multiple males in the short term can increase a woman's fitness, sometimes in the context of an extramarital relationship. Among other benefits, short-term mating can secure immediate resources in direct exchange
for sex; produce children when a woman's mate is infertile; obscure paternity, which may secure investment from multiple males; and help women
gain access to better quality genes than those of their current partners,[24]
and provide women with genetic diversity.

But a key point in understanding women's evolved political psychology is that women tend to prefer different traits when selecting

short-term versus long-term mating partners. For example, in one study, women were presented with photos of an attractive man, with a description portraying qualities of a poor parent and poor cooperator:

> 5 inches taller than you. . . . Rainy weekends are great for reading up on pieces in his weapon collection. Sunny ones are best for playing rugby or rock climbing. Any time's great for jamming on guitars with the guys.[25]

Women were also shown an image of a less-attractive man described as a potentially good parent and good cooperator:

> 2 inches taller than you. . . . Likes carpentry, usually to build things for the house. Listening to live music in a pub with a close group of friends is also a favorite. Summer weekends are great for romantic walks on nearby trails and winter ones for downhill skiing.

Consistent with other studies, women were more likely to choose the taller, more attractive, less cooperative man over the shorter, less attractive, more cooperative man as an extra-pair mate, and the opposite for a long-term mate.

Another kind of short-term mating occurs in the context of extra-pair copulations. Research finds that when it comes to adultery, women tend to prefer masculine men, especially when they are ovulating.[26] This strategy has been observed in other social primates, such as female macaques and chimpanzees, who may mate with lesser males when less fertile, in order to confuse paternity, which would secure protection or favors such as grooming. These same females show a strong preference for dominant males when ovulating.[27]

Aside from the fitness benefits of resources and reproductive choices, liberal policies can also counterbalance the reproductive strategies of men when, by their own success, they begin to impinge on the strategies of women. Certainly both men and women have a reproductive interest in provisioning children, and in general, men and women work well together toward that enterprise—if they hadn't, we wouldn't have made it as a species. However, when given the opportunity, men will leverage sharing to impose sexual control.

For one, conservative men tend to prefer "traditional" households, where men are the primary breadwinners and women stay home to raise children. Accordingly, conservative men show less support of equal pay for women, paid maternity leave, and other resources that would promote financial independence from men. In ultraconservative societies, women are forbidden to work, and under Sharia law, the testimony of women counts half that of men in property cases, and women get half the inheritance as men.[28] All such policies ensure women's financial dependence on men, which men can use to secure women's submission to male reproductive goals—high birth rates and monogamy, the antithesis of short-term mating. As we have discussed before, these arrangements come at a far greater cost to women than to men.

Moreover, male financial control also creates economic disincentives for women who wish to leave them. In many social animals, including chimpanzees, the inability to leave a community—due to factors such as high risk of predation, violence from rival communities, or difficulty acquiring food—often forces physically weaker individuals to endure despotic relationships.[29] Rejecting liberal policies like equal pay, or social welfare, artificially creates environmental difficulties, whereas supporting such policies allows women economic independence from men, and a potential route of egress. Accordingly, we see the greatest opposition to divorce (a legal route of egress) in the most politically conservative societies. Recall too that in the prior chapter we explored the cruelties that are possible, including femicide, in societies where women are not allowed to leave their male "guardians." Divorce and social welfare, on the other hand, safeguard against the brutalities of male overcontrol by giving women alternate means to feed themselves.

In summary, women may adapt their reproductive strategy to environmental circumstances, as shaped by their access to resources, their current partnership status, and their own fertility. When women are economically dependent on men, they are more likely to engage in strict monogamy. When they have greater economic freedom, they may be more likely to mate with more males to increase genetic diversity. Thus the ideologies of conservatism and liberalism are aligned with specific mating strategies and also *create the conditions for them*. Conservative ideology places higher moral value on monogamy, while also encouraging policies that create greater economic dependence for women. Liberal ideology is less sexually restrictive, while also supporting policies that encourage greater social and economic equality, allowing women more freedom in their choice of partner(s).

Seen through the lens of evolutionary science, the utility of liberalism to the female reproductive mission is clear and parsimonious. Nurturing human infants through the construction of their wondrous brains requires a marathon of provisioning, which is served by liberal policies. Liberal policies also inhibit the tendencies of men to use violence, oppression, or financial control to privilege male-typical fitness goals (more mates, less provisioning) at the cost of female-typical ones (greater stability, more provisioning). They also allow women to acquire good genes and genetic variation. On the surface, conservatism might seem anathema to the female endeavor. In some instances it is, and in some cultures women are forced to either adopt or feign conservative values. However, other women are drawn to conservatism freely and with some enthusiasm. The coming section will explore some of the reasons *why*.

WHY ALL WOMEN AREN'T DEMOCRATS

Germs

Despite the fact that women tend to lean liberal,[30] clearly not all women are liberal—there are many millions of politically conservative women in the world today. While various factors influence conservatism among women, our evolved reproductive psychology lies at the heart of them. Across history, infectious disease has posed one of the greatest threats to child survival and, therefore, to successful transmission of genes to the next generation. The fight against microorganisms itself plays a role in women's mate selection.

Testosterone, which drives both dominance behaviors and the formation of masculine features, is also an immunosuppressant.[31] High testosterone, then, can signal not only physical prowess but also resistance to disease, another crucial marker of genetic fitness.[32] In other words, if you're able to maintain high levels of testosterone, your immune system has to be strong enough to fight off diseases even while hampered by excess testosterone. This strong immune system is a desirable trait for potential offspring. Research has found that germ resistance is something humans subconsciously look for in mates. For example, American psychologists Steven Gangestad and David Buss examined mate preference among men and women in twenty-nine cultures around the world.[33] They found that a higher prevalence of pathogens predicted greater emphasis on mates who were physically attractive, which suggests physical health. Tellingly, in another study Gangestad also found pathogen prevalence was *negatively* correlated with women's desire for attributes associated with greater parental investment: "dependable character," "pleasing disposition," "emotional stability and maturity," and "desire for home and children"— all characteristic of empathic, "feminine," lower-testosterone, liberal men, as we have been discussing.[34] This suggests that in high-pathogen environments, women may trade off parental investment for fit genes. A similar study of 186 societies found that higher-pathogen prevalence is associated with greater polygyny.[35] Researchers have argued this is evidence of women trading off *exclusive* parental investment for disease-resistant offspring.[36] Perhaps not surprising then, we see more polygyny practiced in the world's most male-oriented, most politically conservative societies. Finally, one large worldwide study (4,794 women across thirty countries) found that in nations with poorer health, as measured by various indices including death from communicable diseases, women preferred men with more masculine faces.[37] Microbes may be tiny, but their moral, sexual, and political influence is not.

Let's pause for a moment to briefly summarize the complex interplay between germs and our reproductive and political psychologies. As we discussed in chapter 2, germy environments drive conservatism—conservatives tend to be more germophobic and fearful of potential human vectors of disease. The further we move from high-pathogen environments, the more people show personality traits associated with political liberalism, such as sexual openness among women. Germ-ridden environments also can drive women's attraction to high-testosterone males. But seeking a high-testosterone mate comes at a cost: higher testosterone is also associated with lower parenting effort and higher likelihood of having multiple partners (including through polygyny), meaning that women in high-pathogen environments may exchange a degree of male investment for disease-resistant children. Women may also exert more sexual restraint in high-pathogen environments to avoid disease. Germs, in other words, fuel conservatism in women by multiple pathways—encouraging choice of higher-testosterone mates, giving disease-resistant males greater advantage in the mating market, and also by increasing monogamous sexual behavior.

Women and Their Male Alliances

Another font of women's conservatism is *female* mate competition. Women are increasingly bringing financial capital to the mating exchange. But women also bring genes, and fertility, including the physical attributes required to endure the high risks of pregnancy and childbirth. For most of our history, the most reliable route to assessing these assets in women has been physical appearance, which explains the relatively high value men place on good looks.[38] The fact that women use their beauty to compete for mates is uncontroversial. However, what is less known is that beauty among women often translates to political conservatism. Does this mean all conservative women are gorgeous or that all liberal women are not? Certainly not. But beauty and conservatism are linked nonetheless, and by competition.

In one study, researchers measured sex-typical features among congresswomen in the 111th US House of Representatives.[39] The researchers found that Republican congresswomen had far more feminine faces than Democratic counterparts—what became known as the *Michele Bachman* effect, after the attractive and feminine former Republican representative from Minnesota.[40] In addition, the researchers also discovered that the more feminine the congresswoman's face, the more conservative her voting record. Remarkably, the researchers also found that among faces that were previously rated as highly masculine or highly feminine, undergrads could *guess* congresswomen's political affiliation with high accuracy.

But what do we make of these findings? Why would feminine, attractive congresswomen be more conservative—or, conversely, why would women with masculine faces affiliate with liberal parties or support liberal policies? Research consistently finds that people belonging to ethnic or racial groups that hold more power, or those in higher socioeconomic classes, tend to endorse more favorable views of social inequality.[41] The idea is that if you have an advantage, you are inclined to support the conditions that help you maintain it. Research even finds that this effect can be experimentally manipulated—when subjects are assigned to a hypothetical economically advantaged group, they endorse higher social dominance orientation (SDO).[42]

Just as belonging to a privileged ethnic group or economic class can provide a competitive advantage, so can good looks. Research finds, for example, that "beautiful" men and women get hired faster, move up in the corporate ranks more, and make more money.[43] And so, as with money or power, people will use beauty to their advantage in competition. This sort of nature-driven opportunism translates into politically conservative ideology, which is generally positioned against redistribution and in preserving high rank status. Conversely, if you have fewer assets—whether power, social class, money, *or beauty*—you are more likely to support redistribution, share resources, and reject group-based hierarchies.[44]

In another study, subjects rated the attractiveness of both male and female politicians in Australia, the European Union, Finland, and the United States. Across this wide breadth of political cultures, politicians on the Right were rated as significantly more attractive than those on the Left.[45] This study also found that when information is limited, voters use beauty as a cue for candidates' political ideology and that voters will infer that more beautiful candidates fall more to the Right. In other words, we seem to know, instinctively, that beauty means conservatism, which may translate to "social dominance."

Indeed, one study found that both men and women who rate *themselves* as more attractive tend to score higher on SDO.[46] This relationship was also found when self-perceived beauty was manipulated. The researchers primed subjects' perception of their own attractiveness by having them write an essay recalling a time when they felt attractive or a time when they felt unattractive. Subjects primed to feel attractive were more likely to feel that they had more power, higher social class, and greater status, and they scored higher on SDO. In addition, these manipulations appeared to impact one's attitudes about economic inequality; subjects primed to feel attractive were more likely to claim dispositional reasons for inequality, such as "ability and skills," "money management," "hard work," "ambition," "talent," and "effort," whereas those primed to feel less attractive tended to claim contextual reasons, such as "economic policy," "prejudice and discrimination," "political influence," and "inheritance." Moreover, the researchers found that those primed to see themselves as more beautiful were less likely to donate to a hypothetical social equality movement.

So women's good looks translate to better-paying jobs, which may induce support for conservative policies that allow women to maintain their hierarchical advantage. But women's route to higher socioeconomic status doesn't always come by way of the job market—it may also come from wealthy men. Unequal pay for women, discrimination in the workplace, the absence of social services such as paid maternity leave or childcare, and the time and energy demands of child-rearing all may contribute to women choosing wealthy men as a route to acquiring resources. In such circumstances, rather than supporting liberal policies that benefit women, women may be inclined to support policies that benefit their husbands. Indeed, longitudinal research has found that after women get married, they tend to develop more socially conservative attitudes.[47] Marriage may lead to different voting habits as well, with married women tending to vote conservative more often than unmarried women.[48]

In many cases around the world, married women are influenced or coerced into adopting their husbands' conservative political views. But this is not the whole story. Research has found that married women tend to see their fate as less linked to that of other women, asking them questions such as, "Do you think that what happens generally to women in this country will have something to do with what happens in your life?"[49] In the words of our competitive biology, when women form alliances with men in the context of marriage, the politics they espouse may shift toward those based on male alliances (i.e., conservatism), sometimes at the expense of single women, who may have a greater incentive to lobby for resource redistribution. Once again, attractiveness connotes good genes, which have bargaining power.

But the demands of child-rearing, disease, and female mate competition have not been the only pressures shaping the political psychology of women. Women have also had to contend with male violence. Men have developed groupish, hierarchy-favoring, authoritarian psychologies in order to contend with the tyranny of outside males—men who would gladly kill them and sexually enchain their wives and daughters. But the same psychologies also evolved to perpetrate such tyrannies. The resulting cycles of war and oppression have in turn shaped the political psychology of women. In many ways, women's political psychology reflects efforts to survive the maelstrom that male competition has always been.

Sexy Sons: How Women Can Love a Despot

Donald Trump has had a complex relationship with women, and one that has left mouths agape across the political spectrum. In January 2017, millions of women in the United States marched in the streets to protest Trump's election, fearing he and the Republican-led Congress posed a credible threat to reproductive, civil, and human rights. Millions of women around the globe joined the march in solidarity. Throughout the campaign that preceded his election, Trump's history with women was also a bone of contention. Adding to the groping, and trying to bed married women, in a 1991 interview with *Esquire* magazine, Trump said of the media, "You know, it doesn't really matter what [the media] write as long as you've got a young and beautiful piece of ass." In an interview with *New York Magazine*, Trump said of women, "You have to treat them like shit!"[50]

Trump's ownership of the Miss Universe and Miss USA pageants also drew scrutiny. For instance, in a radio interview with Howard Stern, Trump bragged that he used his high status to gain entrance to contestant dressing rooms while they were naked: "You know they're standing there with no clothes. Is everybody OK? And you see these incredible looking women. And so I sort of get away with things like that."[51]

One of the contestants, Tasha Dixon, who was eighteen years old at the time, complained that Trump's employees pressured the girls to "fawn over him, go walk up to him, talk to him, get his attention" before fully dressing. Dixon told CBS that she believed Trump owned the pageant for so long (nineteen years) because he could "utilize his power around beautiful women" and that there was no one above him to make him stop.[52] Alicia Machado, the Miss Universe 1996 pageant winner, complained that Trump continually demeaned her about her ethnicity and weight, calling her "Miss Housekeeping" and "Miss Piggy." Twenty years later during the 2016 campaign, Machado said, "This man behaved like a tyrant when I was Miss Universe and has behaved like a potential despot during this campaign."[53]

There have been far different reactions to Trump. For one, he won 42 percent of the women's vote,[54] and for many women Trump had a mesmerizing draw. As one example, before the 2016 election, an NBC reporter interviewed two women at a Trump rally in Novi, Michigan, both wearing pink T-shirts reading, "Trumpette." The reporter asked the Trumpettes to weigh in on Trump's history with Machado. One replied, "It doesn't matter. She got overweight. It's true. He wasn't lying." The other woman added, "So we finally have this god who's going to come down and help us all." Seeming incredulous, the reporter replied, "You just referred to Trump as a god." Smiling, she responded, "Yes, he is. Well, like she just said, *Jesus, then Trump.*"[55] How can some women see men like Trump as despots while others see them as gods? Once again the answer may lie in our genes.

In 1930, British biologist Ronald Fisher realized that, across the animal kingdom, females choose mates whose genes would produce male offspring with the greatest potential for reproductive success, sons who in turn would deliver the most copies of her genes into the gene pool (for all the reasons we've discussed, male offspring have an exponentially larger potential to disperse genes than female offspring).[56] This became known as the *sexy son hypothesis*. A common example is the male peacock, which drags a weighty, enormous, but brilliantly iridescent tail plume behind him. The ability to maintain such a costly display signifies good health, which peahens prefer. If the peahen chooses the male with the most impressive plume, she is more likely to have impressively plumaged, sexy sons. Her future sons are more likely to be successful in mate competition, attracting peahens with their sexy tails and passing on her genes in turn.

"Sexy sons" provide a fitness advantage to female humans as well. This advantage may explain the seeming paradox of how some women may deify Trump, despite his unsavory track record with women. First, mate competition requires dispensing with rivals. Research has found that during the most fertile phases of their menstrual cycles, women tend to prefer men displaying competitive behaviors, such as derogating their rivals.[57] Recall that Trump called his competitors, variously, "pussy," "little Marco," and "weak" on live television.[58] Also during the fertile phase, women rate the odors of men scoring high on measures of social dominance as more arousing and more masculine.[59] Research also finds that women who rate their partners as being dominant have more frequent and sooner orgasms,[60] a pattern associated with greater sperm retention,[61] which may suggest a similar sort of "alpha son" effect in which domineering men would on average produce more competitive male offspring. In this light, Trump's braggadocio, while repellent to many women, may suggest future fitness in male mate competition.

Because successful male mate competitions involve acquiring females, for some women Trump's womanizing may also be viewed as a sign of fitness. *Mate copying* is a widely observed pattern among nonhuman animals in which females prefer males who have previously mated, and reject males that other females have rejected.[62] Research has consistently found similar patterns among humans,[63] with mate copying more pronounced in women.[64] Studies also show that women rate photographs of men who are surrounded by women as more attractive than photographs of men who are alone,[65] and that women's attraction to men increases when they are seen with attractive women.[66] And so, Trump's association with models and beauty contestants, his multiple wives, and all his other womanizing behaviors may convey signals of great interest to female reproductive psychology. The brutal truth of nature is that mating with a womanizing man has the potential to produce womanizing sons with a greater capacity to pass on a woman's DNA. Mating with a dud, however, runs the risk of producing sexually timid, awkward, or otherwise unappealing sons ill-equipped to pass on a woman's genes.

However disturbing it is to ponder, similar evolutionary fitness advantages have been suggested of sexually aggressive men. Female sexual resistance has been examined as a strategy for mate selection among nonhuman species.[67] The idea is that males who demonstrate high motivation for sex by pushing past some degree of sexual resistance may have

SEX, POWER, AND PARTISANSHIP

a selective advantage to be passed on to their sons. American psychologist Linda Mealey has put forward the possibility that "male coercive sexuality is actually selected through the process of female choice." She goes on to propose that whatever traits led to this form of mate choice among women would be passed on to daughters, which would benefit their fitness as well. Continues Mealey,

> Evidence that this form of selection might occur in humans rests in the fact that an identifiable minority of women (women labeled "hyperfeminine" based on their scores on personality and sex roles questionnaires) are specifically attracted to "macho" and "sexually coercive men."

Canadian psychologist Martin Lalumiére further explains how a trait for sexual coerciveness might persist:

> Compared with other women, those who preferentially mated with men who exhibited the ability to overcome some degree of female resistance had more offspring, who also had more offspring than other women; and therefore the tendency for women to "test" their potential sexual partners became widespread in the population.

Importantly, Lalumiére goes on to note,

> The hypothesis really says little about the subjective feelings of women when doing the testing. Finally, even if this testing sometimes occurs, it remains absolutely appropriate for society to legally and morally proscribe the use of sexual coercion and force by men.

Of course, Lalumiére is correct—even if there were evidence for this kind of mate testing among humans, it would in no way suggest that it is somehow morally acceptable for men to ignore sexual boundaries. But this dynamic could at least partially explain why a man who bragged of grabbing women "by the pussy" without consent, forcing his way into women's dressing rooms, and trying to sleep with married women could garner such a large percentage of women voters.[68]

By this same dark logic, taken to its fullest extreme, females also stand to gain from mating with infanticidal males, even after those males kill their offspring. The evidence for this conclusion is worth repeating here, if only to show how deeply the psychology of women seems to have been shaped by the selective pressure of violent male mate competition.

Like our chimpanzee cousins, our species' past was characterized by frequent, savage regime changes, and our female ancestors were pressured to adapt to these changes. Many mammals, numerous monkey species, all the great apes, and humans are all known to commit infanticide. This is almost exclusively a male behavior, and it most commonly occurs during takeovers. As we've already discussed, males stand to gain by killing off potential competitors to their offspring. Killing them sends females into estrus more quickly, and also removes the males' offspring's potential competitors from the gene pool. This is startling but effective evolutionary logic.

In the 1950s, Hilda Margaret Bruce discovered that pregnant mice will spontaneously abort fetuses upon exposure to outside males.[69] The *Bruce Effect*, as this phenomenon became known, has also been found to occur in other animals, including nonhuman primates, when a new male overthrows the reigning alpha.[70] The most common explanation for this effect is that in species where females risk infanticide by usurper males, spontaneous abortion allows females to avoid investing precious time and energy in offspring with a high likelihood of being killed.[71]

Research has found a significant *male* birth decline in humans in times of stress, such as periods of economic downturns or collapse, or war.[72] More recent male birth declines have allowed researchers to identify causes. For example, there were significant declines in male births across the United States after the 9/11 attacks, and research has tied those declines to an increase in the deaths of male fetuses.[73] We humans have a long history in which male children have been killed in human warfare, whereas female children were taken as spoils. Jettisoning male fetuses, then, while costly, is less costly than pouring resources into a male infant likely to be murdered.

The takeaway message is that women's reproductive biology is tied to the vicissitudes of living among violent males. The ugly math of evolution, driven by the violent history of our species, has imparted women with the capacity to, under the right circumstances, opt for womanizing, sexually aggressive, or even infanticidal males. The high and bloody stakes of male competition have forced that preference.

Rape Fears

Getting raped comes at fitness cost to women, particularly those made pregnant by rape. Researchers Sandra Petralia and Gordon Gallup have enumerated those costs: "(1) inability to exercise mate choice, (2) lack of provisioning and protection by the father, (3) possible abandonment or punishment by her current mate, and (4) reduced likelihood of attracting future mates."[74]

Rape by out-group males appears to have been common enough in our ancestral history that today women's rape fears are linked to fear of outside men. And so another path to women's conservatism may be the same path as for men—xenophobia.

One study by American anthropologist Carlos Navarette and his colleagues presented white women with a scale designed to measure fear of being raped; it included agreement on statements such as, "I am wary of men," and "I am afraid of being sexually assaulted."[75] The researchers also presented scales measuring race bias and fear of out-group men—e.g., "Black men are dangerous." The researchers then gave subjects an identical version of the out-group men scale but replaced "black men" with "white men, white women, and black women." The researchers found that black men were more fear inducing than the other demographic categories, and that fear of being raped uniquely explained fear of black men. Also revealing, one study found that during the fertile phase of their cycles, women showed more unconscious bias against an outside race, rated men from an outside race more frightening than men from the in-group, and rated out-group men as less attractive.[76]

Another study found that the impulse to avoid out-group rape is so strong that it extends to arbitrary, meaningless group differences. In this study, women who filled out a rape fear questionnaire were randomly assigned to either a red, blue, or yellow group, and wore corresponding colored T-shirts. The researchers then digitally enhanced a photo of an attractive man to include either a red, blue, or yellow border. The women chatted online with confederates posing as the attractive man, who, following a script, asked the women on a date. When fertile, women with high rape fear were less likely to date men from a different-color category. Interestingly, rape fear was positively associated with willingness to date the "in-group" member.[77]

How can this fear translate into political stances? Ann Coulter, a hardline conservative political commentator, offers one striking example. Coulter has gained a rather notorious reputation for her racially charged comments, as well as her enthusiasm for attacks on the out-group—after 9/11, for example, she suggested, "We should invade their countries, kill their leaders and convert them to Christianity."[78] Coulter also wrote a book about Donald Trump. With a play on the maxim "In God We Trust," Coulter titled her book *In Trump We Trust*.[79] In an interview, she disclosed that Trump's alpha god status stems from a single issue—his protection from rape by outsiders: "My worship for him is like the people of North Korea worship their Dear Leader—blind loyalty. Once he gave that Mexican rapist speech, I'll walk across glass for him. That's basically it."[80]

Coulter's writing suggests high rape fear. In Coulter's earlier book, *Adios America: The Left's Plan to Turn America into a Third World Nightmare*,[81] she argued that "America is just bringing in a lot of rapists." The book is full of references to "Latin American rape culture" and "the gusto for gang rape, incest and child rape of our main immigrant groups." She even writes, "The rape of little girls isn't even considered a crime in Latino culture" and "Another few years of our current immigration policies, and we'll all have to move to Canada to escape the rapes." Sidling next to Trump, in the context of Coulter's rape fears, then, makes sense, since she perceives him as a strong man who can protect her from what she perceives as threats from an out-group.

The impulse to seek the protection of alpha males is old and observable not just in Ann Coulter but also among other female primates. For example, primatologist Frans de Waal reported of chimpanzees that "a female who is feeling threatened may run to the most dominant male and sit down beside him, whereupon the attacker will not dare proceed."[82] Primatologist Barbara Smuts reported female savanna baboons will befriend and offer sex to males who protect them and their offspring.[83]

It should be no surprise, then, that women tend to be attracted to larger, more physically formidable men, particularly in the fertile phase of their menstrual cycle.[84] These men would likely be more able to provide protection. Studies have also found that women prefer men with light facial scars,[85] which suggests a fighting history, and soldiers, particularly if the soldier had won a medal of honor for bravery in combat, the most brutal form of competition between rival males.[86] In this light, Donald Trump's boisterous promise to protect against rape has ancient, emotionally intuitive appeal that may have drawn in xenophobic females.

WOMEN IN GOVERNMENT

Before we explore the choices women make when they govern, it is worth remembering that men have historically blocked women from the political process. It was only recently that women were allowed a voice in US politics—the Nineteenth Amendment to the Constitution, which granted women equal voting rights, was ratified in 1920. In other parts of the world, women's suffrage was granted far later. Waiting until 2015, Saudi Arabia was the last nation to give women the right to vote.

This comparatively limited tenure in the political world has constrained our time frame to empirically examine how women govern. Moreover, women are often expected to assimilate to the traditionally masculine political cultures they join. These social pressures may obscure women's true political nature. Yet what we have learned in recent years about women in government is consistent with evolutionary theory.

There is a notorious trope that if you ever go to prison, the first thing you need to do is go up to the biggest, meanest-looking inmate and punch him in the face. In starting this fight, you establish a place in the prison hierarchy. This advice seems to show a keen understanding of primate psychology. In the brutal world of male hierarchies, men will fight for rank, and if you are pegged as weak, you risk being forced down to the very lowest rung on the ladder. In prison, as in the chimpanzee troop, this is assuredly not where you want to be.

In a similar vein, scholars have observed that women entering political leadership positions often display excessive hawkishness, which may help to establish themselves within the male primate hierarchy that politics has always been. US secretaries of state Madeline Albright and Hillary Clinton, and British prime ministers Margaret Thatcher and Theresa May, and Indian prime minister Indira Gandhi, among others, all gained reputations for a hawkish male style in dealing with other states. When we recall that women politicians may dress in a manner that makes them appear "broad-shouldered," we can begin to appreciate the value of primal strength displays within the ranks of male primates. We can also see why female leaders may at times adopt strategies that seem more similar to men's.

But most other times, women across all levels of society are less hawkish. A large body of research shows that women citizens are less likely to support the use of military force.[87] Perhaps not surprising, then, research has found that when the ratio of women in legislatures increases, *nations* are less likely to use military force to solve conflicts with other nations.[88] In one study, researchers examined defense spending and conflict behavior of twenty-two nations over a thirty-year span (between 1970 and 2000) and made a number of interesting findings.[89] First, as the number of women legislators increased, nations were less likely to engage in an extensive list of conflict behaviors with other nations, such as threats, sanctions, demands, or actual military engagements. The researchers also calculated Right-Left orientation of nations based on the percentage of government seats that parties held. As we might expect, Right-oriented nations spent more on defense overall. But as the percentage of women legislators increased, defense spending decreased. This decrease occurred at the same rate across nations that were Right-oriented, such as the United States, and those that were Left-oriented, such as Norway, and the results were quantifiable. For example, in 2000, every 1 percent increase in women legislators in the United States produced a $314 million reduction in defense spending (out of $311 billion in total military spending that year). Similarly, a 1 percent increase in women legislators in Norway saw a $3.34 million decrease (out of $3.3 billion that year).

The study also found that when women were in chief executive (or ministers of defense) positions, there was an *increase* in defense spending and conflict behavior with other nations, demonstrating the compulsory hawkishness noted above. However, when there were more women legislators, women chief executives were *less* likely to spend money on defense or engage in conflict behavior. Surrounded by men, which is often the case for women executives, women may be pressured to display their toughness. But when bolstered by the presence of other women, women may feel less obligated to play by male rules. These findings suggest that if women were freer to behave politically according to their evolved inclinations, the gap between the political behaviors of men and women would broaden.

Rwanda offers a case study of women in control of government. In 1994, Hutu tribesmen took to the streets to slaughter rival Tutsis with machetes, bashing them with clubs, seizing Tutsi land, and raping an estimated 250,000 women. Over a short one hundred days, more than 800,000 Rwandans lay dead, most of them hacked to pieces.[90] In the end, Hutus more than tripled the death toll wrought by American atomic bombs in Japan during World War II, using cheap, Chinese-made machetes. One result of this blot on humanity was a population comprised of over 70 percent women. In the years following the genocide, women began filling the power vacuum left by their dead men, and by 2008 Rwanda became the first nation in history to have a female majority in parliament.[91]

The shift of power to women resulted in laws to limit male sexual control. Domestic violence became illegal, and harsh prison sentences were legislated for rape. Further, birth rates and maternal mortality dropped, doors were opened for women to own land and open bank accounts, daughters were allowed to inherit property, and the percentage of women in the labor force surged. In 2009, the women-led government mandated basic education for all Rwandan children.[92] In 2016, the World Economic Forum's *Global Gender Gap Report* ranked Rwanda fifth in the world on gender equality (again, the United States ranks forty-fifth).[93]

Before male competition destroyed 20 percent of Rwandan males, it oppressed Rwandan women. In the years leading up to the massacre, women lived under patriarchal control. Women's property ownership was practically unheard of, literacy among women was low, and maternal mortality was high. Evolutionary science suggests there is an important lesson to learn here—namely that much of the suffering that humans force on one another, whether oppression or genocide, can be attributed ultimately to male mate competition.

But a population of men need not be decimated to improve conditions for women. Scandinavian countries, which do exceptionally well at gender equality—Iceland, Finland, Norway, and Sweden show the greatest gender equality on the World Economic Forum's *Global Gender Gap Report*—use quotas for women. Norwegian law, for example, requires that all public companies listed on the Norwegian stock exchange must appoint boards that include at least 40 percent women. The same goes for state-owned companies.[94] These countries tend to score high on a large number of measures of societal health, such as life expectancy at birth, years of education, gross national income per capita, gross domestic product, crime, literacy, healthcare, rate of university enrollment, years of education, and political stability.[95]

A clear conclusion of the scientific literature is that when women are allowed greater political and economic power, which is inseparable from the power to control their own reproduction, quality of life measurably improves for everyone. Affording that power requires placing thoughtful limits on male reproductive drives, which too often result in violence and oppression. This empirical observation is in direct contrast to foundational cultural doctrines that portray women's sexual agency as the cause of the world's misfortunes, as the story of Eve, who dared taste forbidden fruit. Once we see that those stories are based on male mate competition, a path to more stable human societies comes into greater focus.

CHAPTER 8

ON BLIND TRIBES AND BECOMING SIGHTED

A critical understanding of our political orientations requires that we envision an existence that predates our own. Our distant ancestors made their living directly from a hostile and uncertain natural environment. As relatively small, slow, weak, naked apes, with limited technology, their survival was far more at the mercy of nature than ours today. The basic necessities of life were often scarce, and between-group competition for resources was savage, in ways that most of us can only imagine. Because of their greater size, strength, and aggression, men were often tasked with securing scarce resources for the tribe, which they regularly won through the instrumental violence of male coalitions. Above and beyond any risk of starvation or attack, evolution's pitiless algorithms have imparted males with fitness incentives to massacre men from the rival group, capture their women, and commandeer their territory. This was the game of living in the days of our predecessors. And the pressures of living this way gave the rest of the clan fitness incentives to promote the tribe's interests and to support the groupish, aggressive males at its ruddy spearhead. Clearly it is better to be on the giving than the receiving end of intergroup raids, and in such a treacherous environment, a psychological bias favoring the in-group would have its advantages. Such were the dynamics that gave modern humans our ancient tribalistic psychology and its contemporary expression through political parties.

While today most of us aren't presented daily with the life-or-death reality of needing one another, the urgency to turn inward to the group has been so essential that today our in-group biases can be irrational, sometimes taking primacy over our stated ideologies, our self-interest, or even our deepest moral principles. It is of great concern that our in-group biases blind us to corrective information and present barriers to rationally examining our political choices, for at their worst those blinders can turn a functioning society against itself.

BLINDNESS

Psychological researchers have demonstrated that we are far from natural Bayesian reasoners—that is, rational thinkers who start off with a hypothesis, then update our level of acceptance or rejection of that hypothesis based on incoming evidence. Rather, our thinking is clouded by an expansive array of biases that distort external reality. Of particular interest for political psychology is a kind of bias called *motivated reasoning*—the tendency to use reasoning strategies, such as rebutting factual information (simply ignoring it), in order to arrive at a prior or emotionally preferred conclusion. Typically, this evading of information to self-delude is performed outside of conscious awareness, and is used to fend off negative emotions.

A growing body of research is revealing that voters' decisions to support a given candidate or policy descend easily into the fog of motivated reasoning.[1] Instead of updating one's position upon receiving new information, the voting populace deflects information in order to support emotionally preferred political stances. Indeed, research suggests that Donald Trump may have been onto something, figuratively speaking, when at a campaign rally in Iowa during the 2016 run for president he bragged, "I could stand in the middle of Fifth Avenue and shoot somebody and I wouldn't lose any voters."[2]

In one study conducted before the 2004 US presidential election, researchers presented highly partisan Republican and Democratic subjects with (partly fictional or edited) scenarios depicting either George

W. Bush or John Kerry clearly contradicting their prior positions.[3] For instance, a quote attributed to George W. Bush about Enron—an energy company run by CEO Kenneth Lay that became synonymous with corporate corruption when in 2001 its fraudulent financial practices were revealed—read,

> First of all, Ken Lay is a supporter of mine. I love the man. I got to know Ken Lay years ago, and he has given generously to my campaign. When I'm President, I plan to run the government like a CEO runs a country. Ken Lay and Enron are a model of how I'll do that.

These quotes were followed by contradictory stances, such as, "Mr. Bush now avoids any mention of Ken Lay and is critical of Enron when asked." Following this information, the researchers had subjects rate how much they felt the candidates had contradicted themselves and how much they agreed with an exculpatory statement. For example, "People who know the President report that he feels betrayed by Ken Lay, and was genuinely shocked to find that Enron's leadership had been corrupt." Perhaps not surprisingly, the researchers found that both liberal and conservative subjects were less likely to agree that their candidate self-contradicted, and more likely to agree that the rival candidate did. They were also more likely to agree with statements that gave their preferred candidate a pass on his inconsistency. However, what is even more interesting about this study is that it was conducted in an MRI machine. The researchers found that while engaging in motivated reasoning, subjects' brains were not activated in the regions associated with "cold" reasoning, or reasoning relatively free from emotional content, but in those parts associated with processing the experience of punishment, pain, fear, and the appraisal of threatening information.

One real-world example of motivated reasoning occurred when in 2018 it was revealed that Donald Trump had an affair with porn star Stormy Daniels shortly after his third wife, Melania, gave birth to their son, and that Trump (or, reportedly, his attorney) paid Daniels $130,000 to keep her quiet. Instead of rebuking Trump for so flagrantly violating such an assortment of cherished Christian values, Evangelicals widely gave Trump a pass.[4] Even Tony Perkins—head of the Family Research Council, an Evangelical nonprofit that has spoken out against the human papillomavirus (HPV) vaccine on the basis that it gives women license to engage in premarital sex,[5] and suggested to the Justice Department that the availability of pornography in hotels violates obscenity laws[6]— said only, "All right, you get a mulligan [a golf reference, where a player is allowed to replay a stroke]. You get a do-over here."[7]

It is easy to see the moral hypocrisy in such scenarios without fully appreciating its underlying psychology. Here is where evolutionary theory can help us make better sense of our political biases. Motivated reasoning is a way to avert threatening emotions. A basic evolved function of emotions is to mediate our interactions with the environment. For example, if we see a poisonous snake, we may experience fear, which helps us to avoid being bitten. The problem with relying on emotional reasoning, however, is that the emotion centers of our brain are ancient, often outdated, and prone to false-positive appraisals. As noted in chapter 2, snake phobias persist at relatively high base rates even in environments where the probability of encountering a poisonous snake is practically nil.

But here the fear is not about snakes. The fear-driven motivated reasoning we see in politics is all too often tied to the instinctive need for tribal belonging. In the days of our distant ancestors, being rejected by the group would have been a death sentence. To put the need for the group into perspective, imagine how long it would take for the ravages of nature to kill you if you were dropped off naked and alone in the middle of the Serengeti. Moreover, the unity of the tribe was also necessary to survive other tribes. But today we carry our tribalistic psychology over into politics, despite living in increasingly interconnected societies in which insular thinking has arguably become more of a liability than an asset. And we have known for some time that group thinking can distort basic realities.

In a classic 1951 study, social psychologist Soloman Asch showed us just how much our brains can be influenced to conform to group consensus.[8] Working in the aftermath of World War II, when much of the world was struggling to make sense of how ordinary people could have perpetuated the horrors of the Holocaust, Asch became interested in understanding the impact of social pressure to conform. He ran an experiment based on a visual task, presenting subjects with two cards. On the first card there was one black line. On the second card there were three black lines, one of which was obviously the same size as the line on the first card, the other two obviously different. The subjects' task was to match the line on the first card according to length with one of the three on the second card. Easy enough.

But at this point, Asch sat eight men in a circle. Seven of those men were confederates instructed to *match up the wrong lines*. Asch arranged for the real subject in this experiment to always rate last, which meant that he was regularly put in the position of having to directly contradict the seven men before him. What Asch found is that while a majority of subjects (68 percent) responded correctly in the face of confederate mismatching, an astonishing percentage (32 percent) did not. When interviewed afterward, some "independent" subjects explained the social pressure to conform: "I do not deny that at times I had the feeling: 'to go with it, I'll go along with the rest.'" One conforming subject replied, "I suspected about the middle [line]—but tried to push it out of my mind." Asch concluded that those who understood they were wrong yielded due to an overwhelming need to not appear different or defective in the eyes of the group. Remarkably, a minority of the conforming subjects was completely unaware that the confederates' answers were incorrect.

Importantly, Asch's findings suggest that conformity can be an unconscious impulse and that it can blind us to reality. His work also shows how at other times conformity may arise as a result of emotional pressure, all of which suggest that conforming to the group may have been important to survival in our evolutionary past. More research shows how our tribal blinders extend seamlessly into our political identities, and how easily we dispense with our deeply held convictions in order to belong.

For example, in one study, researchers presented highly partisan liberals and conservatives with two fabricated newspaper reports on welfare programs.[9] One "program" was exorbitantly generous for the time, offering families with one child eight hundred dollars per month, two hundred dollars for every additional child, housing and daycare subsidies, job training, two years' paid tuition at a community college, and two thousand dollars' worth of food stamps. Another program, far more stringent than the first, was also presented to subjects—$250 monthly, fifty dollars for each additional child, partial medical insurance, and an eighteen-month limit with no possibility of reinstating aid. The researchers queried which of the programs subjects supported. Given what we have learned, you may already have some ideas about who supported which policy. However, before subjects rated their support, they were either told that House Republicans (or Democrats) strongly endorsed either of the two welfare policies (they were also told that the rival party rejected the policy). What the researchers found was that if subjects believed their political tribe supported the policy, they too supported it, even when it went against the well-established ideological stances of their respective party and presumably their own. In other words, liberals tended to support the stringent welfare policy if they believed House Democrats backed it, and conservatives supported the lavish welfare policy when told House Republicans backed it. Another experiment in the same study found that after presenting subjects with similar scenarios, and getting similar results, subjects reported believing that their own perspectives on government influenced them the most and that the perspectives of the lawmakers influenced them least, despite going with the group in a way that so obviously countered their values. Put more simply, the subjects were blind to their own tribalistic blindness.

Once again, ancient dangers shape contemporary fears, and the primeval risks of alienating the tribe underlie our contemporary political stance-taking. Conversely, conforming to group norms and behaviors demonstrates loyalty to the group, facilitates cooperation, and serves to inoculate against rejection by one's own clan. Essentially, our fraught history living in violently competing tribes makes it feel good to go with the group and terrible to go against it. Moreover, there appears to have been an advantage in such a lifestyle to blocking out information that would jeopardize our standing in the group, however factual, and to simply going with the momentum of the clan, however corrupt. However, it is fair to say that anytime an edifice of civilization has collapsed from the inside, our insular tribalistic psychology played a central role in eroding its pillars. But are there solutions? Does education hold the key? Let us consider this possibility.

HOW FEAR TRUMPS KNOWLEDGE

The relationship between education and partisanship is a complex one, but one of tremendous import. On the surface, one might think that the more education one receives, the more informed and rational one's choices will become. But in many cases, the rational parts of the mind that education nourishes remain under the control of primal, fear-based survival impulses, even when instilled with a greater volume of knowledge. To examine this dynamic, let us consider the ongoing debate in America over climate change.

Global Warming

First, let us acknowledge straightaway that global warming is a reality with virtually unanimous consensus in the scientific community, and that humans are accelerating global warming through the emission of greenhouse gases such as carbon dioxide, methane, and nitrous oxide. Statistical climate predictions project an extended array of extreme weather phenomena: rising global temperatures, increased droughts, heat waves, desert expansion, rising sea levels, heavy rains, flooding, and hurricanes. Species extinction is also predicted, along with mass human migration from shorelines. If unabated, global warming is also predicted to diminish crop yields, threatening food security and resulting in societal unrest as humans compete for resources.

Given conservatives' overall greater threat sensitivity, one might expect broad and impassioned acceptance of climate change on the political Right. But this is demonstrably not the case. In 2008, Pew Research, for example, found that despite near universal scientific consensus among the world's climate experts that global warming is caused by human activity, there was a deep divide in agreement on the subject between Republicans (27 percent) and Democrats (58 percent).[10] Even more striking was the fact that the *more* educated Republicans were, the *less* they believed in climate change, and that the opposite trend was seen among Democrats; among non-college-educated Republicans, 31 percent agreed with the scientific consensus, whereas that number dropped down to 19 percent among Republicans with a college degree. Among non-college-educated Democrats, 52 percent agreed, and that number bumped up to 75 percent among college-educated Democrats.

Another study, looking at nearly a decade of Gallup poll data between 2001 and 2010, found similar results—liberals were more likely than conservatives to agree with the scientific consensus on climate change. This study also found that more education, and higher reported self-understanding of climate change, was associated with greater belief in global warming. But only among liberals. Once again that relationship was either negligible or negative for conservatives,[11] and other studies find this very same negative correlation.[12] These paradoxical results call to mind the words of historian Daniel Boorstin: "The greatest obstacle to discovery is not ignorance—it is the illusion of knowledge."[13]

But how do we acquire illusory knowledge, and how do we make sense of these data? How is it that Americans on the more fearful end of the natural curve are so prone to rejecting global scientific consensus on an issue that portends danger? And why is this more prevalent among the better educated? *Tribalism*—the pull to go with the group is the single best explanation for all these questions. So deep is the impulse to turn to the group when threatened that, faced with the dangers of climate change, the more ardent tribalists among us will make that turn even when the tribe offers no real protections but only simple, group-level denial. Among those with a greater in-group orientation, more education, it appears, gets swept up by motivated reasoning and simply makes people better at rationalizing the tribe's chosen stance.

But again, tribalism emits a familiar male scent, especially from the anti-climate-change position. An increasingly large volume of research is finding a negative correlation between environmentalism and preference for social hierarchy (social dominance orientation)[14] and authority (right-wing authoritarianism).[15] Given what we have learned about how these constructs are rooted in team-based male competition, it is perhaps not surprising to find that men are far less likely to embrace environmentalism than women,[16] nor that a political ideology based on male competition would turn global warming into an *us-versus-them* issue. Indeed, climate change denial has become locked into a badge of tribal commitment.

Even conservative political operatives recognize anti-climate-change stances for what they are. Republican strategist Whit Ayres, who worked for Senator Marco Rubio's 2016 presidential campaign, admits,

> Most Republicans still do not regard climate change as a hoax. But the entire climate change debate has now been caught up in the broader polarization of American politics. In some ways it's become yet another of the long list of litmus test issues that determine whether or not you're a good Republican.[17]

As we might expect, accepting the science can get you ejected from the tribe. During his 2010 reelection campaign, Bob Inglis, a six-term

Republican congressman from South Carolina, admitted on a local radio show that climate change was real. Using this admission to discredit Inglis's commitment to his tribe, his challenger Trey Gowdy smashed Inglis in the election by forty-two percentage points. Inglis later reported that "the most enduring heresy that I committed was saying the climate change is real and let's do something about it."[18]

The thing that places climate change denial even more squarely within our tribal psychology is its very remedy. One study found that when environmentalism was reframed as patriotism, with statements like, "Being pro-environmental allows us to protect and preserve the American way of life. It is patriotic to conserve the country's natural resources," those especially prone to justify in-group norms were more likely to adopt a pro-environmental stance.[19]

But how did an anti-climate-change stance become such an education-retardant conservative badge? Billionaires with stock in the petroleum industry have a vested financial interest in ensuring that we continue to burn fossil fuels unabated, and they have actively supported anti-climate-change propaganda. Those with the most to gain from the status quo have also ensured that conservative oil lobbyists and climate denialists are appointed to head key environmental cabinet positions. The propaganda keeps the anti-climate-change base loyal while the powerful, already so drenched in oil money, continue to amass profane fortunes. Crucially, in the days of our distant ancestors, when in-group biases resulted in resource gains, those gains were dispersed among the clan. Today, the windfall profits won by the petroleum industry are simply not passed on to those who deny climate change in support of the tribe. Their homes continue to get swept away by hurricanes and flooding, and their children continue to face a hotter, climatically turbulent future. All based on a ruse that abuses the Right's information-resistant tribal psychology.

As one piece of evidence that anti-climate-change stances are socially engineered, powerhouse conservative political consultant Frank Luntz has given written instructions on how to dupe the American electorate on climate change. In a 2002 memo to President George W. Bush, titled "The Environment: A Cleaner, Safer, Healthier America," he advised, "A compelling story, even if factually inaccurate, can be more emotionally compelling than a dry recitation of the truth." He went on to write,

> The scientific debate is closing [against us] . . . but not yet closed. There is still a window of opportunity to challenge the science. . . . Voters believe that there is no consensus about global warming within the scientific community. Should the public come to believe that the scientific issues are settled, their views about global warming will change accordingly. Therefore, you need to continue to make the lack of scientific certainty a primary issue in the debate.[20]

At the time, this strategy relied on the general population's scientific naïveté. But even as the science of climate change has expanded, as noted above, acceptance of climate change has decreased among the conservative populace in America, and rejecting science has become a badge of tribal commitment. As it happens, the same tribalistic, fear-based motivated reasoning that results in climate change denial also results in denying evolution.

Evolution

In general, higher education is associated with greater acceptance of evolution.[21] However, like climate change, this relationship is complex. Crucially, anti-evolutionary stances also show resistance to increasing education. For example, for those who take the stance that the Bible should be taken literally (stances concentrated among political conservatives), education is associated with decreasing acceptance of evolutionary principles, and the opposite for those taking non-literalist stances.[22] Research has found similar influences for political identity. One study of Mormons—who among their religious counterparts in the United States report nearly the lowest acceptance that humans evolved as a result of natural processes[23]—found that as education increased so did acceptance of evolution, but once again only among liberals.[24] More educated Mormon conservatives tended to reject evolution.

It is concerning that politics-based rejection of science puts Americans behind the rest of the world. Research finds not only that public acceptance of evolution in the United States is significantly lower by comparison to other industrialized nations but also that acceptance has been on a slight decline since the 1980s.[25] This trend runs against the current of an ever-increasing knowledge base in the evolutionary sciences. Evolution has been politicized in the United States to an extent not seen in other westernized nations, and the Republican Party has developed creationism as a platform to consolidate their political base in red states. In other words, like global warming, Republicans have turned rejecting evolutionary science into a badge of tribal identity. And as education increases, conservatives or biblical literalists, to borrow from sociologist Joseph Baker, "are more likely to confront issues of evolution directly and reinforce their working knowledge of rhetorical defenses of creationism."[26]

Fear, tribalism, and rejecting evolutionary principles run deep together. Godless Darwinism challenges long-standing religious beliefs that, by promising eternal life, give human beings a salve for the terror of their own mortality. Indeed, a branch of research examining fear-based motivated reasoning, called terror management theory (TMT), has found ways to induce mortality fears in the lab. Many studies in this area have subjects write essays on their own death, whereas controls write innocuous essays on food or television. When death fears are experimentally primed, people gravitate more toward religion, God, and the belief in an afterlife.[27] The ability of religion to allay death fears is intuitive; many scholars, myself included, would argue that this is among religion's primary functions. But it is important to remember that religious worship is a tribalistic experience, and tribalism thrives on group consensus. Consider one example in 1 Corinthians among a nearly endless number of scriptures across religious traditions: "I appeal to you, brothers and sisters, in the name of our Lord Jesus Christ, that all of you agree with one another in what you say and that there be no divisions among you, but that you be perfectly united in mind and thought."[28]

And so in churches, mosques, synagogues, or any other place of worship, the faithful inject themselves with an emotionally potent sense of unity. In unison, the pious recite immortality scriptures, passages promising protection from death itself. Coming together to reject evolution, in this sense, is just another way of coming together in agreement against death, something intuitive to the human brain and an exercise regularly practiced in religious traditions. Yet being "perfectly united in mind and thought" can be dangerous, particularly when the thought is erroneous—from the notion that women should be burned as witches to the idea that climate change is a liberal conspiracy. Maintaining group consensus that evolution is false is also deeply concerning. Apart from dispensing with evolutionary science's crucial insights, waving it away creates other vulnerabilities.

HOW OUR EVOLVED PSYCHOLOGY IS USED TO EXPLOIT US

One fact that I wish to convey to all readers, liberal or conservative, is that if you fail to understand your evolved psychology, others will use it to exploit you. Typically this is achieved by prodding our evolved fears, particularly our inborn fear of outsiders. Moreover, there is empirical evidence to suggest that conservatives, those on the threat-sensitive end of the natural curve, may be more vulnerable to this sort of manipulation.

One study examining credulity, for example, presented subjects with a series of false statements connoting danger, such as, "Sharks pose a significant risk to beachgoers," and "Terrorist attacks have increased in the U.S. since Sept. 11, 2001," along with false statements with a positive valence, such as, "When flying on major airlines, you are more likely to be upgraded from economy to business class if you ask at the gate."[29] Subjects were then asked how much they felt the statements were believable. Conservative subjects were significantly more likely to believe false information than liberals when the misinformation posited a threat. This led the researchers to conclude that "some individuals are more sensitive to the possibility of threats, and correspondingly pay higher precautionary costs; other people are less sensitive to this possibility, and pay higher costs when hazards are encountered."

The tendency to have a greater emotional or behavioral reaction to negative information, called *negativity bias*, is a universally shared trait shaped by the dangers of our ancestral environment. When our ancestors heard rustling in the bushes, it benefitted them to think, *Bear*, and respond accordingly, even when it was just the wind. In other words, negativity bias kept us alive in the cases when it really *wasn't* just the wind. It's not that liberals don't ever have this bias—it's just that conservatives have a greater tendency for it.

Unfortunately, negativity bias is also an easily manipulable trait, frequently used for profit by the sharks of the business world. One striking example comes from a company that owns a number of fake news sites, under the brazen moniker *Disinfomedia*. Disinfomedia's owner, Californian liberal Democrat Jestin Coler, peddles fake news stories for advertising dollars. Coler reportedly started the company to punish right-wing news outlets by selling them misinformation, with the goal of later exposing them for using it.[30] In keeping with the research above, Coler stated that he tried to write fake new stories for liberal outlets but was unsuccessful—that is, liberals wouldn't buy them. Here he boasts about how easy it was to bilk conservatives: "It was just anybody with a blog can get on there and find a big, huge Facebook group of kind of rabid Trump supporters just waiting to eat up this red meat that they're about to get served."

While Coler wouldn't disclose exact numbers, he stated that other fake news sites' $10,000 to $30,000 monthly earnings apply to him. One example of his for-profit fabricated news is a story with an ominous headline reading, "FBI Agent Suspected in Hillary Clinton Email Leaks Found Dead in Apparent Murder-Suicide."

A nascent but growing scientific literature is finding that Coler's observations were accurate—conservatives believe and share fake news on social media more than liberals. In one study examining "extremist, sensationalist, conspiratorial, masked commentary, fake news and other forms of junk news" on Facebook and Twitter, a team of Oxford researchers found that the highest percentage of sharing and circulation of these kinds of misinformation was concentrated on the political Right, in particular by Donald Trump supporters, and extreme Right social media pages.[31] Similarly, in a report summarizing the research on fake news, a team of Harvard scholars recently remarked that "while any group can come to believe false information, misinformation is currently predominantly a pathology of the right."[32] This vulnerability is not limited to rejecting evolution or global warming. Falsehoods widely popularized by conservative media outlets and politicians have included ideas such as the Obama administration's healthcare included "death panels" to decide on euthanizing patients,[33] and that President Obama is a Muslim,[34] both of which were false but believed more commonly within the conservative Right. But again, if, as I suggest, conservatism evolved in response to the pressures of violent group-based male coalitions, falsehoods about death panels or about a black president being from the outside tribe's religion would have high incendiary value. Theoretically, those fears could be exploited to kill popular support for a healthcare plan by those with financial interests in seeing the plan fail.

In chapter 2, we examined research linking xenophobia and fear of pathogens to conservatism. Conservative radio show host and conspiracy theorist Alex Jones has demonstrated that he clearly understands these links, and he has used this knowledge in a conservative fear-for-profit scam. In one segment, he brought on a young man whom he introduced as Dr. Edward Group III, who claimed to be an MIT alumnus. As it turns out, Dr. Group was a chiropractor with no undergraduate degree and his

MIT degree was flatly refuted by the university. Here is a transcript of "Dr." Group selling Jones's supplement, "Harmful Organisms Cleansing Dietary Supplement":

> If you're suffering from abdominal pain, allergies, even like headaches, anemia, weakened immune system, gut problems, depression, hair loss, excess gas, muscle pain, nervousness, I mean all these things. If you look at some of these conditions, and then us opening up our borders, and all the other countries opening up their borders. You're just dealing with mass amount of parasites or harmful organisms. You can type in "refugees spreading disease," I mean the CDC is going crazy right now.[35]

By intentionally tapping into our evolved fear of germs and outsiders, which is concentrated among his conservative viewership, Jones makes a fortune using preposterous claims to sell worthless products. (In describing a key ingredient in one of his supplements, Jones once stated, "This stuff is only found in comets . . . with trace amounts in blueberries.")

Producing fear and subsequently providing a "solution" to force a behavior is a common grifter's technique, known by researchers as the "fear-then-relief social influence technique," and it has been studied in the lab. Research has confirmed that subjects are more likely to comply with various requests when fear followed promptly by relief is experimentally manipulated.[36] Interestingly this manipulation impairs the ability to process emotional expressions in faces[37]—a task on which conservatives perform more poorly than liberals but which is invaluable in detecting falsehoods. But again, the feared stimulus in this kind of manipulation is often the threat of an outside tribe, as we see in the case of Jones's bogus supplements.

During the 2016 presidential debates, Donald Trump frequently used this same misdirection tactic. In the example below, Trump was attempting to deflect attention away from a newly released recording of him bragging about grabbing women's genitals by highlighting the threat of ISIS, followed promptly by his promise to make America safe:[38]

Moderator Anderson Cooper: You described kissing women without consent, grabbing their genitals. That is sexual assault. You bragged that you have sexually assaulted women. Do you understand that?

Trump: No, I didn't say that at all. I don't think you understood what was said. This was locker room talk. I am not proud of it. I apologize to my family, I apologized to the American people. Certainly, I am not proud of it. But this is locker room talk. You know, when we have a world where you have ISIS chopping off heads, where you have them, frankly, drowning people in steel cages, where you have wars and horrible, horrible sights all over and you have so many bad things happening, this is like medieval times. We haven't seen anything likes [*sic*] this. The carnage all over the world and they look and they see, can you imagine the people that are frankly doing so well against us with ISIS and they look at our country and see what's going on. Yes, I am very embarrassed by it and I hate it, but it's locker room talk and it's one of those things. I will knock the hell out of ISIS. We are going to defeat ISIS. ISIS happened a number of years ago in a vacuum that was left because of bad judgment. And I will tell you, I will take care of ISIS. We need to get on to much more important and bigger things.

At this point, Anderson Cooper ignores Trump's smoke screen and doggedly returns to the question at hand, but Trump quickly reverts to the threat of ISIS:

Cooper: For the record, are you saying that what you said on the bus 11 years ago, that you did not actually kiss women without consent or grope women without consent?

Trump: I have great respect for women. Nobody has more respect for women than I do.

Cooper: So for the record, you're saying you never did that?

Trump: Frankly, you hear these things. They are said. And I was embarrassed by it. But I have respect for women.

Cooper: Have you ever done those things?

Trump: And they have respect for me. And I will tell you, no I have not.

> And I will tell you, that I'm going to make our country safe and we're going to have borders, which we don't have now. People are pouring into our country and they're coming in from the Middle East and other places. We're gonna make America safe again, we're gonna make America great again but we're gonna make America safe again and we're gonna make America wealthy again. Because if you don't do that, it just, it sounds harsh to say, but we have to build up the wealth of our nation. Other nations are taking our job and they're taking our wealth.

So it is that tyrants rise to power, as James Madison wrote, "on some favorable emergency."[39]

The use of fear as a leverage point can be far more sinister. One notorious example concerns the Iraq War. In 2003, US troops were sent into Iraq based on faulty or manufactured intelligence reports that Iraq's leader, Saddam Hussein, was harboring weapons of mass destruction. Because the move played upon the lingering fear of outsiders generated by the 9/11 attacks, which were less than two years fresh in the minds of the American populace, the invasion gained wide popular support. Here is how then president George W. Bush framed the threat on March 17, 2003: "We are now acting because the risks of inaction would be far greater. In one year, or five years, the power of Iraq to inflict harm on all free nations would be multiplied many times over. . . . We choose to meet that threat now, where it arises, before it can appear suddenly in our skies and cities."[40] What was not broadcast was the fact that then vice president Dick Cheney was also the former CEO of the mammoth energy company Halliburton, a company that Cheney failed to fully divest himself of after he assumed office. One Halliburton subsidiary, KBR, made nearly forty billion dollars in a *no-bid contract* for reconstruction, private security, and feeding the troops in Iraq. Cheney and his friends made a personal fortune off the Iraq War. To a great extent, the fear of attack was the wool pulled over the eyes of the American public, and it made many powerful men very rich. Indeed, TMT research conducted during this time found that when death fears were primed, subjects across the political spectrum were more likely to support Bush's foreign policy, and that reminders of 9/11 boosted support for Bush.[41]

The great irony is that outsiders can also harm us not just by invading but also by using our irrational fear of outsiders to make us turn on one another. Political orientation is so persistently tribal that it is frequently imputed based on patterns of online behavior—shopping habits, likes, browsing history, responses to seemingly innocuous online question-naires or quizzes (e.g., "How well do you know your guns; test your fire-arms knowledge"). Foreign interests have made a new kind of warfare out of targeting specific internet users by launching politically divisive memes. This includes publicizing entirely fabricated stories about the opposing party or enflaming sensitive social issues around race, or guns, for example.

As one example, in 2013, the Black Lives Matter movement formed in America to protest racially biased police killings. To support the movement, in 2016, NFL quarterback Colin Kaepernick began kneeling at games during the national anthem. For its basis in equal rights, liberals widely sup-ported this gesture, whereas those on the extreme Right railed that it meant Kaepernick was a traitor to the United States. Emboldened by Donald Trump's election, white supremacy groups began counter-protesting the Black Lives Matter movement at rallies, shouting racist taunts and waving Nazi and Confederate flags. The ensuing turmoil turned into fistfights in the streets and resulted in one young woman's death when a white suprema-cist sped his vehicle into a crowd of liberal protestors.[42]

This rupture had some help. US intelligence agencies have linked fake Twitter and Facebook accounts to Russian bots. With knowledge of what is most likely to infuriate a liberal or conservative, the Russian govern-ment and possibly others have taken to spraying the fires of discontent with incendiary misinformation. In the Kaepernick case, bots blew up the controversy by spreading fake news and opposing memes (with hashtags such as #standforouranthem, and #takeaknee) across social media, making the posts look as though they came from American activists.[43] Intel agencies also discovered that a flood of automated fake news stories about the candidates in the 2016 US presidential election was instrumental in Donald Trump's win, and that foreign bots continue to target socially divisive partisan issues in the United States. It is concerning that two billion individuals around the globe (close to one-third of the global human population) currently use Facebook and a high proportion use social media as a news source.[44] This spectacular connectivity amounts to a worldwide arid field ready to take flame. Even more concerning is that the flood of fake, divisive news so intelligently targets our evolved tribalistic psychology, already primed for taking irrational stances against the rival tribe and for deflecting corrective information.

BECOMING SIGHTED

Knowing what we now know about how tribalism can blind us, what do we do? In coming to the realization of how profoundly our public discourse is shaped by evolved and fear-driven biases, it becomes clear that education about how to manage those biases is an important part of the solution. (Note that in the discussion of education above, the findings merely spoke to the amount of education received, not the quality or content of that education.) One of the most important steps toward rational political decision-making would be to make critical thinking a mandatory component of public education. Without the ability to think critically, to be fiercely rational, we are simply far more vulnerable—to our most primitive instincts and to those who would commandeer them for their own uses. But what is critical thinking? Here is one description offered by an organization called, no less, the Foundation for Critical Thinking:

They [critical thinkers] are keenly aware of the inherently flawed nature of human thinking when left unchecked. They strive to diminish the power of their egocentric and sociocentric tendencies. They use the intellectual tools that critical thinking offers—concepts and principles that enable them to analyze, assess, and improve thinking. . . . They realize that no matter how skilled they are as thinkers, they can always improve their reasoning abilities and they will at times fall prey to mistakes in reasoning, human irrationality, prejudices, biases, distortions, uncritically accepted social rules and taboos, self-interest, and vested interest.[45]

In other words, properly trained critical thinkers are able to better evaluate not only the information put before them but also their own responses to that information. Thus while our instincts can blind us to reality, critical thinking can help us to become sighted and to enjoy greater freedom—the freedom to not simply respond to our most reactive impulses but to pause, to consider.

Scientific inquiry must be primary among the intellectual tools used for critical thinking because it is arguably the best means to arrive at unbiased information. Although the scientific method is in no way perfect, it has built-in mechanisms designed to help its practitioners maintain objectivity in their quest for knowledge. Cognitive psychology is also key, offering a detailed study of our emotionally motivated biases. It is self-evident that if we don't understand our biases, we are more likely to enact them. Teaching students how to thoughtfully challenge authority figures is also invaluable. This was a central aim of the "denazification" efforts in post-WWII Germany intended to forestall the rise of another Hitler. These efforts gave the Germans a counterweight to the kind of primitive, unreasoned consensus that opens the door to despots.[46] In the (false) information age, a deep curriculum in information literacy—that is, how to obtain accurate facts amid a rising sea of false information[47]—is increasingly essential. Political literacy would also be desired. Surveys consistently show that high numbers of Americans are ignorant to elementary facts about US government, such as the name of the vice president, the name of a single Supreme Court justice, or the specific rights guaranteed by the First Amendment to the US Constitution.[48]

In reality, none of these measures, either alone or in combination, will completely erase motivated reasoning from the political realm. But there is little question that our educational shortcomings leave us literally more primitive in our thinking. Lastly, and perhaps most crucially, critical thinking must involve teaching the evolutionary sciences in the public school system, with a particular focus on evolutionary psychology. For its unmatched utility in exposing the ultimate reasons for what we think and do, including our political impulses, evolutionary science must have a protected place in the conversation about who we are.

CLOSING THOUGHTS

Thinking is our most foundational adaptation as human beings. Once we commit ourselves to doing more of it, a crucial question becomes, "How do we achieve an effective balance between liberal and conservative adaptations in contemporary life, toward the goals of reducing conflict, increasing effective dialogue, and ensuring flourishing societies?" John Stuart Mill once remarked, "A party of order or stability, and a party of progress or reform, are both necessary elements of a healthy state of political life."[49] This claim may have some basis in evolutionary science. Among humans, as among other animals, a spectrum of traits reflects a population's adaptability. Teddy Roosevelt once made a similar observation when he advised that we "speak softly, and carry a big stick." As a diplomat, but also a fervent outdoorsman and naturalist, Roosevelt seemed to have a keen understanding of human and animal behavior. And he may have a point—we cannot dispense with the martial, acquisitive, territorial male imperatives of our human ancestry altogether, yet, because our enemies will not be allayed with compassion alone. But loudly chest-thumping while carrying a big stick is an invitation for trouble. To create functioning nations, and to adapt to an increasingly interconnected world, the face of a nation must employ great diplomacy and rise above its most primal impulses.

Since Mill and Roosevelt, psychological science has been steadily accelerating, and our understanding of our evolutionary psychology is beginning to blossom. As we have learned, our spectrum of political orientations reflects the pressures of an ancestral environment that, with the help of our technology, we have for the most part left far behind. But on an evolutionary timescale we were in that environment only yesterday, and we continue to operate using the ancient psychology that helped our ancestors survive. Without understanding the evolved purpose of our political spectrum, we handicap our ability to think rationally about which of our adaptations to put forward and which to scale back.

The need to see human offspring through their unparalleled period of dependency drove our capacity for compassion, to understand other minds, and to share. The need to immigrate to new lands, and to acquire new genes and technologies from outside groups, gave us xenophilia. We still need to raise human offspring. And as we continue to evolve into a global community of nations, entwining into a single interdependent economic, technological, and cultural network, our xenophilia may be more necessary than ever. Certainly, this impulse must know some limits. Opening the doors indiscriminately also lets in those who would do us harm, and extreme empathy would potentially blind us to real danger.

On the other end of the natural curve, the continuous and deadly threat of starvation, predators, human-borne pathogens, and murderous outside clans gave us fear of germs, a toleration for in-group hierarchies, a tendency for submitting to large and aggressive male authorities, group-oriented thinking, and even in-group moral biases that sometimes blind us to reality. Without our ability to form coalitions, with all their inherent biases, we likely would not have survived our ancestral past, when our existence was at the mercy of nature.

But today, nature is at our mercy. We have the great fortune of a large, thinking brain that allows us to harness the earth's energies in order to make the human experience more livable. Having in so many ways surpassed our ancestral environment, important questions remain. To what extent does it serve humanity to collaborate on a global scale, openly sharing technology, information, and wealth? To what extent do we more fully thrive in smaller, competing tribes? How do we organize our communities, societies, and global networks in order to ensure their stability? These are difficult questions to answer. We may be able to take lessons from some of our forebears.

The Iroquois had two forms of government. One was for wartime, the other for peace.[50] The *sachems*, the peacetime leaders, men who were often elected by women, had total control over the internal affairs of the tribe. It was only when war erupted that the war leaders took over, with the sole purpose of dispensing with the enemy threat. When the enemy tried to negotiate a peace settlement, they did so with the sachems. If the terms were agreed upon, the war leaders stepped down and the female-elected sachems took the helm once again. This arrangement certainly seems intelligent. If we are going to make use of male adaptations for territorial gain, hierarchy, violence, and suppressing empathy, war is the time to do so. But holstering those men when wartime is over is a simple, yet brilliantly pragmatic strategy. Letting the warrior class among us administer civil affairs—we already know what happens. Driven by male primate reproductive ambitions, warrior-driven governments have historically been oppressive and misogynistic, prone to forming in-groups, promoting unhealthy respect for authority, and encouraging winner-take-all economic policies that destabilize societies and destroy our natural environment. Moreover, as a means to ensure the hierarchy remains unquestioned, these authoritarians have either forbidden questioning altogether or, more recently, crippled our ability to question by drowning us with false information. But questioning, no matter how difficult the answer, is the only way to keep evolving. Here I recall the words of Thomas Jefferson when he said, "There is not a truth existing which I fear, or would wish unknown to the whole world."[51]

In all of this focus on what divides us, one intellectually gripping fact about humanity is that we appear to get along best when faced with an outside threat. This response, which has reliably been documented across the world's bloody conflicts, reveals just how far cooperation was shaped by male coalitionary psychology and its propensity for making war. The question remains, Can we truly come together in the absence of an outside enemy? Or will we be forever destined to create those enemies if for nothing more than the intoxicating sense of unity we experience when standing together? Could we transpose the hostile outside tribe for something else? Hunger? Ignorance? Human limitation? If we are ever to stop fighting one another, it will require understanding where we came from. Only then can we transcend the fears and sufferings of our Stone Age ancestors. Only then can we fully evolve into the worlds we create.

ACKNOWLEDGMENTS

First, I would like to thank Avi Tuschman for his comments and for his foundational book *Our Political Nature*. His work greatly stimulated my thinking. Thanks, too, to Benjamin Purzycki for his ever-insightful perspectives, and to Jessica McCutcheon for her careful editing. Rose McDermott's research and her energetic feedback on a significant section of this book were tremendously valuable. Melissa M. McDonald graciously shared her expertise in evolutionary psychology and provided a thoughtful review, for which I owe a debt of gratitude. I am deeply grateful to Sebastian Junger for a generous exchange of ideas, and for encouraging me to pull the trigger on this book when it was still in the formulation stage. This and his inspiring writing took me a long way.

Erin—this book would not be possible without your support, which you provided in every conceivable way, not the least of which being your tireless, incisive review of every page. Engaging with your exceptional mind improves my work, nourishes my intellectual growth, and is one of life's greatest pleasures.

NOTES

CHAPTER 1: EVOLUTIONARY POLITICS

1. Christopher Matthews, "Mommy's Love and Daddy's Protection," *Baltimore Sun*, May 14, 1991, http://articles.baltimoresun.com/1991-05-14/news/1991134061_1_liberal-democrats-gulf-war-mommy.

2. Bob Burnett, "Republicans Are from Mars; Democrats Are from Venus," *Huffington Post*, December 10, 2016, https://www.huffingtonpost.com/bob-burnett/republicans-are-from-mars_1_b_8770824.html.

3. "Ann Coulter on Her Feud with Elizabeth Edwards," Fox News, June 29, 2007, https://www.foxnews.com/story/ann-coulter-on-her-feud-with-elizabeth-edwards.

4. Monika L. McDermott, *Masculinity, Femininity, and American Political Behavior* (repr.; New York: Oxford University Press, 2016).

5. Steve Sailer, "Q&A: Steven Pinker of 'Blank Slate,'" United Press International, October 30, 2002, https://www.upi.com/QA-Steven-Pinker-of-Blank-Slate/26021035991232/.

6. Ibid.

7. L. Cosmides and J. Tooby, "Beyond Intuition and Instinct Blindness: Toward an Evolutionarily Rigorous Cognitive Science," *Cognition* 50, no. 1–3 (June 1994): 41–77.

8. William James, *The Principles of Psychology*, vol. 1, rev. ed. (New York: Dover Publications, 1950).

9. John R. Alford, Carolyn L. Funk, and John R. Hibbing, "Are Political Orientations Genetically Transmitted?" *American Political Science Review* 99, no. 2 (May 2005): 153–67, https://doi.org/10.1017/S0003055405051579.

10. Robert Altemeyer, *The Authoritarian Specter*, 1st ed. (Cambridge, MA: Harvard University Press, 1996).

11. Thomas J. Bouchard and Matt McGue, "Genetic and Environmental Influences on Human Psychological Differences," *Journal of Neurobiology* 54,

no. 1 (January 2003): 4–45; Thomas J. Bouchard et al., "Sources of Human Psychological Differences: The Minnesota Study of Twins Reared Apart," *Science* 250, no. 4798 (1990): 223–28.

12. John R. Alford and John R. Hibbing, "The Origin of Politics: An Evolutionary Theory of Political Behavior," *Perspectives on Politics* 2, no. 4 (2004): 707–23, https://www.cambridge.org/core/journals/perspectives-on-politics/article/origin-of-politics-an-evolutionary-theory-of-political-behavior/0A5EDA700EE2022AC9DFB5AE1CAA7C4D; Peter K. Hatemi et al., "Genetic Influences on Political Ideologies: Twin Analyses of 19 Measures of Political Ideologies from Five Democracies and Genome-Wide Findings from Three Populations," *Behavior Genetics* 44, no. 3 (May 2014): 282–94, https://doi.org/10.1007/s10519-014-9648-8.

13. John T. Jost, "The End of the End of Ideology.," *American Psychologist* 61, no. 7 (2006): 651–70, https://doi.org/10.1037/0003-066X.61.7.651.

14. Peter Mair, "Left–Right Orientations," in *Oxford Handbook or Political Behavior*, ed. Russell J Dalton and Hans-Dieter Klingemann (Oxford, England: Oxford University Press, 2007), 206–22, http://www.oxfordhandbooks.com/view/10.1093/oxfordhb/9780199270125.001.0001/oxfordhb-9780199270125-e-011.

CHAPTER 2: LEFT, RIGHT, AND MOTHER NATURE

1. K. L. Jang, W. J. Livesley, and P. A. Vernon, "Heritability of the Big Five Personality Dimensions and Their Facets: A Twin Study," *Journal of Personality* 64, no. 3 (September 1996): 577–91.

2. Robert R. McCrae and Antonio Terracciano, "Universal Features of Personality Traits from the Observer's Perspective: Data from 50 Cultures," *Journal of Personality and Social Psychology* 88, no. 3 (March 2005): 547–61, https://doi.org/10.1037/0022-3514.88.3.547.

3. Anton Aluja, Óscar García, and Luis F. García, "A Comparative Study of Zuckerman's Three Structural Models for Personality through the NEO-PI-R, ZKPQ-III-R, EPQ-RS and Goldberg's 50-Bipolar Adjectives," *Personality and Individual Differences* 33, no. 5 (October 5, 2002): 713–25, https://doi.org/10.1016/S0191-8869(01)00186-6.

4. Marvin Zuckerman, *Behavioral Expressions and Biosocial Bases of Sensation Seeking*, 1st ed. (Cambridge; New York: Cambridge University Press, 1994).

5. Ronnie L. McGhee et al., "The Relation between Five-Factor Personality Traits and Risk-Taking Behavior in Preadolescents," *Psychology* 3, no. 8 (August 23, 2012): 558, https://doi.org/10.4236/psych.2012.38083.

6. Jack Block and Jeanne H. Block, "Nursery School Personality and Political Orientation Two Decades Later," *Journal of Research in Personality* 40, no. 5 (October 2006): 734–49, https://doi.org/10.1016/j.jrp.2005.09.005.

7. Dana R. Carney et al., "The Secret Lives of Liberals and Conservatives: Personality Profiles, Interaction Styles, and the Things They Leave Behind," *Political Psychology* 29, no. 6 (December 1, 2008): 807–40, https://doi.org/10.1111/j.1467-9221.2008.00668.x; John T. Jost and David M. Amodio, "Political Ideology as Motivated Social Cognition: Behavioral and Neuroscientific Evidence," *Motivation and Emotion* 36, no. 1 (March 2012): 55–64, https://doi.org/10.1007/s11031-011-9260-7; Samuel D. Gosling, Peter J. Rentfrow, and William B. Swann, "A Very Brief Measure of the Big-Five Personality Domains," *Journal of Research in Personality* 37, no. 6 (December 1, 2003): 504–28, https://doi.org/10.1016/S0092-6566(03)00046-1; Alain Van Hiel and Ivan Mervielde, "Openness to Experience and Boundaries in the Mind: Relationships with Cultural and Economic Conservative Beliefs," *Journal of Personality* 72, no. 4 (August 2004): 659–86, https://doi.org/10.1111/j.0022-3506.2004.00276.x; Alain van Hiel, Malgorzata Kossowska, and Ivan Mervielde, "The Relationship between Openness to Experience and Political Ideology," *Personality and Individual Differences* 28, no. 4 (April 1, 2000): 741–51, https://doi.org/10.1016/S0191-8869(99)00135-X.

8. Alan S. Gerber et al., "Personality and Political Attitudes: Relationships across Issue Domains and Political Contexts," *American Political Science Review* 104, no. 1 (February 2010): 111–33, https://doi.org/10.1017/S0003055410000031.

9. Ibid.

10. Carney et al., "Secret Lives of Liberals and Conservatives."

11. Time Staff, "Here's Donald Trump's Presidential Announcement Speech," *Time*, June 16, 2015, http://time.com/3923128/donald-trump-announcement-speech/.

12. Nina Totenburg, "Who Is Judge Gonzalo Curiel, the Man

Trump Attacked for His Mexican Ancestry?" NPR, June 7, 2016, http://www.npr.org/2016/06/07/481140881/who-is-judge-gonzalo -curiel-the-man-trump-attacked-for-his-mexican-ancestry.

13. Jessica Taylor, "Trump Calls For 'Total and Complete Shutdown of Muslims Entering' US," NPR, December 7, 2015, https://www.npr.org/ 2015/12/07/458836388/trump-calls-for-total-and-complete -shutdown-of-muslims-entering-u-s.

14. Maggie Haberman and Richard Pérez-Peña, "Donald Trump Sets Off a Furor with Call to Register Muslims in the US," *New York Times*, November 20, 2015, https://www.nytimes.com/2015/11/21/us/politics/donald-trump-sets-off -a-furor-with-call-to-register-muslims-in-the-us.html.

15. John R. O'Donnell and James Rutherford, *Trumped! The Inside Story of the Real Donald Trump—His Cunning Rise and Spectacular Fall* (New York: Simon & Schuster, 1991).

16. Mark Bowden, "The Art of the Donald," *Playboy*, May 1997.

17. Holly Yan, Kristina Sgueglia, and Kylie Walker, "'Make America White Again': Hate Speech and Crimes Post-Election," CNN.com, December 22, 2016, https://www.cnn.com/2016/11/10/us/post-election-hate-crimes-and-fears-trnd/ index.html.

18. "British PM Cameron Stands by 'Divisive, Stupid and Wrong' Comment on Trump: Spokesman," *Reuters*, May 16, 2016, https://www.reuters.com/article/ us-usa-election-trump-britain-cameron-idUSKCN0Y7116.

19. Adam Taylor, "61 Not-Very-Positive Things Foreign Leaders Have Said about Donald Trump," *Washington Post*, July 19, 2016, https://www .washingtonpost.com/news/worldviews/wp/2016/05/06/47-not-very-positive -things-foreign-leaders-have-said-about-donald-trump/.

20. David O. Sears, James Sidanius, and Lawrence Bobo, eds., *Racialized Politics: The Debate about Racism in America*, Studies in Communication, Media, and Public Opinion (Chicago: University of Chicago Press, 2000), http://www .press.uchicago.edu/ucp/books/book/chicago/R/bo3617330.html.

21. Agustín Echebarria-Echabe and Emilia Fernández Guede, "A New Measure of Anti-Arab Prejudice: Reliability and Validity Evidence," *Journal of Applied Social Psychology* 37, no. 5 (May 1, 2007): 1077–91, https://doi.org/ 10.1111/j.1559-1816.2007.00200.x.

22. Thomas Pettigrew, "Systematizing the Predictors of Prejudice," in *Racialized Politics: The Debate about Racism in America*, ed. David O. Sears, Jim

Sidanius, and Lawrence Bobo (Chicago: University of Chicago Press, 2000), pp. 280–301.

23. Avi Tuschman, *Our Political Nature: The Evolutionary Origins of What Divides Us* (Amherst, NY: Prometheus Books, 2013).

24. Richard E. Green et al., "A Draft Sequence of the Neandertal Genome," *Science* 328, no. 5979 (May 7, 2010): 710–22, https://doi.org/10.1126/science.1188021.

25. Nancy Wilmsen Thornhill, ed., *The Natural History of Inbreeding and Outbreeding: Theoretical and Empirical Perspectives*, 1st ed. (Chicago: University of Chicago Press, 1993).

26. Eric M. Poolman and Alison P. Galvani, "Evaluating Candidate Agents of Selective Pressure for Cystic Fibrosis," *Journal of The Royal Society Interface* 4, no. 12 (February 22, 2007): 91–98, https://doi.org/10.1098/rsif.2006.0154.

27. Simone Sommer, "The Importance of Immune Gene Variability (MHC) in Evolutionary Ecology and Conservation," *Frontiers in Zoology* 2, no. 16 (October 20, 2005), https://doi.org/10.1186/1742-9994-2-16.

28. Ann Gibbons, "A Denisovan Legacy in the Immune System?" *Science* 333, no. 6046 (August 26, 2011): 1086, https://doi.org/10.1126/science.333.6046.1086.

29. John R. Hibbing, Kevin B. Smith, and John R. Alford, *Predisposed: Liberals, Conservatives, and the Biology of Political Differences* (New York: Routledge, 2013).

30. A. C. Stevenson et al., "Aspects of Pre-Eclamptic Toxaemia of Pregnancy, Consanguinity, Twinning in Ankara," *Journal of Medical Genetics* 13, no. 1 (February 1976): 1–8, http://www.ncbi.nlm.nih.gov/pmc/articles/PMC1013340/.

31. Eva Bianconi et al., "An Estimation of the Number of Cells in the Human body," *Annals of Human Biology* 40, no. 6 (2013), https://doi.org/10.3109/03014460.2013.807878.

32. A. Souther, "Warfare Analogy to Virus Infection," Artificial Intelligence Center, "http://www.ai.sri.com/~rkf/designdoc/souther-analogy.txt.

33. Carlos David Navarrete and Daniel M.T. Fessler, "Disease Avoidance and Ethnocentrism: The Effects of Disease Vulnerability and Disgust Sensitivity on Intergroup Attitudes," *Evolution and Human Behavior* 27, no. 4 (July 2006): 270–82, https://doi.org/10.1016/j.evolhumbehav.2005.12.001.

34. Jason Faulkner et al., "Evolved Disease-Avoidance Mechanisms and

Contemporary Xenophobic Attitudes," *Group Processes & Intergroup Relations* 7, no. 4 (October 2004): 333–53, https://doi.org/10.1177/1368430204046142.

35. Justin H. Park, Mark Schaller, and Christian S. Crandall, "Pathogen-Avoidance Mechanisms and the Stigmatization of Obese People," *Evolution and Human Behavior* 28, no. 6 (November 1, 2007): 410–14, https://doi.org/10.1016/j.evolhumbehav.2007.05.008.

36. Yoel Inbar et al., "Disgust Sensitivity Predicts Intuitive Disapproval of Gays," *Emotion* (Washington, DC) 9, no. 3 (June 2009): 435–39, https://doi .org/10.1037/a0015960.

37. Yoel Inbar, David A. Pizarro, and Paul Bloom, "Conservatives Are More Easily Disgusted than Liberals," *Cognition & Emotion* 23, no. 4 (June 2009): 714–25, https://doi.org/10.1080/02699930802110007; John A. Terrizzi, Natalie J. Shook, and W. Larry Ventis, "Disgust: A Predictor of Social Conservatism and Prejudicial Attitudes toward Homosexuals," *Personality and Individual Differences* 49, no. 6 (October 1, 2010): 587–92, https://doi.org/10.1016/j.paid.2010 .05.024; Yoel Inbar et al., "Disgust Sensitivity, Political Conservatism, and Voting," *Social Psychological and Personality Science* 3, no. 5 (September 2012): 537–44, https://doi.org/10.1177/1948550611429024.

38. Inbar et al., "Disgust Sensitivity, Political Conservatism, and Voting."

39. Gordon Hodson and Kimberly Costello, "Interpersonal Disgust, Ideological Orientations, and Dehumanization as Predictors of Intergroup Attitudes," *Psychological Science* 18, no. 8 (August 1, 2007): 691–98, https://doi .org/10.1111/j.1467-9280.2007.01962.x.

40. Inbar et al., "Disgust Sensitivity, Political Conservatism, and Voting"; Kevin B. Smith et al., "Disgust Sensitivity and the Neurophysiology of Left-Right Political Orientations," *PLOS ONE* 6, no. 10 (October 19, 2011): e25552, https://doi.org/10.1371/journal.pone.0025552.

41. Jüri Allik and Robert R. McCrae, "Toward a Geography of Personality Traits: Patterns of Profiles across 36 Cultures," *Journal of Cross-Cultural Psychology* 35, no. 1 (January 1, 2004): 13–28, https://doi.org/10.1177/ 0022022103260382.

42. Ibid.

43. Douglas R. Oxley et al., "Political Attitudes Vary with Physiological Traits," *Science* 321, no. 5896 (September 19, 2008): 1667–70, https://doi.org/ 10.1126/science.1157627.

44. Ryota Kanai et al., "Political Orientations Are Correlated with Brain

Structure in Young Adults," *Current Biology* 21, no. 8 (April 26, 2011): 677–80, https://doi.org/10.1016/j.cub.2011.03.017.

45. Jacob M. Vigil, "Political Leanings Vary with Facial Expression Processing and Psychosocial Functioning," *Group Processes & Intergroup Relations* 13, no. 5 (September 1, 2010): 547–58, https://doi.org/10.1177/1368430209356930.

46. Andreas Olsson et al., "The Role of Social Groups in the Persistence of Learned Fear," *Science* (New York) 309, no. 5735 (July 29, 2005): 785–87, https://doi.org/10.1126/science.1113551.

47. S. Agras, D. Sylvester, and D. Oliveau, "The Epidemiology of Common Fears and Phobia," *Comprehensive Psychiatry* 10, no. 2 (March 1969): 151–56.

48. Navarrete and Fessler, "Disease Avoidance and Ethnocentrism."

49. Daniel Lieberman, *The Story of the Human Body: Evolution, Health, and Disease* (repr.; New York: Vintage, 2014).

CHAPTER 3: IS CONSERVATISM AN EXTREME FORM OF THE MALE BRAIN?

1. W. Rodzinski, *A History of China* (Oxford: Pergamon, 1979), p. 165.

2. Aaron Sell, Liana S. E. Hone, and Nicholas Pound, "The Importance of Physical Strength to Human Males," *Human Nature* (Hawthorne, NY) 23, no. 1 (March 2012): 30–44, https://doi.org/10.1007/s12110-012-9131-2.

3. Nicholas J. G. Winter, "Masculine Republicans and Feminine Democrats: Gender and Americans' Explicit and Implicit Images of the Political Parties," *Political Behavior* 32, no. 4 (December 2010): 587–618, https://doi.org/10.1007/s11109-010-9131-z.

4. Ibid.

5. Monika L. McDermott, *Masculinity, Femininity, and American Political Behavior* (repr.; New York: Oxford University Press, 2016).

6. Ibid.

7. B. Sinervo and C. M. Lively, "The Rock-Paper-Scissors Game and the Evolution of Alternative Male Strategies," *Nature* 380, no. 6571 (March 21, 1996): 240–43, https://doi.org/10.1038/380240a0.

8. B. Sinervo et al., "Testosterone, Endurance, and Darwinian Fitness: Natural and Sexual Selection on the Physiological Bases of Alternative Male Behaviors in Side-Blotched Lizards," *Hormones and Behavior* 38, no. 4 (December 2000): 222–33, https://doi.org/10.1006/hbeh.2000.1622.

9. Sinervo and Lively, "Rock-Paper-Scissors Game."

10. Simon Baron-Cohen, "The Extreme Male Brain Theory of Autism," *Trends in Cognitive Sciences* 6, no. 6 (June 1, 2002): 248–54.

11. Simon Baron-Cohen, Leda Cosmides, and John Tooby, *Mindblindness: An Essay on Autism and Theory of Mind*, rev. ed. (Cambridge, MA: Bradford Books, 1997).

12. Tony Charman, Ted Ruffman, and Wendy Clements, "Is There a Gender Difference in False Belief Development?" *Social Development* 11, no. 1 (January 1, 2002): 1–10, https://doi.org/10.1111/1467-9507.00183; Sue Walker, "Gender Differences in the Relationship between Young Children's Peer-Related Social Competence and Individual Differences in Theory of Mind," *Journal of Genetic Psychology* 166, no. 3 (September 2005): 297–312, https://doi.org/10.3200/GNTP.166.3.297-312.

13. Mita Banerjee, "Hidden Emotions: Preschoolers' Knowledge of Appearance-Reality and Emotion Display Rules," *Social Cognition* 15, no. 2 (June 1, 1997): 107–32, https://doi.org/10.1521/soco.1997.15.2.107.

14. R. Hatcher et al., "Psychological Mindedness and Abstract Reasoning in Late Childhood and Adolescence: An Exploration Using New Instruments," *Journal of Youth and Adolescence* 19, no. 4 (August 1990): 307–26, https://doi.org/10.1007/BF01537075.

15. Agustin Ibanez et al., "Empathy, Sex and Fluid Intelligence as Predictors of Theory of Mind," *Personality and Individual Differences* 54, no. 5 (April 1, 2013): 616–21, https://doi.org/10.1016/j.paid.2012.11.022.

16. Francesca G. E. Happé, "The Role of Age and Verbal Ability in the Theory of Mind Task Performance of Subjects with Autism," *Child Development* 66, no. 3 (1995): 843–55, https://doi.org/10.2307/1131954.

17. S. Baron-Cohen et al., "Another Advanced Test of Theory of Mind: Evidence from Very High Functioning Adults with Autism or Asperger Syndrome," *Journal of Child Psychology and Psychiatry, and Allied Disciplines* 38, no. 7 (October 1997): 813–22.

18. Ryota Kanai et al., "Political Orientations Are Correlated with Brain Structure in Young Adults," *Current Biology* 21, no. 8 (April 26, 2011): 677–80, https://doi.org/10.1016/j.cub.2011.03.017.

19. K. Vogeley et al., "Mind Reading: Neural Mechanisms of Theory of Mind and Self-Perspective," *NeuroImage* 14, no. 1 (July 2001): 170–81, https://doi.org/10.1006/nimg.2001.0789.

20. Darren Schreiber et al., "Red Brain, Blue Brain: Evaluative Processes Differ in Democrats and Republicans," *PLoS ONE* 8, no. 2 (February 13, 2013): e52970, https://doi.org/10.1371/journal.pone.0052970.

21. M. L. Hoffman, "Sex Differences in Empathy and Related Behaviors," *Psychological Bulletin* 84, no. 4 (July 1977): 712–22; Michele Volbrecht et al., "Examining the Familial Link between Positive Affect and Empathy Development in the Second Year," *Journal of Genetic Psychology* 168, no. 2 (June 2007): 105–29, https://doi.org/10.3200/GNTP.168.2.105-130.

22. Mark H. Davis, *Empathy: A Social Psychological Approach* (Boulder, CO: Westview Press, 1996).

23. Baron-Cohen, "Extreme Male Brain Theory."

24. Clifford P. McCue and J. David Gopoian, "Dispositional Empathy and the Political Gender Gap," *Women & Politics* 21, no. 2 (May 25, 2000): 1–20, https://doi.org/10.1300/J014v21n02_01.

25. Judith A. Hall, "Gender Effects in Decoding Nonverbal Cues," *Psychological Bulletin* 85, no. 4 (1978): 845–57.

26. Jennifer Connellan et al., "Sex Differences in Human Neonatal Social Perception," *Infant Behavior and Development* 23, no. 1 (January 1, 2000): 113–18, https://doi.org/10.1016/S0163-6383(00)00032-1.

27. Ofer Golan, Simon Baron-Cohen, and Jacqueline Hill, "The Cambridge Mindreading (CAM) Face-Voice Battery: Testing Complex Emotion Recognition in Adults with and without Asperger Syndrome," *Journal of Autism and Developmental Disorders* 36, no. 2 (February 2006): 169–83, https://doi.org/10.1007/s10803-005-0057-y; Barbara Montagne et al., "Sex Differences in the Perception of Affective Facial Expressions: Do Men Really Lack Emotional Sensitivity?" *Cognitive Processing* 6, no. 2 (June 1, 2005): 136–41, https://doi.org/10.1007/s10339-005-0050-6; Qazi Rahman, Glenn D. Wilson, and Sharon Abrahams, "Sex, Sexual Orientation, and Identification of Positive and Negative Facial Affect," *Brain and Cognition* 54, no. 3 (April 2004): 179–85, https://doi.org/10.1016/j.bandc.2004.01.002.

28. Ryan McBain, Dan Norton, and Yue Chen, "Females Excel at Basic Face Perception," *Acta Psychologica* 130, no. 2 (February 2009): 168–73, https://doi.org/10.1016/j.actpsy.2008.12.005.

29. C. Jacobs et al., "Carrying Your Heart (and Your Politics) on Your Face: Ideology and Facial Muscle Responses" (paper presented at the Midwest Political Science Association Meeting, Bloomington, IN, 2012).

30. Ibid.

31. James J. Gross and Oliver P. John, "Facets of Emotional Expressivity: Three Self-Report Factors and Their Correlates," *Personality and Individual Differences* 19, no. 4 (October 1, 1995): 555–68, https://doi.org/10.1016/0191-8869(95)00055-B.

32. Svetlana Lutchmaya, Simon Baron-Cohen, and Peter Raggatt, "Foetal Testosterone and Vocabulary Size in 18- and 24-Month-Old Infants," *Infant Behavior and Development* 24, no. 4 (April 18, 2001): 418–24, https://doi.org/10.1016/S0163-6383(02)00087-5.

33. Alejandro Portes and Lingxin Hao, "The Price of Uniformity: Language, Family and Personality Adjustment in the Immigrant Second Generation," *Ethnic and Racial Studies* 25, no. 6 (2002): 889–912, https://www.tandfonline.com/doi/abs/10.1080/0141987022000009368; Yvette Lapayese, Karen Huchting, and Olga Grimalt, "Gender and Bilingual Education: An Exploratory Study of the Academic Achievement of Latina and Latino English Learners," *Journal of Latinos and Education* 13, no. 2 (2014): 152–60.

34. Douglas D. Burman, Tali Bitan, and James R. Booth, "Sex Differences in Neural Processing of Language among Children," *Neuropsychologia* 46, no. 5 (April 2008): 1349–62, https://doi.org/10.1016/j.neuropsychologia.2007.12.021.

35. David J. Martin and H. D. Hoover, "Sex Differences in Educational Achievement: A Longitudinal Study," *Journal of Early Adolescence* 7, no. 1 (March 1, 1987): 65–83, https://doi.org/10.1177/0272431687071007; Johan Olav Undheim and Hilmar Nordvik, "Socio-Economic Factors and Sex Differences in an Egalitarian Educational System: Academic Achievement in 16-Year-Old Norwegian Students," *Scandinavian Journal of Educational Research* 36, no. 2 (January 1, 1992): 87–98, https://doi.org/10.1080/0031383920360201.

36. M. L. Bleecker et al., "Age-Related Sex Differences in Verbal Memory," *Journal of Clinical Psychology* 44, no. 3 (May 1988): 403–11; R. Portin et al., "Education, Gender and Cognitive Performance in a 62-Year-Old Normal Population: Results from the Turva Project," *Psychological Medicine* 25, no. 6 (November 1995): 1295–98.

37. M. F. Elias et al., "Role of Age, Education, and Gender on Cognitive Performance in the Framingham Heart Study: Community-Based Norms," *Experimental Aging Research* 23, no. 3 (September 1997): 201–35, https://doi.org/10.1080/03610739708254281.

38. Chris McComb, "About One in Four Americans Can Hold a

Conversation in a Second Language," Gallup, Washington, DC, April 6, 2001, http://www.gallup.com/poll/1825/About-One-Four-Americans-Can-Hold-Conversation-Second-Language.aspx.

39. Markus Kemmelmeier, "Is There a Relationship between Political Orientation and Cognitive Ability? A Test of Three Hypotheses in Two Studies," *Personality and Individual Differences* 45, no. 8 (December 1, 2008): 767–72, https://doi.org/10.1016/j.paid.2008.08.003.

40. Gerhard Meisenberg, "Verbal Ability as a Predictor of Political Preferences in the United States, 1974–2012," *Intelligence* 50 (May 1, 2015): 135–43, https://doi.org/10.1016/j.intell.2015.03.004.

41. Peter Leeson, Patrick C. L. Heaven, and Joseph Ciarrochi, "Revisiting the Link between Low Verbal Intelligence and Ideology," *Intelligence* 40, no. 2 (March 1, 2012): 213–16, https://doi.org/10.1016/j.intell.2011.11.006.

42. Andrew P. Bayliss, Giuseppe di Pellegrino, and Steven P. Tipper, "Sex Differences in Eye Gaze and Symbolic Cueing of Attention," *Quarterly Journal of Experimental Psychology Section A* 58, no. 4 (May 1, 2005): 631–50, https://doi.org/10.1080/02724980443000124.

43. Kåre S. Olafsen et al., "Joint Attention in Term and Preterm Infants at 12 Months Corrected Age: The Significance of Gender and Intervention Based on a Randomized Controlled Trial," *Infant Behavior & Development* 29, no. 4 (December 2006): 554–63, https://doi.org/10.1016/j.infbeh.2006.07.004.

44. S. Lutchmaya, S. Baron-Cohen, and P. Raggatt, "Foetal Testosterone and Eye Contact in 12-Month Old Infants," *Infant Behavior and Development* 25 (2002): 327–35.

45. Simon Baron-Cohen et al., "Are Children with Autism Blind to the Mentalistic Significance of the Eyes?" *British Journal of Developmental Psychology* 13, no. 4 (November 1, 1995): 379–98, https://doi.org/10.1111/j.2044-835X.1995.tb00687.x; H. Roeyers, P. Van Oost, and S. Bothuyne, "Immediate Imitation and Joint Attention in Young Children with Autism," *Development and Psychopathology* 10, no. 3 (1998): 441–50.

46. Michael D. Dodd, John R. Hibbing, and Kevin B. Smith, "The Politics of Attention: Gaze-Cuing Effects Are Moderated by Political Temperament," *Attention, Perception, & Psychophysics* 73, no. 1 (January 2011): 24–29, https://doi.org/10.3758/s13414-010-0001-x.

47. Luciano Carraro, Mario Dalmaso, Luigi Castelli, and Giovanni Galfano, "The Politics of Gaze Cuing Contextualized: Gaze but Not Arrow Cuing of

Attention Is Moderated by Political Temperament," *Cognitive Processing* 16, no. 3 (2015): 309–14.

48. W. R. Charlesworth and C. Dzur, "Gender Comparisons of Preschoolers' Behavior and Resource Utilization in Group Problem Solving," *Child Development* 58, no. 1 (February 1987): 191–200.

49. E. E. Maccoby, "Gender and Relationships: A Developmental Account," *American Psychologist* 45, no. 4 (April 1990): 513–20.

50. Ibid.; Penelope Brown and Stephen C. Levinson, *Politeness: Some Universals in Language Usage* (Cambridge: Cambridge University Press, 1987).

51. Joyce F. Benenson and Henry Markovits, *Warriors and Worriers: The Survival of the Sexes* (Oxford; New York: Oxford University Press, 2014).

52. Ibid.

53. Janet Lever, "Sex Differences in the Games Children Play," *Social Problems*, 1976; Janet Lever, "Sex Differences in the Complexity of Children's Play and Games," *American Sociological Review* 43, no. 4 (1978): 471–83, https://doi.org/10.2307/2094773.

54. Costas Panagopoulos, "Occupy Wall Street Survey Results October 2011," Fordham University, October 14–18, 2011, https://www.fordham.edu/download/downloads/id/2538/occupy_wall_street_survey.pdf.

55. Jesse Graham et al., "Mapping the Moral Domain," *Journal of Personality and Social Psychology* 101, no. 2 (2011): 366–85, https://doi.org/10.1037/a0021847.

56. John T. Jost et al., "Political Conservatism as Motivated Social Cognition," *Psychological Bulletin* 129, no. 3 (May 2003): 339–75.

57. S. M. Lindberg, J. S. Hyde, et al., "New Trends in Gender and Mathematics Performance: A Meta-Analysis," *Psychological Bulletin* 136, no. 6 (2010): 1123–35, http://dx.doi.org/10.1037/a0021276; Diane F. Halpern, Camilla P. Benbow, David C. Geary, et al., "The Science of Sex Differences in Science and Mathematics," *Psychological Science in the Public Interest* 8, no. 1 (August 2007): 1–51, doi: 10.1111/j.1529-1006.2007.00032.x.

58. Simon Baron-Cohen et al., "Is There a Link between Engineering and Autism?" *Autism* 1, no. 1 (July 1, 1997): 101–109, https://doi.org/10.1177/1362361397011010; Kinga Morsanyi et al., "Are Systemizing and Autistic Traits Related to Talent and Interest in Mathematics and Engineering? Testing Some of the Central Claims of the Empathizing-Systemizing Theory," *British Journal of Psychology* (London, England) 103, no. 4 (November 2012): 472–96, https://

doi.org/10.1111/j.2044-8295.2011.02089.x; Emily Ruzich et al., "Sex and STEM Occupation Predict Autism-Spectrum Quotient (AQ) Scores in Half a Million People," *PLoS ONE* 10, no. 10 (October 21, 2015), https://doi.org/10.1371/journal.pone.0141229.

59. Baron-Cohen, "Extreme Male Brain Theory."

60. Stanley Rothman, S. Robert Lichter, and Neil Nevitte, "Politics and Professional Advancement among College Faculty," *Forum* 3, no. 1 (2005); Ingrid Nilsson, Bo Ekehammar, and Jim Sidanius, "Education and Sociopolitical Attitudes," *Scandinavian Journal of Educational Research* 29, no. 1 (March 1, 1985): 1–15, https://doi.org/10.1080/0031383850290101.

61. John T. Jost et al., "Political Conservatism as Motivated Social Cognition," *Psychological Bulletin* 129, no. 3 (May 2003): 339–75; Samuel D Gosling, Peter J Rentfrow, and William B Swann, "A Very Brief Measure of the Big-Five Personality Domains," *Journal of Research in Personality* 37, no. 6 (December 1, 2003): 504–28, https://doi.org/10.1016/S0092-6566(03)00046-1; Alain Van Hiel and Ivan Mervielde, "Openness to Experience and Boundaries in the Mind: Relationships with Cultural and Economic Conservative Beliefs," *Journal of Personality* 72, no. 4 (August 2004): 659–86, https://doi.org/10.1111/j.0022-3506.2004.00276.x; Alain van Hiel, Malgorzata Kossowska, and Ivan Mervielde, "The Relationship between Openness to Experience and Political Ideology," *Personality and Individual Differences* 28, no. 4 (April 1, 2000): 741–51, https://doi.org/10.1016/S0191-8869(99)00135-X.

62. Dana R. Carney et al., "The Secret Lives of Liberals and Conservatives: Personality Profiles, Interaction Styles, and the Things They Leave Behind," *Political Psychology* 29, no. 6 (December 1, 2008): 807–40, https://doi.org/10.1111/j.1467-9221.2008.00668.x.

63. Alain Van Hiel, Emma Onraet, and Sarah De Pauw, "The Relationship between Social-Cultural Attitudes and Behavioral Measures of Cognitive Style: A Meta-Analytic Integration of Studies," *Journal of Personality* 78, no. 6 (December 2010): 1765–99, https://doi.org/10.1111/j.1467-6494.2010.00669.x; Jost et al., "Political Conservatism as Motivated Social Cognition."

64. Lever, "Sex Differences in the Games Children Play"; Lever, "Sex Differences in the Complexity of Children's Play and Games."

65. Beverly I. Fagot, "Beyond the Reinforcement Principle: Another Step Toward Understanding Sex Role Development," *Developmental Psychology* 21, no. 6 (1985): 1097–1104.

66. Joyce F. Benenson and Henry Markovits, *Warriors and Worriers: The Survival of the Sexes* (Oxford University Press, 2014).

67. Hulda Thorisdottir et al., "Psychological Needs and Values Underlying Left-Right Political Orientation: Cross-National Evidence from Eastern and Western Europe," *Public Opinion Quarterly* 71, no. 2 (January 1, 2007): 175–203, https://doi.org/10.1093/poq/nfm008.

68. Carney et al., "Secret Lives of Liberals and Conservatives."

69. John T. Jost, "The End of the End of Ideology," *American Psychologist* 61, no. 7 (2006): 651–70, https://doi.org/10.1037/0003-066X.61.7.651; Jost et al., "Political Conservatism as Motivated Social Cognition."

70. Stanley Feldman and Karen Stenner, "Perceived Threat and Authoritarianism," *Political Psychology* 18, no. 4 (1997): 741–70, https://doi.org/10.2307/3792208; Stewart J. H. McCann, "Societal Threat, Authoritarianism, Conservatism, and U.S. State Death Penalty Sentencing (1977-2004)," *Journal of Personality and Social Psychology* 94, no. 5 (May 2008): 913–23, https://doi.org/10.1037/0022-3514.94.5.913.

71. Thomas G. Power, "Mother- and Father-Infant Play: A Developmental Analysis," *Child Development* 56, no. 6 (1985): 1514–24, https://doi.org/10.2307/1130470.

72. Dave Grossman, *On Killing: The Psychological Cost of Learning to Kill in War and Society*, rev. ed. (New York: Back Bay Books, 2009).

73. Patricia A. Resick, Candice M. Monson, and Kathleen M. Chard, *Cognitive Processing Therapy for PTSD: A Comprehensive Manual*, 1st ed. (New York: Guilford Press, 2016).

74. Irwin Silverman, Jean Choi, and Michael Peters, "The Hunter-Gatherer Theory of Sex Differences in Spatial Abilities: Data from 40 Countries," *Archives of Sexual Behavior* 36, no. 2 (April 2007): 261–68, https://doi.org/10.1007/s10508-006-9168-6.

75. Jonathan Wai, David Lubinski, and Camila Person Benbow, "Spatial Ability for STEM Domains: Aligning Over 50 Years of Cumulative Psychological Knowledge Solidifies Its Importance - Semantic Scholar," *Journal of Educational Psychology* 101, no. 4 (2009): 817–35, /paper/Spatial-Ability-for-STEM-Domains%3A-Aligning-Over-50-Wai-Lubinski/ca3d6205ffb8cab6724fb0828634826e2e87ead7.

76. Donald Kolakowski and Robert M. Malina, "Spatial Ability, Throwing Accuracy and Man's Hunting Heritage," *Nature* 251, no. 5474 (October 1974): 410–12, https://doi.org/10.1038/251410a0.

77. Rosemary Jardine and N. G. Martin, "Spatial Ability and Throwing Accuracy," *Behavior Genetics* 13, no. 4 (July 1, 1983): 331–40, https://doi.org/10.1007/BF01065771; Neil Watson and Doreen Kimura, "Nontrivial Sex Differences in Throwing and Intercepting: Relation to Psychometrically-Defined Spatial Functions," *Personality and Individual Differences* 12, no. 5 (1991): 375–85.

78. J. R. Thomas and K. E. French, "Gender Differences across Age in Motor Performance a Meta-Analysis," *Psychological Bulletin* 98, no. 2 (September 1985): 260–82.

CHAPTER 4: EQUALITY VERSUS HIERARCHY

1. Mike Allen and Edward Walsh, "Presidential Rivals Feast on Jokes, Jabs," *Washington Post*, October 20, 2000, https://www.washingtonpost.com/archive/politics/2000/10/20/presidential-rivals-feast-on-jokes-jabs/aab5a86a-28f2-4ab7-b1db-85716c55fe68/?noredirect=on&utm_term=.ca2256ce215e.

2. Christopher Boehm, *Hierarchy in the Forest: The Evolution of Egalitarian Behavior*, rev. ed. (Cambridge, MA: Harvard University Press, 2001).

3. Richard Borshay Lee, *The !Kung San: Men, Women and Work in a Foraging Society*, 1st ed. (Cambridge, England; New York: Cambridge University Press, 1979).

4. Boehm, *Hierarchy in the Forest*.

5. Napoleon A. Chagnon, *Yanomamo: The Fierce People*, 3rd ed. (New York: Holt McDougal, 1984).

6. Raymond Hames, "Costs and Benefits of Monogamy and Polygyny for Yanomamö Women," *Ethology and Sociobiology* 17 (1996): 181–99.

7. Jared M. Diamond, *Guns, Germs, and Steel: The Fates of Human Societies*, 1st edition (New York: W. W. Norton, 1999).

8. Monika Karmin et al., "A Recent Bottleneck of Y Chromosome Diversity Coincides with a Global Change in Culture," *Genome Research* 25, no. 4 (April 2015): 459–66, https://doi.org/10.1101/gr.186684.114.

9. Felipe Guaman Poma de Ayala, *The First New Chronicle and Good Government on the History of the World and the Incas up to 1615*, trans. and ed. Roland Hamilton (Austin: University of Texas Press, 2009), https://utpress.utexas.edu/books/guafir.

10. Thomas Jefferson, "To George Washington from Thomas Jefferson,

16 April 1784," Founders Online, http://founders.archives.gov/documents/ Washington/04-01-02-0215.

11. James Madison, "From James Madison to Jacob De La Motta, [Post–7] August 1820," Founders Online, http://founders.archives.gov/documents/ Madison/04-02-02-0089.

12. Lyndon B. Johnson (speech, US House of Representatives, Washington, DC, November 26, 1963), https://www.senate.gov/artandhistory/history/ resources/pdf/JointSession1963.pdf. Italics author's.

13. David P. Watts and John C. Mitani, "Boundary Patrols and Intergroup Encounters in Wild Chimpanzees," *Behaviour* 138, no. 3 (2001): 299–327, https://doi.org/10.1163/15685390152032488.

14. Jane Goodall, *The Chimpanzees of Gombe: Patterns of Behavior* (Cambridge, MA: Belknap Press, 1986); Watts and Mitani, "Boundary Patrols and Intergroup Encounters."

15. Toshisada Nishida et al., "Group Extinction and Female Transfer in Wild Chimpanzees in the Mahale National Park, Tanzania," *Zeitschrift für Tierpsychologie* 67, no. 1–4 (January 12, 1985): 284–301, https://doi.org/10 .1111/j.1439-0310.1985.tb01395.x; Jennifer M. Williams et al., "Why Do Male Chimpanzees Defend a Group Range?" *Animal Behaviour* 68, no. 3 (September 1, 2004): 523–32, https://doi.org/10.1016/j.anbehav.2003.09.015.

16. J. C. Mitani and D. P. Watts, "Demographic Influences on the Hunting Behavior of Chimpanzees," *American Journal of Physical Anthropology* 109, no. 4 (August 1999): 439–54, https://doi.org/10.1002/(SICI)1096-8644 (199908)109:4<439::AID-AJPA2>3.0.CO;2-3.

17. Martin N. Muller and John C. Mitani, "Conflict and Cooperation in Wild Chimpanzees," *Advances in the Study of Behavior* 35 (January 1, 2005): 275– 331, https://doi.org/10.1016/S0065-3454(05)35007-8.

18. Michael Greshko, "In Rare Killing, Chimpanzees Cannibalize Former Leader," *National Geographic*, January 30, 2017, http://news.nationalgeographic .com/2017/01/chimpanzees-murder-cannibalism-senegal/.

19. Dale Peterson and Richard Wrangham, *Demonic Males: Apes and the Origins of Human Violence*, October 15, 1997 ed. (Boston: Mariner, 1997).

20. Lawrence H. Keeley, "War Before Civilization—15 Years On," in *The Evolution of Violence*, ed. Todd K. Shackelford and Ranald D. Hansen (New York: Springer New York, 2014), pp. 23–31, https://doi.org/10.1007/978-1-4614-9314-3_2.

21. US Census Bureau, "21.3 Percent of US Participates in Government

Assistance Programs Each Month," press release, May 28, 2015, https://www.census.gov/newsroom/press-releases/2015/cb15-97.html; Rich Morin, "The Politics and Demographics of Food Stamp Recipients," Pew Research Center, Washington, DC, July 12, 2013, http://www.pewresearch.org/fact-tank/2013/07/12/the-politics-and-demographics-of-food-stamp-recipients/.

22. Martin Gilens, "Racial Attitudes and Opposition to Welfare," *Journal of Politics* 57, no. 4 (1995): 994–1014, https://doi.org/10.2307/2960399; Martin Gilens, "'Race Coding' and White Opposition to Welfare," *American Political Science Review* 90, no. 3 (1996): 593–604, https://doi.org/10.2307/2082611.

23. David M. Buss, *The Evolution of Desire: Strategies of Human Mating*, 3rd ed. (New York: Basic Books, 2003).

24. Ibid.

25. Russell D. Clark and Elaine Hatfield, "Gender Differences in Receptivity to Sexual Offers," *Journal of Psychology & Human Sexuality* 2, no. 1 (August 7, 1989): 39–55, https://doi.org/10.1300/J056v02n01_04.

26. Glenn D. Wilson, "Gender Differences in Sexual Fantasy: An Evolutionary Analysis," *Personality and Individual Differences* 22, no. 1 (January 1, 1997): 27–31, https://doi.org/10.1016/S0191-8869(96)00180-8.

27. Bruce J. Ellis and Donald Symons, "Sex Differences in Sexual Fantasy: An Evolutionary Psychological Approach," *Journal of Sex Research* 27, no. 4 (1990): 527–55, https://doi.org/10.1080/00224499009551579.

28. Buss, *Evolution of Desire*; Rosemary L. Hopcroft, "Sex, Status, and Reproductive Success in the Contemporary United States," *Evolution and Human Behavior* 27, no. 2 (March 1, 2006): 104–20, https://doi.org/10.1016/j.evolhumbehav.2005.07.004.

29. M. Teschler-Nicola et al., "Evidence of Genocide 7000 BP--Neolithic Paradigm and Geo-Climatic Reality," *Collegium Antropologicum* 23, no. 2 (December 1999): 437–50.

30. Will Durant, *The Story of Civilization*, vol. 4, *The Age of Faith: A History of Medieval Civilization—Christian, Islamic, and Judaic—From Constantine to Dante: A.D. 325–1300* (New York: Simon & Schuster, 1950).

31. Dominick Busnot, *History of the Reign of Muley Ismael, the Present King of Morocco* (Bronx, NY: Ishi Press, 2015).

32. Elisabeth Oberzaucher and Karl Grammer, "The Case of Moulay Ismael: Fact or Fancy?" *PLOS ONE* 9, no. 2 (February 14, 2014): e85292, https://doi.org/10.1371/journal.pone.0085292.

33. Laura L. Betzig, ed., *Despotism and Differential Reproduction: A Darwinian View of History*, 1st ed. (Piscataway, NJ: Routledge, 2008).

34. Janine di Giovanni, Leah McGrath Goodman, and Damien Sharkov, "How Does ISIS Fund Its Reign of Terror?" *Newsweek*, November 6, 2014, http://www.newsweek.com/2014/11/14/how-does-isis-fund-its-reign-terror-282607.html.

35. Rukmini Callimachi, "ISIS Enshrines a Theology of Rape," *New York Times*, August 13, 2015, https://www.nytimes.com/2015/08/14/world/middleeast/isis-enshrines-a-theology-of-rape.html.

36. Atika Shubert and Bharati Naik, "ISIS 'Forced Pregnant Yazidi Women to Have Abortions,'" CNN.com, October 6, 2015, https://www.cnn.com/2015/10/06/middleeast/pregnant-yazidis-forced-abortions-isis/index.html.

37. Lei Chang et al., "The Face That Launched a Thousand Ships: The Mating-Warring Association in Men," *Personality and Social Psychology Bulletin* 37, no. 7 (July 2011): 976–84, https://doi.org/10.1177/0146167211402216.

38. Michael E. Price et al., "Muscularity and Attractiveness as Predictors of Human Egalitarianism," *Personality and Individual Differences* 50, no. 5 (April 2011): 636–40, https://doi.org/10.1016/j.paid.2010.12.009.

39. Samuel Bendahan et al., "Leader Corruption Depends on Power and Testosterone," *Leadership Quarterly* 26, no. 2 (April 1, 2015): 101–22, https://doi.org/10.1016/j.leaqua.2014.07.010.

40. Paul J. Zak et al., "Testosterone Administration Decreases Generosity in the Ultimatum Game," *PloS One* 4, no. 12 (December 16, 2009): e8330, https://doi.org/10.1371/journal.pone.0008330.

41. Raphael S. Ezekiel, *The Racist Mind: Portraits of American Neo-Nazis and Klansmen* (repr.; New York: Penguin, 1996).

42. Niambi M. Carter, "The Curious Case of Judge Aaron: The Race, the Law, and the Protection of White Supremacy," *Politics, Groups, and Identities* 1, no. 3 (September 1, 2013): 370–79, https://doi.org/10.1080/21565503.2013.820137.

43. David A. Graham, "Paul LePage's Racist Fearmongering on Drugs," *Atlantic*, January 8, 2016, https://www.theatlantic.com/politics/archive/2016/01/racial-dogwhistling-with-paul-lepage-still-americas-most-outlandish-governor/423246/. Italics author's.

44. Felicia Pratto et al., "Social Dominance Orientation: A Personality Variable Predicting Social and Political Attitudes," *Journal of Personality and Social*

Psychology 67, no. 4 (1994): 741–63, https://doi.org/10.1037/
0022-3514.67.4.741.

45. Ibid.

46. Jim Sidanius and James H. Liu, "The Gulf War and the Rodney King Beating: Implications of the General Conservatism and Social Dominance Perspectives," *Journal of Social Psychology* 132, no. 6 (December 1, 1992): 685–700, https://doi.org/10.1080/00224545.1992.9712099; Jim Sidanius, Felicia Pratto, and Joshua L. Rabinowitz, "Gender, Ethnic Status, and Ideological Asymmetry: A Social Dominance Interpretation," *Journal of Cross-Cultural Psychology* 25, no. 2 (June 1, 1994): 194–216, https://doi.org/10.1177/0022022194252003; Bob Altemeyer, "The Other 'Authoritarian Personality,'" *Advances in Experimental Social Psychology* 30 (January 1, 1998): 47–92, https://doi.org/10.1016/S0065-2601(08)60382-2; Jim Sidanius, Felicia Pratto, and Lawrence Bobo, "Social Dominance Orientation and the Political Psychology of Gender: A Case of Invariance?," *Journal of Personality and Social Psychology* 67, no. 6 (1994): 998–1011, https://doi.org/10.1037/0022-3514.67.6.998.

47. Jim Sidanius, Shana Levin, James Lui, and Felicia Pratto, "Social Dominance Orientation, Anti- Egalitarianism and the Political Psychology of Gender: An Extension and Cross-Cultural Replication," *European Journal of Social Psychology* 30 (2000): 41–67.

48. Sam G. McFarland, "On the Eve of War: Authoritarianism, Social Dominance, and American Students' Attitudes toward Attacking Iraq," *Personality & Social Psychology Bulletin* 31, no. 3 (March 2005): 360–67, https://doi.org/10.1177/0146167204271596; Felicia Pratto et al., "Social Dominance Orientation: A Personality Variable Predicting Social and Political Attitudes.," *Journal of Personality and Social Psychology* 67, no. 4 (1994): 741–63, https://doi.org/10.1037/0022-3514.67.4.741; J. Christopher Cohrs et al., "Personal Values and Attitudes Toward War," *Peace and Conflict: Journal of Peace Psychology* 11, no. 3 (September 1, 2005): 293–312, https://doi.org/10.1207/s15327949pac1103_5.

49. Pratto et al., "Social Dominance Orientation."

50. Ibid.; Patrick C. L. Heaven, "Attitudes toward Women's Rights: Relationships with Social Dominance Orientation and Political Group Identities," *Sex Roles* 41, no. 7–8 (October 1, 1999): 605–14, https://doi.org/10.1023/A:1018851606423.

51. R. I. M. Dunbar, "Coevolution of Neocortical Size, Group Size and Language in Humans," *Behavioral and Brain Sciences* 16, no. 4 (December 1993): 681–94, https://doi.org/10.1017/S0140525X00032325.

52. Chris Cantor, *Evolution and Posttraumatic Stress: Disorders of Vigilance and Defence*, 1st ed. (Hove, East Sussex; New York: Routledge, 2005).

53. Dunbar, "Coevolution of Neocortical Size."

54. I.-Ching Lee, Felicia Pratto, and Blair T. Johnson, "Intergroup Consensus/Disagreement in Support of Group-Based Hierarchy: An Examination of Socio-Structural and Psycho-Cultural Factors," *Psychological Bulletin* 137, no. 6 (November 2011): 1029–64, https://doi.org/10.1037/a0025410.

55. George A. Bonanno and John T. Jost, "Conservative Shift among High-Exposure Survivors of the September 11th Terrorist Attacks," *Basic and Applied Social Psychology* 28, no. 4 (December 1, 2006): 311–23, https://doi.org/10.1207/s15324834basp2804_4.

56. Yesilernis Peña and Jim Sidanius, "US Patriotism and Ideologies of Group Dominance: A Tale of Asymmetry," *Journal of Social Psychology* 142, no. 6 (December 2002): 782–90, https://doi.org/10.1080/00224540209603936.

57. Carroll Doherty, "Who Flies the Flag? Not Always Who You Might Think," Pew Research Center, Washington, DC, June 27, 2007, http://www.pewresearch.org/2007/06/27/who-flies-the-flag-not-always-who-you-might-think/; "American Values Survey: Question Database; 40i I Am Very Patriotic," Pew Research Center, Washington, DC, 2013, http://www.people-press.org/values-questions/q40i/i-am-very-patriotic/#party.

58. Arnold K. Ho et al., "Social Dominance Orientation: Revisiting the Structure and Function of a Variable Predicting Social and Political Attitudes," *Personality and Social Psychology Bulletin* 38, no. 5 (May 1, 2012): 583–606, https://doi.org/10.1177/0146167211432765.

59. Jane Goodall, *The Chimpanzees of Gombe: Patterns of Behavior* (Cambridge, MA: Belknap Press, 1986).

60. Margo Wilson and Martin Daly, *Homicide* (New York: Aldine Transaction, 1988); Peterson and Wrangham, *Demonic Males*.

61. Richard Dawkins, *The Selfish Gene: 40th Anniversary Edition*, 4th ed. (New York: Oxford University Press, 2016).

62. Jennifer Ackerman, *Chance in the House of Fate: A Natural History of Heredity*, 1st ed. (Boston: Mariner, 2002).

63. George Peter Murdock, *Atlas of World Cultures* (Pittsburgh, PA: University of Pittsburgh Press, 1981).

64. Peterson and Wrangham, *Demonic Males*.

65. William Tulio Divale and Marvin Harris, "Population, Warfare, and the

Male Supremacist Complex," *American Anthropologist* 78, no. 3 (September 1, 1976): 521–38, https://doi.org/10.1525/aa.1976.78.3.02a00020.

66. Peterson and Wrangham, *Demonic Males.*

67. John C. Mitani, David P. Watts, and Martin N. Muller, "Recent Developments in the Study of Wild Chimpanzee Behavior," *Evolutionary Anthropology: Issues, News, and Reviews* 11, no. 1 (January 1, 2002): 9–25, https://doi.org/10.1002/evan.10008.

68. UNODC Research and Trend Analysis Branch, Division of Policy Analysis and Public Affairs, *The Global Study on Homicide 2013* (Vienna, Austria: United Nations, 2013), http://www.unodc.org/documents/gsh/pdfs/2014 _GLOBAL_HOMICIDE_BOOK_web.pdf.

69. Lawrence Keeley, *War before Civilization* (Oxford: Oxford University Press, 1996).

70. Dave Grossman, *On Killing: The Psychological Cost of Learning to Kill in War and Society*, rev. ed. (New York: Back Bay Books, 2009).

71. Mark Van Vugt, David De Cremer, and Dirk P. Janssen, "Gender Differences in Cooperation and Competition: The Male-Warrior Hypothesis," *Psychological Science* 18, no. 1 (January 1, 2007): 19–23, https://doi.org/10.1111/j.1467-9280.2007.01842.x.

CHAPTER 5: ON BIG APES AND PRESIDENTS

1. Associated Press, "Leaked DNC Emails Reveal Details of Anti-Sanders Sentiment," *Guardian*, July 24, 2016, https://www.theguardian.com/us-news/2016/jul/23/dnc-emails-wikileaks-hillary-bernie-sanders.

2. Adam Taylor, "61 Not-Very-Positive Things Foreign Leaders Have Said about Donald Trump," *Washington Post*, July 19, 2016, https://www.washington post.com/news/worldviews/wp/2016/05/06/47-not-very-positive-things -foreign-leaders-have-said-about-donald-trump/; Patrick Wintour, "'A Revolting Slug': What Politicians Said before Trump Got Elected," *Guardian*, November 9, 2016, http://www.theguardian.com/us-news/2016/nov/09/ a-revolting-slug-what-politicians-said-before-trump-got-elected.

3. Taylor, "61 Not-Very-Positive Things."

4. Aaron Blake, "19 Things Donald Trump Knows Better than Anyone Else,

According to Donald Trump," *Washington Post*, October 4, 2016, https://www.washingtonpost.com/news/the-fix/wp/2016/10/04/17-issues -that-donald-trump-knows-better-than-anyone-else-according-to-donald -trump/?utm_term=.72e843f55ce7; Oliver Noble, "24 Things Nobody Does Better than Trump (According to Trump)," Vice News, February 22, 2017, https://news.vice.com/en_us/article/nedxnm/24-things -nobody-does-better-than-trump-according-to-trump.

5. Charles Krauthammer, "It's Not the 'Locker-Room' Talk. It's the 'Lock Her up' Talk," *Washington Post*, October 13, 2016, https://www .washingtonpost.com/opinions/its-not-the-locker-room-talk-its-the-lock-her-up -talk/2016/10/13/9dd5fbea-9172-11e6-9c85-ac42097b8cc0_story.html.

6. John W. L. Berry, "Donald Trump: On the Road to War," *Patheos: Progressive American*, March 1, 2017, http://www.patheos.com/blogs/ progressiveamerican/2017/03/donald-trump-road-war/.

7. Jonathan Haidt, "Trump Calls for 'Hell of a Lot Worse than Waterboarding,'" *The Hill*, February 6, 2016, http://thehill.com/blogs/ballot-box/ gop-primaries/268530-trump-calls-for-hell-of-a-lot-worse-than-waterboarding.

8. Taylor, "61 Not-Very-Positive Things."

9. "Pope Francis Warns against Rise in Populism," BBC News, January 22, 2017, http://www.bbc.com/news/world-europe-38708485.

10. Jessica Taylor, "Trump Gets Mixed Response from Conservative Liberty University," NPR, January 18, 2016, http://www.npr.org/ 2016/01/18/463503852/ trump-gets-mixed-response-from-conservative-liberty-university.

11. "Transcript: Donald Trump's Taped Comments about Women," *New York Times*, October 8, 2016, https://www.nytimes.com/2016/10/08/us/donald -trump-tape-transcript.html.

12. J. Antonakis and O. Dalgas, "Predicting Elections: Child's Play!" *Science* 323, no. 5918 (February 27, 2009): 1183, https://doi.org/10.1126/ science.1167748.

13. Fred H. Willhoite, "Primates and Political Authority: A Biobehavioral Perspective," *American Political Science Review* 70, no. 4 (1976): 1110–26, https:// doi.org/10.2307/1959377; Julie A. Johnson, "Dominance Rank in Juvenile Olive Baboons, *Papio anubis*: The Influence of Gender, Size, Maternal Rank and Orphaning," *Animal Behaviour* 35, no. 6 (December 1, 1987): 1694–708, https:// doi.org/10.1016/S0003-3472(87)80062-3; Frans de Waal, *Chimpanzee Politics:*

Power and Sex among Apes, 25th anniversary ed. (Baltimore, MD: Johns Hopkins University Press, 2007).

14. Gregg R. Murray and J. David Schmitz, "Caveman Politics: Evolutionary Effects on Political Preferences" (paper presented at the Annual Meeting of the MPSA Annual National Conference, Chicago IL, April 4–7, 2008).

15. Gregg R. Murray and J. David Schmitz, "Caveman Politics: Evolutionary Leadership Preferences and Physical Stature: Evolutionary Leadership Preferences and Physical Stature," *Social Science Quarterly*, 92, no. 5 (October 2011): 1215–35, https://doi.org/10.1111/j.1540-6237.2011.00815.x.

16. Anne Case and Christina Paxson, "Stature and Status: Height, Ability, and Labor Market Outcomes," *Journal of Political Economy* 116, no. 3 (2008): 499–532, https://doi.org/10.1086/589524.

17. M. Vaz, S. Hunsberger, and B. Diffey, "Prediction Equations for Handgrip Strength in Healthy Indian Male and Female Subjects Encompassing a Wide Age Range," *Annals of Human Biology* 29, no. 2 (January 1, 2002): 131–41, https://doi.org/10.1080/03014460110058962.

18. Christopher Von Rueden, Michael Gurven, and Hillard Kaplan, "The Multiple Dimensions of Male Social Status in an Amazonian Society," *Evolution and Human Behavior: Official Journal of the Human Behavior and Evolution Society* 29, no. 6 (November 2008): 402–15, https://doi.org/10.1016/j.evolhumbehav.2008.05.001.

19. B. Pawlowski, R. I. Dunbar, and A. Lipowicz, "Tall Men Have More Reproductive Success," *Nature* 403, no. 6766 (January 13, 2000): 156, https://doi.org/10.1038/35003107.

20. Melissa Fares, "Canadian PM Trudeau Slips from Political Ring to Boxing Ring," Reuters, April 21, 2016, https://www.reuters.com/article/us-usa-canada-trudeau-gym/canadian-pm-trudeau-slips-from-political-ring-to-boxing-ring-idUSKCN0XI2RL.

21. Heather Saul, "Democratic Debate: Jim Webb Gives the Most Awkward Answer of the Evening," *Independent*, October 14, 2015, https://www.independent.co.uk/news/people/democratic-debate-jim-webb-gives-the-most-awkward-answer-of-the-evening-a6693361.html.

22. Eric Bradner, "Ben Carson's Violent Past: Bricks, Bats, Hammers," CNN, October 26, 2015, http://www.cnn.com/2015/10/25/politics/ben-carson-violent-past-donald-trump/index.html.

23. Nick Corasaniti and Maggie Haberman, "Donald Trump on Protester:

'I'd Like to Punch Him in the Face,'" *New York Times*, February 23, 2016, https://www.nytimes.com/politics/first-draft/2016/02/23/donald-trump-on-protester-id-like-to-punch-him-in-the-face/.

24. Sebastian Junger, "How Donald Trump Could Stop Being a Coward: There Is a Simple Reason Trump Is Placating Putin Even as He Has Attacked Assad," *Vanity Fair*, April 25, 2007, https://www.vanityfair.com/news/2017/04/donald-trump-putin-sebastian-junger.

25. Ben Jacobs, "Trump Repeats Crowd Member's 'Pussy' Insult as New Hampshire Votes," *Guardian*, February 9, 2016, https://www.theguardian.com/us-news/2016/feb/08/trump-repeats-insult-from-crowd-member-calling-cruz-a-pussy.

26. "Donald Trump Running for President," Fox News, June 17, 2015, http://www.foxnews.com/transcript/2015/06/17/donald-trump-running-for-president.html. Italics author's.

27. Aaron Sell, Liana S. E. Hone, and Nicholas Pound, "The Importance of Physical Strength to Human Males," *Human Nature* (Hawthorne, NY) 23, no. 1 (March 2012): 30–44, https://doi.org/10.1007/s12110-012-9131-2.

28. Jonathan Chait, "Mike Pence Strongly Believes Donald Trump's Shoulder Width Guarantees His Foreign-Policy Acumen," *Daily Intelligencer*, August 22, 2017, http://nymag.com/daily/intelligencer/2017/08/12-times-mike-pence-praised-donald-trumps-shoulders.html.

29. James Fallows, "When Donald Meets Hillary: Who Will Win the Debates? Trump's Approach Was an Important Part of His Strength in the Primaries. But Will It Work When He Faces Clinton Onstage?" *Atlantic*, October 2016, https://www.theatlantic.com/magazine/archive/2016/10/who-will-win/497561/.

30. Ian S. Penton-Voak and Jennie Y. Chen, "High Salivary Testosterone Is Linked to Masculine Male Facial Appearance in Humans," *Evolution and Human Behavior* 25, no. 4 (July 1, 2004): 229–41, https://doi.org/10.1016/j.evolhumbehav.2004.04.003.

31. Alexander Todorov et al., "Social Attributions from Faces: Determinants, Consequences, Accuracy, and Functional Significance," *Annual Review of Psychology* 66 (January 3, 2015): 519–45, https://doi.org/10.1146/annurev-psych-113011-143831.

32. Ulrich Mueller and Allan Mazur, "Facial Dominance of West Point Cadets as a Predictor of Later Military Rank," *Social Forces* 74, no. 3 (1996): 823–50, https://doi.org/10.2307/2580383.

33. Daniel E. Re et al., "Facial Cues to Perceived Height Influence Leadership Choices in Simulated War and Peace Contexts," *Evolutionary Psychology: An International Journal of Evolutionary Approaches to Psychology and Behavior* 11, no. 1 (January 31, 2013): 89–103.

34. Ibid.; Anthony C. Little et al., "Facial Appearance Affects Voting Decisions," *Evolution and Human Behavior* 28, no. 1 (January 1, 2007): 18–27, https://doi.org/10.1016/j.evolhumbehav.2006.09.002.

35. Brian R. Spisak et al., "Facing the Situation: Testing a Biosocial Contingency Model of Leadership in Intergroup Relations Using Masculine and Feminine Faces," *Leadership Quarterly*, Biology of Leadership, 23, no. 2 (April 1, 2012): 273–80, https://doi.org/10.1016/j.leaqua.2011.08.006.

36. Mark Van Vugt and Brian R. Spisak, "Sex Differences in the Emergence of Leadership during Competitions within and between Groups," *Psychological Science* 19, no. 9 (September 2008): 854–58, https://doi.org/10.1111/j.1467-9280.2008.02168.x.

37. Gregory A. Smith and Jessica Martínez, "How the Faithful Voted: A Preliminary 2016 Analysis," Pew Research Center, Washington, DC, November 9, 2016, http://www.pewresearch.org/fact-tank/2016/11/09/how-the-faithful-voted-a-preliminary-2016-analysis/.

38. Exod. 15:3 (International Standard Version).

39. Hector A. Garcia, *Alpha God: The Psychology of Religious Violence and Oppression* (Amherst, NY: Prometheus Books, 2015).

40. Exod. 34:24 (New International Version).

41. Exod. 16:4 (King James Version).

42. Ps. 111:5 (King James Version).

43. Ps. 22:19–21 (New International Version).

44. Harriet Sinclair, "Trump Has Authority from God to Wage War with North Korea, His Religious Adviser Claims," *Newsweek*, August 9, 2017, http://www.newsweek.com/trumps-religious-adviser-says-god-has-given-president-authority-take-north-648974.

45. Julian Borger, "How Born-Again George Became a Man on a Mission," *Guardian*, October 7, 2005, https://www.theguardian.com/world/2005/oct/07/usa.georgebush.

46. "With God on Our Side," *Washington Post*, October 18, 2003, https://www.washingtonpost.com/archive/opinions/2003/10/18/with-god-on-our-side/d918315c-eaab-41c2-af73-6fa27b556c9e/.

47. Case and Paxson, "Stature and Status."

48. Avi Tuschman, *Our Political Nature: The Evolutionary Origins of What Divides Us* (Amherst, NY: Prometheus Books, 2013).

49. "Profile: Kim Jong-Il," BBC News, January 16, 2009, http://news.bbc .co.uk/2/hi/asia-pacific/1907197.stm.

50. Jim Powell, *Wilson's War: How Woodrow Wilson's Great Blunder Led to Hitler, Lenin, Stalin, and World War II* (New York: Crown, 2007).

51. Edgar Snow, "A Conversation with Mao Tse-Tung," *LIFE*, April 30, 1971.

52. Tang Tsou, *The Cultural Revolution and Post-Mao Reforms: A Historical Perspective* (Chicago: University of Chicago Press, 1999).

53. Frederic Wakeman, *History and Will: Philosophical Perspectives of Mao Tse-Tung's Thought* (Berkeley: University of California Press, 1973).

54. Frank Dikötter, *Mao's Great Famine: The History of China's Most Devastating Catastrophe, 1958–1962* (London: Bloomsbury, 2011).

55. Steven Pinker, *The Better Angels of Our Nature: Why Violence Has Declined* (New York: Viking, 2011).

56. Timothy Snyder, *Bloodlands: Europe between Hitler and Stalin.* (New York: Basic Books, 2010).

57. Harrison E. Salisbury, *The New Emperors: China in the Era of Mao and Deng* (Boston: Little, Brown, 1992).

58. Juan Reinaldo Sanchez and Axel Gyldén, *The Double Life of Fidel Castro: My 17 Years as Personal Bodyguard to El Lider Maximo*, trans. Catherine Spencer (repr.; New York: St. Martin's Griffin, 2016).

59. Ann Louise Bardach, *Without Fidel: A Death Foretold in Miami, Havana and Washington*, 1st ed. (New York: Scribner, 2009).

60. Kenji Fujimoto, "I Was Kim Jong Il's Cook," *Atlantic*, February 2004, https://www.theatlantic.com/magazine/ archive/2004/01/i-was-kim-jong-ils-cook/308837/.

61. *Inside North Korea*, dir. Peter Jost, featuring Lisa Ling (Washington, DC: National Geographic, 2006).

62. Peter Singer, *A Darwinian Left: Politics, Evolution, and Cooperation* (New Haven, CT: Yale University Press, 2000).

63. Robert Altemeyer, *The Authoritarian Specter*, 1st ed. (Cambridge, MA: Harvard University Press, 1996).

64. Sam G. McFarland, Vladimir S. Ageyev, and Mariana A. Abalakina-Paap, "Authoritarianism in the Former Soviet Union," *Journal of Personality and Social*

Psychology 63, no. 6 (1992): 1004–10, http://dx.doi.org/10.1037/0022
-3514.63.6.1004; Sam G. McFarland, Vladimir S. Ageyev, and Mariana Abalakina,
"The Authoritarian Personality in the United States and the Former Soviet Union:
Comparative Studies," in *Strength and Weakness: The Authoritarian Personality
Today*, ed. W.F. Stone, G. Lederer, and R. Christie (New York: Springer, 1993).

65. Bob Altemeyer, *The Authoritarians*, unabridged ed. (Ramona, CA: Cherry
Hill, 2008).

66. Joachim C. Fest, *Hitler*, 1st ed. (San Diego: Mariner, 2002).

67. Josh Aronson and Denise George, *Orchestra of Exiles: The Story of
Bronislaw Huberman, the Israel Philharmonic, and the One Thousand Jews He
Saved from Nazi Horrors*, 1st ed. (New York: Berkley, 2016).

68. Fest, *Hitler*.

69. Bob Altemeyer, *Right-Wing Authoritarianism* (Winnipeg: University of
Manitoba Press, 1981), p. 148.

70. J. Christopher Cohrs and Frank Asbrock, "Right-Wing Authoritarianism,
Social Dominance Orientation and Prejudice against Threatening and Competitive Ethnic Groups," *European Journal of Social Psychology* 39, no. 2 (March 1,
2009): 270–89, https://doi.org/10.1002/ejsp.545; Bernard E. Whitley Jr., "Right-
Wing Authoritarianism, Social Dominance Orientation, and Prejudice," *Journal of
Personality and Social Psychology* 77, no. 1 (1999): 126–34, https://doi
.org/10.1037/0022-3514.77.1.126.

71. Bill E. Peterson and Marian D. Lane, "Implications of Authoritarianism
for Young Adulthood: Longitudinal Analysis of College Experiences and Future
Goals," *Personality and Social Psychology Bulletin* 27, no. 6 (June 1, 2001): 678–90,
https://doi.org/10.1177/0146167201276004.

72. John T. Jost et al., "Political Conservatism as Motivated Social
Cognition," *Psychological Bulletin* 129, no. 3 (May 2003): 339–75.

73. Bob Altemeyer, "The Other 'Authoritarian Personality,'" *Advances in
Experimental Social Psychology* 30 (January 1, 1998): 47–92, https://doi.org/
10.1016/S0065-2601(08)60382-2.

74. Whitley, "Right-Wing Authoritarianism."

75. Altemeyer, "Other 'Authoritarian Personality.'"

76. Jost et al., "Political Conservatism."

77. Altemeyer, "Other 'Authoritarian Personality'"; Alain Van Hiel, Mario
Pandelaere, and Bart Duriez, "The Impact of Need for Closure on Conservative
Beliefs and Racism: Differential Mediation by Authoritarian Submission and

Authoritarian Dominance," *Personality & Social Psychology Bulletin* 30, no. 7 (July 2004): 824–37, https://doi.org/10.1177/0146167204264333; John Duckitt, "A Dual-Process Cognitive-Motivational Theory of Ideology and Prejudice," *Advances in Experimental Social Psychology* 33 (January 1, 2001): 41–113, https://doi.org/ 10.1016/S0065-2601(01)80004-6.

78. John L. Genz and David Lester, "Military Service, Education and Authoritarian Attitudes of Municipal Police Officers," *Psychological Reports* 40, no. 2 (April 1977): 402, https://doi.org/10.2466/pr0.1977.40.2.402; Sharon E. Robinson Kurpius and A. Leigh Lucart, "Military and Civilian Undergraduates: Attitudes toward Women, Masculinity, and Authoritarianism," *Sex Roles* 43, no. 3–4 (August 1, 2000): 255–65, https://doi.org/10.1023/A:1007085015637.

79. Bert Hölldobler and Edward O. Wilson, *Journey to the Ants: A Story of Scientific Exploration*, rev. ed. (London: Belknap Press, 1994).

80. Ibid.

81. E. O. Wilson, *Success and Dominance in Ecosystems: The Case of the Social Insects* (Oldendorf, Germany: Ecology Institute, 1990), https://www.cabdirect .org/cabdirect/abstract/19920232190.

82. Hölldobler and Wilson, *Journey to the Ants.*

83. Anna Maria Manganelli Rattazzi, Andrea Bobbio, and Luigina Canova, "A Short Version of the Right-Wing Authoritarianism (RWA) Scale," *Personality and Individual Differences* 43, no. 5 (October 1, 2007): 1223–34, https://doi.org/ 10.1016/j.paid.2007.03.013.

84. Tom Vanden Brook, "Army Demotes 'Swinging General' after Investigation into Affairs, Lifestyle," *USA Today*, December 16, 2016, https:// www.usatoday.com/story/news/politics/2016/12/16/army-demotes -swinging-general-david-haight/95493058/.

85. B. Smuts, "Male Aggression against Women: An Evolutionary Perspective," *Human Nature* (Hawthorne, NY) 3, no. 1 (March 1992): 1–44, https://doi.org/10.1007/BF02692265.

86. Kevin B. Smith et al., "Political Orientations May Vary with Detection of the Odor of Androstenone" (paper presented at annual meeting of the Midwest Political Science Association, Chicago, IL, 2011).

87. John D. Wagner, Mark V. Flinn, and Barry G. England, "Hormonal Response to Competition among Male Coalitions," *Evolution and Human Behavior* 23, no. 6 (November 1, 2002): 437–42, https://doi.org/10.1016/ S1090-5138(02)00100-9.

88. Mark V. Flinn, Davide Ponzi, and Michael P. Muehlenbein, "Hormonal Mechanisms for Regulation of Aggression in Human Coalitions," *Human Nature* 23, no. 1 (March 1, 2012): 68–88, https://doi.org/10.1007/s12110-012-9135-y.

89. Deut. 20:13–15 (New International Version).

90. Matt. 12:25 (New International Version).

91. Sebastian Junger, *Tribe: On Homecoming and Belonging*, 1st ed. (New York: Twelve, 2016).

92. George A. Bonanno and John T. Jost, "Conservative Shift among High-Exposure Survivors of the September 11th Terrorist Attacks," *Basic and Applied Social Psychology* 28, no. 4 (December 1, 2006): 311–23, https://doi.org/10.1207/s15324834basp2804_4.

93. John T. Jost and Jim Sidanius, eds., *Political Psychology (Key Readings in Social Psychology)* (New York: Psychology Press; 2004).

94. De Waal, *Chimpanzee Politics*.

CHAPTER 6: THE POLITICS OF SEXUAL CONTROL

1. David M. Buss, *The Evolution of Desire: Strategies of Human Mating*, 3rd ed. (New York: Basic Books, 2003).

2. Ibid.

3. Martin N. Muller and Richard W. Wrangham, eds., *Sexual Coercion in Primates and Humans: An Evolutionary Perspective on Male Aggression against Females*, 1st ed. (Cambridge, MA: Harvard University Press, 2009).

4. D. Singh and P. M. Bronstad, "Female Body Odour Is a Potential Cue to Ovulation," *Proceedings of the Royal Society B: Biological Sciences* 268, no. 1469 (April 22, 2001): 797–801, https://doi.org/10.1098/rspb.2001.1589.

5. Steven W. Gangestad, Randy Thornhill, and Christine E Garver, "Changes in Women's Sexual Interests and Their Partners' Mate-Retention Tactics across the Menstrual Cycle: Evidence for Shifting Conflicts of Interest," *Proceedings of the Royal Society B: Biological Sciences* 269, no. 1494 (May 7, 2002): 975–82, https://doi.org/10.1098/rspb.2001.1952.

6. Buss, *Evolution of Desire*.

7. Ibid.

8. Donatella Barazzetti, Franca Garreffa, and Rosaria Marsico, *Daphne Project Proposing New Indicators: Measure Violence's Effects. GVEI* (Rende, Italy:

University of Calabria, Centre Women's Studies, July 2007), http://www.surt.org/gvei/docs/national_report_italy.pdf.

9. United Nations Committee on the Elimination of Discrimination against Women, *Consideration of Reports Submitted by States Parties under Article 18 of the Convention on the Elimination of All Forms of Discrimination against Women Combined Fourth, Fifth, Sixth and Seventh Periodic Reports of States Parties Uruguay*, https://documents-dds-ny.un.org/doc/UNDOC/GEN/N07/408/93/PDF/N0740893.pdf?OpenElement.

10. Ronald F. Inglehart, "The Worldviews of Islamic Publics in Global Perspective," in *Values and Perceptions of the Islamic and Middle Eastern Publics*, ed. Mansoor Moaddel (New York: Palgrave Macmillan, 2007), pp. 25–46, https://doi.org/10.1057/9780230603332_2.

11. M. Steven Fish, "Islam and Authoritarianism," *World Politics* 55, no. 1 (October 2002): 4–37, https://doi.org/10.1353/wp.2003.0004.

12. *The Global Gender Gap Report 2016* (Geneva, Switzerland: World Economic Forum, 2016), http://reports.weforum.org/global-gender-gap-report-2016/.

13. Elham Manea, "Yemen," in *Women's Rights in the Middle East and North Africa: Progress Amid Resistance*, ed. Sanja Kelly and Julia Breslin (New York: Lanham MD: Freedom House/Rowman & Littlefield, 2010).

14. Kristine Beckerle, *Boxed In: Women and Saudi Arabia's Male Guardianship System* (New York: Human Rights Watch, July 16, 2016), https://www.hrw.org/report/2016/07/16/boxed/women-and-saudi-arabias-male-guardianship-system.

15. Samuel Osborne, "Saudi Arabia Jails Man for a Year after He Publically Called for End of Male Control over Women," *Independent*, December 30, 2016, http://www.independent.co.uk/news/world/middle-east/saudi-arabia-jail-man-public-call-for-end-of-male-dominance-women-misogyny-sexism-a7501651.html.

16. Courtney Howland, ed., *Religious Fundamentalisms and the Human Rights of Women* (1999; New York: Palgrave Macmillan, 2001).

17. Manea, "Yemen."

18. UNICEF, *Regional Overview for the Middle East and North Africa: MENA Gender Equality Profile*, October 2011, https://www.unicef.org/gender/files/REGIONAL-Gender-Eqality-Profile-2011.pdf.

19. Sūrat l-nisāa 4:34.

20. United Nations, "World Population Prospects 2017 Revision," Sex Ratio

by Region, Subregion, and Country, 1950–2100, https://esa.un.org/unpd/wpp/Download/Standard/Population/.

21. *2002 Women of Our World* (Washington, DC: Population Reference Bureau, 2002), http://www.onlinewomeninpolitics.org/womenofworld02.pdf.

22. Laura K. Weir, James W. A. Grant, and Jeffrey A. Hutchings, "The Influence of Operational Sex Ratio on the Intensity of Competition for Mates," *American Naturalist* 177, no. 2 (February 2011): 167–76, https://doi.org/10.1086/657918.

23. Hector A. Garcia, *Alpha God: The Psychology of Religious Violence and Oppression* (Amherst, NY: Prometheus Books, 2015).

24. Ronald Inglehart and Pippa Norris, "The True Clash of Civilizations," *Foreign Policy*, no. 135 (2003): 63–70, http://www.jstor.org/stable/3183594.

25. *Global Gender Gap Report 2016*.

26. Buss, *Evolution of Desire*.

27. Geoffrey R. Stone, *Sex and the Constitution: Sex, Religion, and Law from America's Origins to the Twenty-First Century*, 1st ed. (New York: Liveright, 2017).

28. Ibid.

29. Ibid.

30. Elaine Tyler May, "Promises the Pill Could Never Keep," *New York Times*, April 24, 2010, https://www.nytimes.com/2010/04/25/opinion/25may.html.

31. Lucy Madison, "Foster Friess: In My Day, Women 'Used Bayer Aspirin for Contraceptives,'" CBS News, February 17, 2012, https://www.cbsnews.com/news/foster-friess-in-my-day-women-used-bayer-aspirin-for-contraceptives/.

32. Kyle Munzenrieder, "Rep. Allen West: Activist Women Are 'Neutering American Men,'" *Miami New Times*, April 26, 2011, http://www.miaminewtimes.com/news/rep-allen-west-activist-women-are-neutering-american-men-6553902.

33. Joe Anderson et al., "Gun Owners, Ethics, and the Problem of Evil: A Response to the Las Vegas Shooting," *HAU: Journal of Ethnographic Theory* 7, no. 3 (December 22, 2017): 39–65, https://doi.org/10.14318/hau7.3.003.

34. John Ingold, "Senator Doesn't Regret Comments on HIV," *Denver Post*, February 26, 2009, https://www.denverpost.com/2009/02/26/senator-doesnt-regret-comments-on-hiv/.

35. "Public Divided over Birth Control Insurance Mandate," Pew Research Center, Washington, DC, February 14, 2012, http://www.people-press.org/2012/02/14/public-divided-over-birth-control-insurance-mandate/.

36. Russell Shorto, "Contra-Contraception," *New York Times*, May 7, 2006, https://www.nytimes.com/2006/05/07/magazine/07contraception.html.

37. 1 Cor. 6:13.

38. 1 Cor. 7–9.

39. Col. 3:18.

40. Jeffrey F. Peipert et al., "Preventing Unintended Pregnancies by Providing No-Cost Contraception," *Obstetrics and Gynecology* 120, no. 6 (December 2012): 1291–97, https://www.ncbi.nlm.nih.gov/pmc/articles/PMC4000282/.

41. Malcolm Potts and Thomas Hayden, *Sex and War: How Biology Explains Warfare and Terrorism and Offers a Path to a Safer World* (Dallas, TX: BenBella Books, 2008).

42. Conservapedia, s.v. "Abortion and Promiscuity," last modified July 11, 2016, http://www.conservapedia.com/Abortion_and_promiscuity.

43. Hosea 5:3.

44. Hosea 7:4.

45. Hosea 9:16.

46. Hosea 13:16.

47. Stone, *Sex and the Constitution*.

48. Charlie Savage, "Nixon Comments Disclosed on Abortion and Watergate," *New York Times*, June 23, 2009, https://www.nytimes.com/2009/06/24/us/politics/24nixon.html.

49. Sarah R. Hayford and S. Philip Morgan, "Religiosity and Fertility in the United States: The Role of Fertility Intentions," *Social Forces: A Scientific Medium of Social Study and Interpretation* 86, no. 3 (2008): 1163–88, https://doi.org/10.1353/sof.0.0000; Nitzan Peri-Rotem, "Religion and Fertility in Western Europe: Trends across Cohorts in Britain, France and the Netherlands," *European Journal of Population* 32 (2016): 231–65, https://doi.org/10.1007/s10680-015-9371-z.

50. Gen. 38: 8–10.

51. Gen. 1:28. Italics author's.

52. Conrad Hackett and David McClendon, "Christians Remain World's Largest Religious Group, but They Are Declining in Europe," Pew Research Center, Washington, DC, April 5, 2017, http://www.pewresearch.org/fact-tank/2017/04/05/christians-remain-worlds-largest-religious-group-but-they-are-declining-in-europe/.

53. Conrad Hackett and David McClendon, "The Changing Global Religious Landscape," Pew Research Center, April 5, 2017, http://www.pewforum.org/2017/04/05/the-changing-global-religious-landscape/.

54. John T. Noonan Jr., *Contraception: A History of Its Treatment by the Catholic Theologians and Canonists*, enlarged ed. (Cambridge, MA: Harvard University Press, 1986).

55. Merry Wiesner-Hanks, *Christianity and Sexuality in the Early Modern World: Regulating Desire, Reforming Practice*, 2nd ed. (London; New York: Routledge, 2010).

56. "The Global Catholic Population," Pew Research Center', Washington, DC, February 13, 2013, http://www.pewforum.org/2013/02/13/the-global -catholic-population/.

57. Ibid.

58. Julian R. Homburger et al., "Genomic Insights into the Ancestry and Demographic History of South America," *PLOS Genetics* 11, no. 12 (December 4, 2015): e1005602, https://doi.org/10.1371/journal.pgen.1005602; Katarzyna Bryc et al., "Genome-Wide Patterns of Population Structure and Admixture among Hispanic/Latino Populations," *Proceedings of the National Academy of Sciences* 107, supp. 2 (May 11, 2010): 8954–61, https://doi.org/10.1073/pnas.0914618107.

59. "1976: Government Admits Forced Sterilization of Indian Women," US National Library of Medicine, https://www.nlm.nih.gov/nativevoices/timeline/543.html.

60. P. 127: 3–5.

61. Barbara B. Hagerty, "In Quiverfull Movement, Birth Control Is Shunned," NPR, March 5, 2009, https://www.npr.org/templates/story/story .php?storyId=102005062.

62. Margaret Sanger, *Woman and the New Race* (New York: Brentano's Publishers, 1920).

63. Potts and Hayden, *Sex and War*.

64. Theodore Schleifer, "King Doubles down on Controversial 'Babies' Tweet," CNN, March 14, 2017, http://www.cnn.com/2017/03/13/politics/steve -king-babies-tweet-cnntv/index.html.

65. Potts and Hayden, *Sex and War*.

66. Christian G. Mesquida and Neil I. Wiener, "Male Age Composition and Severity of Conflicts," *Politics and the Life Sciences* 18, no. 2 (September 1999): 181–89, https://doi.org/10.1017/S0730938400021158.

67. Lawrence E. Cohen and Kenneth C. Land, "Age Structure and Crime: Symmetry versus Asymmetry and the Projection of Crime Rates through the

1990s," *American Sociological Review* 52, no. 2 (1987): 170–83, https://doi.org/10.2307/2095446.

68. John Bock, "Evolutionary Demography and Intrahousehold Time Allocation: School Attendance and Child Labor among the Okavango Delta Peoples of Botswana," *American Journal of Human Biology: The Official Journal of the Human Biology Council* 14, no. 2 (April 2002): 206–21, https://doi.org/10.1002/ajhb.10040.

69. Vladas Griskevicius et al., "The Financial Consequences of Too Many Men: Sex Ratio Effects on Saving, Borrowing, and Spending," *Journal of Personality and Social Psychology* 102, no. 1 (January 2012): 69–80, https://doi.org/10.1037/a0024761.

70. Margo Wilson and Martin Daly, "Competitiveness, Risk Taking, and Violence: The Young Male Syndrome," *Ethology and Sociobiology* 6, no. 1 (January 1, 1985): 59–73, https://doi.org/10.1016/0162-3095(85)90041-X.

71. Ellis Lee and Anthony Walsh, *Criminology: A Global Perspective*, 1st ed. (Boston: Allyn & Bacon, 2000).

72. Wilson and Daly, "Competitiveness, Risk Taking, and Violence."

73. Anindya Sen, "Does Increased Abortion Lead to Lower Crime? Evaluating the Relationship between Crime, Abortion, and Fertility," *B.E. Journal of Economic Analysis & Policy* 7, no. 1 (2007), https://doi.org/10.2202/1935-1682.1537; Hans Forssman and Inga Thuwe, "One Hundred and Twenty Children Born after Application for Therapeutic Abortion Refused: Their Mental Health, Social Adjustment and Educational Level up to the Age of 21," *Acta Psychiatrica Scandinavica* 42, no. 1 (March 1, 1966): 71–88, https://doi.org/10.1111/j.1600-0447.1966.tb01915.x; John J. Donohue and Steven D. Levitt, "The Impact of Legalized Abortion on Crime," *Quarterly Journal of Economics* 116, no. 2 (May 1, 2001): 379–420, https://doi.org/10.1162/00335530151144050.

74. *Conservapedia*, s.v. "Population Control," last modified December 1, 2017, http://www.conservapedia.com/Population_control.

75. Andrew C. Revkin, "C.I.A. Chief Lists Population as a Top Concern," *Dot Earth* (blog), *New York Times*, May 1, 2018, https://dotearth.blogs.nytimes.com/2008/05/01/cia-chief-lists-population-as-a-top-concern/.

76. Potts and Hayden, *Sex and War*.

77. Ibid.

78. Ibid.

79. Prescott Bush, "To Preserve Peace Let's Show Russia How Strong We Are," *Readers Digest*, July 1959, pp. 25–30.

80. Potts and Hayden, *Sex and War*.

81. Thomas H. Kean and Lee H. Hamilton, *The 9/11 Report: The National Commission on Terrorist Attacks Upon the United States* (New York: St. Martin's, 2004).

CHAPTER 7: WOMEN, SEX, AND POLITICS

1. Ashley Montagu, *Touching: The Human Significance of the Skin*, 3rd ed. (New York: William Morrow Paperbacks, 1986).

2. David M. Buss, *The Evolution of Desire: Strategies of Human Mating*, 3rd ed. (New York: Basic Books, 2003).

3. M. D. Botwin, D. M. Buss, and T. K. Shackelford, "Personality and Mate Preferences: Five Factors in Mate Selection and Marital Satisfaction," *Journal of Personality* 65, no. 1 (March 1997): 107–36; Pat Barclay, "Altruism as a Courtship Display: Some Effects of Third-Party Generosity on Audience Perceptions," *British Journal of Psychology* (London, England) 101, no. 1 (February 2010): 123–35, https://doi.org/10.1348/000712609X435733.

4. Kristen Hawkes and Rebecca Bliege Bird, "Showing off, Handicap Signaling, and the Evolution of Men's Work," *Evolutionary Anthropology: Issues, News, and Reviews* 11, no. 2 (January 1, 2002): 58–67, https://doi.org/10.1002/evan.20005.

5. Daniel Farrelly, Paul Clemson, and Melissa Guthrie, "Are Women's Mate Preferences for Altruism Also Influenced by Physical Attractiveness?" *Evolutionary Psychology* 14, no. 1 (February 24, 2016): 147470491562369, https://doi.org/10.1177/1474704915623698.

6. A. C. Little et al., "Partnership Status and the Temporal Context of Relationships Influence Human Female Preferences for Sexual Dimorphism in Male Face Shape," *Proceedings of the Royal Society B: Biological Sciences* 269, no. 1496 (June 7, 2002): 1095–100, https://doi.org/10.1098/rspb.2002.1984.

7. D. I. Perrett et al., "Effects of Sexual Dimorphism on Facial Attractiveness," *Nature* 394, no. 6696 (August 27, 1998): 884–87, https://doi.org/10.1038/29772.

8. Victor S. Johnston et al., "Male Facial Attractiveness: Evidence for Hormone-Mediated Adaptive Design," *Evolution and Human Behavior* 22, no. 4 (July 1, 2001): 251–67, https://doi.org/10.1016/S1090-5138(01)00066-6.

9. Lee T. Gettler et al., "Longitudinal Evidence That Fatherhood Decreases Testosterone in Human Males," *Proceedings of the National Academy of Sciences* 108, no. 39 (September 27, 2011): 16194–99, https://doi.org/10.1073/pnas.1105403108; Anne E. Storey et al., "Hormonal Correlates of Paternal Responsiveness in New and Expectant Fathers," *Evolution and Human Behavior* 21, no. 2 (March 1, 2000): 79–95, https://doi.org/10.1016/S1090-5138(99)00042-2.

10. Samuele Zilioli et al., "Interest in Babies Negatively Predicts Testosterone Responses to Sexual Visual Stimuli among Heterosexual Young Men," *Psychological Science* 27, no. 1 (2016): 114–18, http://journals.sagepub.com/doi/abs/10.1177/0956797615615868.

11. J. S. Mascaro, P. D. Hackett, and J. K. Rilling, "Testicular Volume Is Inversely Correlated with Nurturing-Related Brain Activity in Human Fathers," *Proceedings of the National Academy of Sciences* 110, no. 39 (September 24, 2013): 15746–51, https://doi.org/10.1073/pnas.1305579110.

12. Alison S. Fleming et al., "Testosterone and Prolactin Are Associated with Emotional Responses to Infant Cries in New Fathers," *Hormones and Behavior* 42, no. 4 (December 1, 2002): 399–413, https://doi.org/10.1006/hbeh.2002.1840.

13. Paul J. Zak et al., "Testosterone Administration Decreases Generosity in the Ultimatum Game," *PloS One* 4, no. 12 (December 16, 2009): e8330, https://doi.org/10.1371/journal.pone.0008330.

14. Kathryn Kopinak, "Gender Differences in Political Ideology in Canada," *Canadian Review of Sociology/Revue Canadienne de Sociologie* 24, no. 1 (February 1, 1987): 23–38, https://doi.org/10.1111/j.1755-618X.1987.tb01069.x; Riane Eisler and David Loye, "The 'Failure' of Liberalism: A Reassessment of Ideology from a New Feminine-Masculine Perspective," *Political Psychology* 4, no. 2 (June 1983): 375, https://doi.org/10.2307/3790946; Jim Sidanius, B. J. Cling, and Felicia Pratto, "Ranking and Linking as a Function of Sex and Gender Role Attitudes," *Journal of Social Issues* 47, no. 3 (October 1, 1991): 131–49, https://doi.org/10.1111/j.1540-4560.1991.tb01827.x.

15. Robert Y. Shapiro and Harpreet Mahajan, "Gender Differences in Policy Preferences: A Summary of Trends from the 1960s to the 1980s," *Public Opinion Quarterly* 50, no. 1 (1986): 42–61, http://dx.doi.org/10.1086/268958.

16. Richard L. Fox and Zoe Oxley M., "Women's Support for an Active Government," in *Minority Voting in the United States*, ed. Thomas J. Kreider and Thomas J. Baldino (Santa Barbara, CA: Praeger, 2016).

17. Rebecca L. Warner and Brent S. Steel, "Child Rearing as a Mechanism for Social Change: The Relationship of Child Gender to Parents' Commitment to Gender Equity," *Gender & Society* 13, no. 4 (1999): 503–17, http://journals.sagepub.com/doi/abs/10.1177/089124399013004005.

18. Andrew J. Oswald and Nattavudh Powdthavee, "Daughters and Left-Wing Voting," *Review of Economics and Statistics* 92, no. 2 (2010): 213–27, http://www.mitpressjournals.org/doi/abs/10.1162/rest.2010.11436.

19. Ebonya L. Washington, "Female Socialization: How Daughters Affect Their Legislator Fathers' Voting on Women's Issues," *American Economic Review* 98, no. 1 (February 2008): 311–32, https://doi.org/10.1257/aer.98.1.311.

20. S. W. Gangestad and J. A. Simpson, "The Evolution of Human Mating: Trade-Offs and Strategic Pluralism," *Behavioral and Brain Sciences* 23, no. 4 (August 2000): 573–87; discussion 587–644.

21. Buss, *Evolution of Desire*.

22. Michael E. Price, Nicholas Pound, and Isabel M. Scott, "Female Economic Dependence and the Morality of Promiscuity," *Archives of Sexual Behavior* 43, no. 7 (October 2014): 1289–301, https://doi.org/10.1007/s10508-014-0320-4.

23. David P. Schmitt, "Sociosexuality from Argentina to Zimbabwe: A 48-Nation Study of Sex, Culture, and Strategies of Human Mating," *Behavioral and Brain Sciences* 28, no. 2 (2005): 247–75, https://www.cambridge.org/core/journals/behavioral-and-brain-sciences/article/sociosexuality-from-argentina-to-zimbabwe-a-48-nation-study-of-sex-culture-and-strategies-of-human-mating/E6442571B8E524AE8CAF7613BD4CECC8.

24. M. D. Jennions and M. Petrie, "Why Do Females Mate Multiply? A Review of the Genetic Benefits," *Biological Reviews of the Cambridge Philosophical Society* 75, no. 1 (February 2000): 21–64.

25. Joanna E. Scheib, "Context-Specific Mate Choice Criteria: Women's Trade-Offs in the Contexts of Long-Term and Extra-Pair Mateships," *Personal Relationships* 8, no. 4 (December 1, 2001): 371–89, https://doi.org/10.1111/j.1475-6811.2001.tb00046.x.

26. I. S Penton-Voak and D. I Perrett, "Female Preference for Male Faces Changes Cyclically," *Evolution and Human Behavior* 21, no. 1 (January 1, 2000):

39–48, https://doi.org/10.1016/S1090-5138(99)00033-1; Anthony C. Little, Benedict C. Jones, and Robert P. Burriss, "Preferences for Masculinity in Male Bodies Change across the Menstrual Cycle," *Hormones and Behavior* 51, no. 5 (May 1, 2007): 633–39, https://doi.org/10.1016/j.yhbeh.2007.03.006.

27. Dario Maestripieri, *Macachiavellian Intelligence: How Rhesus Macaques and Humans Have Conquered the World*, 1st ed. (Chicago: University of Chicago Press, 2007).

28. Elham Manea, "Yemen," in Sanja Kelly and Julia Breslin, eds., *Women's Rights in the Middle East and North Africa: Progress Amid Resistance* (New York: Freedom House; Lanham, MD: Rowman and Littlefield, 2010).

29. Sandra L. Vehrencamp, "A Model for the Evolution of Despotic versus Egalitarian Societies," *Animal Behaviour* 31, no. 3 (August 1, 1983): 667–82, https://doi.org/10.1016/S0003-3472(83)80222-X.

30. F. Pratto, L. M. Stallworth, and J. Sidanius, "The Gender Gap: Differences in Political Attitudes and Social Dominance Orientation," *British Journal of Social Psychology* 36 (March 1997): 49–68, https://www.ncbi.nlm.nih .gov/pubmed/9114484; J. Sidanius, F. Pratto, and L. Bobo, "Social Dominance Orientation and the Political Psychology of Gender: A Case of Invariance?" *Journal of Personality and Social Psychology* 67 (1994): 998–1011.

31. S. Ansar Ahmed and N. Talal, "Sex Hormones and the Immune System— Part 2. Animal Data," *Baillière's Clinical Rheumatology* 4, no. 1 (April 1, 1990): 13–31, https://doi.org/10.1016/S0950-3579(05)80241-9.

32. Ivar Folstad and Andrew John Karter, "Parasites, Bright Males, and the Immunocompetence Handicap," *American Naturalist* 139, no. 3 (1992): 603–22, https://doi.org/ 10.1086/285346.

33. Steven W. Gangestad and David M. Buss, "Pathogen Prevalence and Human Mate Preferences," *Ethology and Sociobiology* 14, no. 2 (March 1, 1993): 89–96, https://doi.org/10.1016/0162-3095(93)90009-7.

34. S. W. Gangestad, "Sexual Selection and Physical Attractiveness: Implications for Mating Dynamics," *Human Nature* 4 (1993): 205–35.

35. Bobbi S. Low, "Marriage Systems and Pathogen Stress in Human Societies," *American Zoologist* 30, no. 2 (1990): 325–39, https://doi.org/ 10.1093/icb/30.2.325.

36. Gangestad and Simpson, "Evolution of Human Mating."

37. Lisa M. DeBruine, Benedict C. Jones, et al., "The Health of a Nation Predicts Their Mate Preferences: Cross-Cultural Variation in Women's

Preferences for Masculinized Male Faces," *Proceedings of the Royal Society B* 277, no. 1692 (2010): 2405–10, http://rspb.royalsocietypublishing.org/content/early/2010/03/13/rspb.2009.2184#sec-2.

38. Buss, *Evolution of Desire*.

39. Colleen M. Carpinella and Kerri L. Johnson, "Appearance-Based Politics: Sex-Typed Facial Cues Communicate Political Party Affiliation," *Journal of Experimental Social Psychology* 49, no. 1 (January 1, 2013): 156–60, https://doi.org/10.1016/j.jesp.2012.08.009.

40. David Wagner, "The 'Michele Bachmann' Effect; Curiosity Finds a Streambed on Mars," *Atlantic*, September 27, 2012, https://www.theatlantic.com/technology/archive/2012/09/michele-bachmann-effect-curiosity-finds-streambed-mars/323139/.

41. Paul K. Piff et al., "Having Less, Giving More: The Influence of Social Class on Prosocial Behavior," *Journal of Personality and Social Psychology* 99, no. 5 (November 2010): 771–84, https://doi.org/10.1037/a0020092; Michael W. Kraus and Dacher Keltner, "Social Class Rank, Essentialism, and Punitive Judgment," *Journal of Personality and Social Psychology* 105, no. 2 (August 2013): 247–61, https://doi.org/10.1037/a0032895; I.-Ching Lee, Felicia Pratto, and Blair T. Johnson, "Intergroup Consensus/Disagreement in Support of Group-Based Hierarchy: An Examination of Socio-Structural and Psycho-Cultural Factors," *Psychological Bulletin* 137, no. 6 (November 2011): 1029–64, https://doi.org/10.1037/a0025410.

42. Serge Guimond and Michaël Dambrun, "When Prosperity Breeds Intergroup Hostility: The Effects of Relative Deprivation and Relative Gratification on Prejudice," *Personality and Social Psychology Bulletin* 28, no. 7 (July 1, 2002): 900–12, https://doi.org/10.1177/014616720202800704.

43. Daniel S. Hamermesh, *Beauty Pays: Why Attractive People Are More Successful* (Princeton, NJ; Oxford: Princeton University Press, 2013).

44. Peter Belmi and Margaret Neale, "Mirror, Mirror on the Wall, Who's the Fairest of Them All? Thinking That One Is Attractive Increases the Tendency to Support Inequality," *Organizational Behavior and Human Decision Processes* 124, no. 2 (July 1, 2014): 133–49, https://doi.org/10.1016/j.obhdp.2014.03.002; Lee, Pratto, and Johnson, "Intergroup Consensus/Disagreement."

45. Niclas Berggren, Henrik Jordahl, and Panu Poutvaara, "The Right Look: Conservative Politicians Look Better and Voters Reward It," *Journal of Public Economics* 146 (February 2017): 79–86, https://doi.org/10.1016/j.jpubeco.2016.12.008.

46. Belmi and Neale, "Mirror, Mirror on the Wall."

47. Paul William Kingston and Steven E. Finkel, "Is There a Marriage Gap in Politics?" *Journal of Marriage and Family* 49, no. 1 (1987): 57–64, https://doi .org/10.2307/352669.

48. "Presidential Race: 2012 Election Center," CNN, last updated December 10, 2012, http://www.cnn.com/election/2012/results/race/president; "2016 Election Results: Exit Polls," CNN, last updated November 23, 2016, http://www .cnn.com/election/results/exit-polls; "Election Center 2008: President National Exit Poll," CNN, 2008, http://www.cnn.com/ELECTION/2008/results/ polls/#val=USP00p3.

49. Christopher T. Stout, Kelsy Kretschmer, and Leah Ruppanner, "Gender Linked Fate, Race/Ethnicity, and the Marriage Gap in American Politics," *Political Research Quarterly* 70, no. 3 (September 1, 2017): 509–22, https://doi .org/10.1177/1065912917702499.

50. Arwa Mahdawi, "This Is What Rape Culture Looks Like—In the Words of Donald Trump," *Guardian*, October 15, 2016, http://www.theguardian.com/ us-news/2016/oct/15/donald-trump-words-what-rape-culture-looks-like.

51. Rachael Revesz, "Donald Trump Boasted about Meeting Semi-Naked Teenagers in Beauty Pageants," *Independent*, October 12, 2016, http://www .independent.co.uk/news/world/americas/donald-trump-former-miss-arizona -tasha-dixon-naked-undressed-backstage-howard-stern-a7357866.html.

52. Revesz.

53. Janell Ross, "Alicia Machado, the Woman Trump Called Miss Housekeeping, Is Ready to Vote against Donald Trump," *Washington Post*, September 27, 2016, https://www.washingtonpost.com/news/the-fix/ wp/2016/09/27/alicia-machado-the-woman-trump-called-miss-housekeeping-is -ready-to-vote-against-donald-trump/.

54. Alec Tyson and Shiva Maniam, "Behind Trump's Victory: Divisions by Race, Gender, Education," Pew Research Center, November 9, 2016, http://www .pewresearch.org/fact-tank/2016/11/09/behind-trumps-victory -divisions-by-race-gender-education/.

55. "At Rally 'Trumpettes' Talk Machado, Taxes and More," NBC News, September 30, 2016, https://www.nbcnews.com/video/at-rally-trumpettes -talk-machado-taxes-and-more-776866371522.

56. R. A. Fisher, *The Genetical Theory of Natural Selection*, ed. J. H. Bennett, 1st ed. (Oxford: Oxford University Press, 2000).

57. Steven W. Gangestad et al., "Women's Preferences for Male Behavioral Displays Change across the Menstrual Cycle," *Psychological Science* 15, no. 3 (March 2004): 203–207, https://doi.org/10.1111/j.0956-7976.2004.01503010.x.

58. Ryan Teague Beckwith, "Read the Full Transcript of the Sixth Republican Debate in Charleston," *Time*, January 15, 2016, http://time.com/ 4182096/republican-debate-charleston-transcript-full-text/; Ben Jacobs, "Trump Repeats Crowd Member's 'Pussy' Insult as New Hampshire Votes," *Guardian*, February 9, 2016, https://www.theguardian.com/us-news/2016/ feb/08/trump-repeats-insult-from-crowd-member-calling-cruz-a-pussy; "The Fox News GOP Debate Transcript, Annotated," *Washington Post*, March 3, 2016, https://www.washingtonpost.com/news/the-fix/wp/2016/03/03/ the-fox-news-gop-debate-transcript-annotated/?utm_term=.85fb2d30134c.

59. Jan Havlicek, S. Craig Roberts, and Jaroslav Flegr, "Women's Preference for Dominant Male Odour: Effects of Menstrual Cycle and Relationship Status," *Biology Letters* 1, no. 3 (September 22, 2005): 256–59, https://doi.org/10.1098/ rsbl.2005.0332.

60. David A. Puts et al., "Men's Masculinity and Attractiveness Predict Their Female Partners Reported Orgasm Frequency and Timing," *Evolution and Human Behavior* 33, no. 1 (2012): 1–9, http://www.academia.edu/6514194/Mens _masculinity_and_attractiveness_predict_their_female_partners_reported _orgasm_frequency_and_timing.

61. Randy Thornhill, Steven W Gangestad, and Randall Comer, "Human Female Orgasm and Mate Fluctuating Asymmetry," *Animal Behaviour* 50, no. 6 (1995).

62. Lee Alan Dugatkin, "Sexual Selection and Imitation: Females Copy the Mate Choice of Others," *American Naturalist* 139, no. 6 (1992): 1384– 89, https://doi.org/10.1086/285392; Klaudia Witte and Kirsten Ueding, "Sailfin Molly Females (*Poecilia latipinna*) Copy the Rejection of a Male," *Behavioral Ecology* 14, no. 3 (May 1, 2003): 389–95, https://doi.org/10.1093/ beheco/14.3.389.

63. D. Waynforth, "Mate Choice Copying in Humans," *Human Nature* (Hawthorne, NY) 18, no. 3 (September 2007): 264–71, https://doi.org/10.1007/ s12110-007-9004-2.

64. Jessica L. Yorzinski and Michael L. Platt, "Same-Sex Gaze Attraction Influences Mate-Choice Copying in Humans," *PLOS ONE* 5, no. 2 (February 9, 2010): e9115, https://doi.org/10.1371/journal.pone.0009115.

65. Sarah E. Hill and David M. Buss, "The Mere Presence of Opposite-Sex Others on Judgments of Sexual and Romantic Desirability: Opposite Effects for Men and Women," *Personality & Social Psychology Bulletin* 34, no. 5 (May 2008): 635–47, https://doi.org/10.1177/0146167207313728.

66. Waynforth, "Mate Choice Copying in Humans."

67. Martin L. Lalumiére et al., *The Causes of Rape: Understanding Individual Differences in Male Propensity for Sexual Aggression* (Washington, DC: American Psychological Association, 2005).

68. Tyson and Maniam, "Behind Trump's Victory."

69. Hilda M. Bruce, "An Exteroceptive Block to Pregnancy in the Mouse," *Nature* 184, no. 4680 (July 11, 1959): 105, https://doi.org/10.1038/184105a0.

70. E. K. Roberts et al., "A Bruce Effect in Wild Geladas," *Science* 335, no. 6073 (March 9, 2012): 1222–25, https://doi.org/10.1126/science.1213600.

71. Sarah Blaffer Hrdy, "Infanticide among Animals: A Review, Classification, and Examination of the Implications for the Reproductive Strategies of Females," *Ethology and Sociobiology* 1, no. 1 (October 1, 1979): 13–40, https://doi.org/10.1016/0162-3095(79)90004-9; P. L. Schwagmeyer, "The Bruce Effect: An Evaluation of Male/Female Advantages," *American Naturalist* 114, no. 6 (1979): 932–38, https://doi.org/10.1086/283541.

72. Ralph A. Catalano, "Sex Ratios in the Two Germanies: A Test of the Economic Stress Hypothesis," *Human Reproduction* (Oxford, England) 18, no. 9 (September 2003): 1972–75; Ralph A. Catalano and Tim Bruckner, "Economic Antecedents of the Swedish Sex Ratio," *Social Science & Medicine* 60, no. 3 (February 2005): 537–43, https://doi.org/10.1016/j.socscimed.2004.06.008; Branko Zorn et al., "Decline in Sex Ratio at Birth after 10-Day War in Slovenia: Brief Communication," *Human Reproduction* (Oxford, England) 17, no. 12 (December 2002): 3173–77; Jan Graffelman and Rolf F. Hoekstra, "A Statistical Analysis of the Effect of Warfare on the Human Secondary Sex Ratio," *Human Biology* 72, no. 3 (2000): 433–45, https://www.ncbi.nlm.nih.gov/pubmed/10885189.

73. Tim A. Bruckner, Ralph Catalano, and Jennifer Ahern, "Male Fetal Loss in the U.S. Following the Terrorist Attacks of September 11, 2001," *BMC Public Health* 10, no. 1 (2010): 273, https://bmcpublichealth.biomedcentral.com/articles/10.1186/1471-2458-10-273.

74. Tara J. Chavanne and Gordon G. Gallup, "Variation in Risk Taking Behavior among Female College Students as a Function of the Menstrual Cycle,"

Evolution and Human Behavior 19, no. 1 (1998): 27–32, http://www
.sciencedirect.com/science/article/pii/S1090513898000166.

75. Carlos David Navarrete et al., "Prejudice at the Nexus of Race and
Gender: An Outgroup Male Target Hypothesis," *Journal of Personality and Social
Psychology* 98, no. 6 (2010): 933–45, https://doi.org/10.1037/a0017931.

76. Carlos David Navarrete et al., "Race Bias Tracks Conception Risk across
the Menstrual Cycle," *Psychological Science* 20, no. 6 (June 2009): 661–65, https://
doi.org/10.1111/j.1467-9280.2009.02352.x.

77. Melissa M. McDonald et al., "Mate Choice Preferences in an Intergroup
Context: Evidence for a Sexual Coercion Threat-Management System among
Women," *Evolution and Human Behavior* 36, no. 6 (November 2015): 438–45,
https://doi.org/10.1016/j.evolhumbehav.2015.04.002.

78. Jonah Goldberg, "L'Affaire Coulter," *National Review*, October 2,
2001, http://www.nationalreview.com/article/220676/laffaire-coulter-jonah
-goldberg.

79. Ann Coulter, *In Trump We Trust: E Pluribus Awesome!* (New York:
Sentinel, 2016).

80. Michelle Cottle, "The Queen of Trump Conservatives," *Atlantic*,
September 16, 2016, https://www.theatlantic.com/politics/archive/2016/09/
dont-count-out-coulter/500237/.

81. Ann Coulter, *Adios, America: The Left's Plan to Turn Our Country into a
Third World Hellhole* (repr.; Washington, DC: Regnery Publishing, 2016).

82. Frans de Waal, *Chimpanzee Politics: Power and Sex among Apes*, 25th
anniversary ed. (Baltimore, MD: Johns Hopkins University Press, 2007).

83. Barbara B. Smuts, *Sex and Friendship in Baboons*, 1st ed. (New
Brunswick: Routledge, 2007).

84. Boguslaw Pawlowski and Grazyna Jasienska, "Women's Preferences for
Sexual Dimorphism in Height Depend on Menstrual Cycle Phase and Expected
Duration of Relationship," *Biological Psychology* 70, no. 1 (September 1, 2005):
38–43, https://doi.org/10.1016/j.biopsycho.2005.02.002.

85. Robert P. Burriss, Hannah M. Rowland, and Anthony C. Little, "Facial
Scarring Enhances Men's Attractiveness for Short-Term Relationships," *Personality
and Individual Differences* 46, no. 2 (January 1, 2009): 213–17, https://doi.org/
10.1016/j.paid.2008.09.029.

86. Hannes Rusch, Joost M. Leunissen, and Mark van Vugt, "Historical
and Experimental Evidence of Sexual Selection for War Heroism," *Evolution and*

Human Behavior 36, no. 5 (September 2015): 367–73, https://doi.org/10.1016/j.evolhumbehav.2015.02.005.

87. Pamela Johnston Conover and Virginia Sapiro, "Gender, Feminist Consciousness, and War," *American Journal of Political Science* 37, no. 4 (1993): 1079–99, https://doi.org/10.2307/2111544; Richard C. Eichenberg, "Gender Differences in Public Attitudes toward the Use of Force by the United States, 1990–2003," *International Security* 28, no. 1 (2003): 110–41, https://doi.org/10.1162/016228803322427992; Shapiro and Mahajan, "Gender Differences in Policy Preferences"; Clyde Wilcox, Lara Hewitt, and Dee Allsop, "The Gender Gap in Attitudes toward the Gulf War: A Cross-National Perspective," *Journal of Peace Research* 33, no. 1 (1996): 67–82, https://doi.org/10.1177/0022343396033001005.

88. Mary Caprioli, "Gendered Conflict," *Journal of Peace Research* 37, no. 1 (2000): 51–68, https://doi.org/10.1177/0022343300037001003; Mary Caprioli and Mark A. Boyer, "Gender, Violence, and International Crisis," *Journal of Conflict Resolution* 45, no. 4 (August 1, 2001): 503–18, https://doi.org/10.1177/0022002701045004005.

89. Michael T. Koch and Sarah A. Fulton, "In the Defense of Women: Gender, Office Holding, and National Security Policy in Established Democracies," *Journal of Politics* 73, no. 1 (January 2011): 1–16, https://doi.org/10.1017/S0022381610000824.

90. "Rwanda Genocide: 100 Days of Slaughter," BBC, April 7, 2014, https://www.bbc.com/news/world-africa-26875506.

91. Stephanie McCrummen, "Women Run the Show in a Recovering Rwanda," *Washington Post*, October 27, 2008, http://www.washingtonpost.com/wp-dyn/content/article/2008/10/26/AR2008102602197.html.

92. Swanee Hunt and Laura Heaton, "Women in Post-Genocide Rwanda Have Helped Heal Their Country," *National Geographic News*, April 4, 2014, http://news.nationalgeographic.com/news/2014/04/140404-rwanda-genocide-parliament-kigali-rwandan-patriotic-front-world-women-education/.

93. *The Global Gender Gap Report 2016* (Geneva, Switzerland: World Economic Forum, 2016), http://reports.weforum.org/global-gender-gap-report-2016/.

94. United Nations Development Programme, ed., *Human Development Report 2016: Human Development for Everyone* (New York: United Nations Development Programme, 2016).

95. P. Zuckerman, *Society without God* (New York: New York University Press, 2008).

CHAPTER 8: ON BLIND TRIBES AND BECOMING SIGHTED

1. David P. Redlawski, "Motivated Reasoning, Affect, and the Role of Memory in Voter Decision Making," in *Feeling Politics* (New York: Palgrave Macmillan, 2006), pp. 87–107, https://doi.org/10.1057/9781403983114_6; John T. Jost et al., "Political Conservatism as Motivated Social Cognition," *Psychological Bulletin* 129, no. 3 (May 2003): 339–75.

2. Steve Holland and Ginger Gibson, "Confident Trump Says Could 'Shoot Somebody' and Not Lose Voters," Reuters, January 23, 2016, https://www.reuters.com/article/us-usa-election/confident-trump-says-could-shoot-somebody-and-not-lose-voters-idUSMTZSAPEC1NFEQLYN.

3. Drew Westen et al., "Neural Bases of Motivated Reasoning: An FMRI Study of Emotional Constraints on Partisan Political Judgment in the 2004 U.S. Presidential Election," *Journal of Cognitive Neuroscience* 18, no. 11 (November 2006): 1947–58, https://doi.org/10.1162/jocn.2006.18.11.1947.

4. Eugene Scott, "'You Get a Do-Over Here': Evangelical Leaders' Apparent Double-Standard on the Alleged Trump-Daniels Affair," *Washington Post*, January 23, 2018, https://www.washingtonpost.com/news/the-fix/wp/2018/01/23/you-get-a-do-over-here-evangelical-leaders-apparent-double-standard-on-the-alleged-trump-daniels-affair/.

5. Nancy Gibbs, "Defusing the War over the 'Promiscuity' Vaccine," *Time*, June 21, 2006, http://content.time.com/time/nation/article/0,8599,1206813,00.html.

6. Amy Clark, "Hotels Pressured To Halt Porn," CBS News, August 22, 2006, https://www.cbsnews.com/news/hotels-pressured-to-halt-porn/.

7. Scott, "'You Get a Do-Over Here.'"

8. S. E. Asch, "Effects of Group Pressure upon the Modification and Distortion of Judgments," in *Groups, Leadership and Men; Research in Human Relations*, ed. H. Guetzkow (Oxford, England: Carnegie Press, 1951).

9. Geoffrey L. Cohen, "Party over Policy: The Dominating Impact of Group Influence on Political Beliefs," *Journal of Personality and Social Psychology* 85, no. 5 (November 2003): 808–22, https://doi.org/10.1037/0022-3514.85.5.808.

10. "A Deeper Partisan Divide over Global Warming," Pew Research Center, May 8, 2008, http://www.people-press.org/2008/05/08/a-deeper-partisan-divide-over-global-warming/.

11. Aaron M. McCright and Riley E. Dunlap, "The Politicization of Climate Change and Polarization in the American Public's Views of Global Warming, 2001–2010," *Sociological Quarterly* 52, no. 2 (March 2011): 155–94, https://doi.org/10.1111/j.1533-8525.2011.01198.x.

12. Lawrence C. Hamilton, "Education, Politics and Opinions about Climate Change Evidence for Interaction Effects," *Climatic Change* 104, no. 2 (January 1, 2011): 231–42, https://doi.org/10.1007/s10584-010-9957-8; Lawrence C. Hamilton, "Who Cares about Polar Regions? Results from a Survey of U.S. Public Opinion," *Arctic, Antarctic, and Alpine Research* 40, no. 4 (2008): 671–78.

13. Carol Krucoff, "The 6 O'Clock Scholar," *Washington Post*, January 29, 1984, https://www.washingtonpost.com/archive/lifestyle/1984/01/29/the-6-oclock-scholar/eed58de4-2dcb-47d2-8947-b0817a18d8fe/.

14. Felicia Pratto et al., "Social Dominance Orientation: A Personality Variable Predicting Social and Political Attitudes.," *Journal of Personality and Social Psychology* 67, no. 4 (1994): 741–63, https://doi.org/10.1037/0022-3514.67.4.741; Leanne S. Son Hing et al., "Authoritarian Dynamics and Unethical Decision Making: High Social Dominance Orientation Leaders and High Right-Wing Authoritarianism Followers," *Journal of Personality and Social Psychology* 92, no. 1 (January 2007): 67–81, https://doi.org/10.1037/0022-3514.92.1.67.

15. Clara Sabbagh, "Environmentalism, Right-Wing Extremism, and Social Justice Beliefs among East German Adolescents," *International Journal of Psychology* 40, no. 2 (April 1, 2005): 118–31, https://doi.org/10.1080/00207590544000095; Bill E. Peterson, Richard M. Doty, and David G. Winter, "Authoritarianism and Attitudes toward Contemporary Social Issues," *Personality and Social Psychology Bulletin* 19, no. 2 (April 1, 1993): 174–84, https://doi.org/10.1177/0146167293192006.

16. Lynnette C. Zelezny, Poh-pheng Chua, and Christina Aldrich, "Elaborating on Gender Differences in Environmentalism," *Journal of Social Issues*, 56, no. 3 (2000): 443–57; Thomas Dietz, Linda Kalof, and Paul C. Stern, "Gender, Values, and Environmentalism," *Social Science Quarterly* 83, no. 1 (March 1, 2002): 353–64, https://doi.org/10.1111/1540-6237.00088.

17. Coral Davenport and Eric Lipton, "How G.O.P. Leaders Came to View

Climate Change as Fake Science," *New York Times*, June 3, 2017, https://www.nytimes.com/2017/06/03/us/politics/republican-leaders-climate-change.html.

18.   J. M. Breslow, "Bob Inglis: Climate Change and the Republican Party," Frontline, October 23, 2012, http://www.pbs.org/wgbh/frontline/article/bob-inglis-climate-change-and-the-republican-party/.

19.   Irina Feygina, John T. Jost, and Rachel E. Goldsmith, "System Justification, the Denial of Global Warming, and the Possibility of 'System-Sanctioned Change,'" *Personality and Social Psychology Bulletin* 36, no. 3 (March 1, 2010): 326–38, https://doi.org/10.1177/0146167209351435.

20.   Oliver Burkeman, "Memo Exposes Bush's New Green Strategy," *Guardian*, March 4, 2003, http://www.theguardian.com/environment/2003/mar/04/usnews.climatechange.

21.   Allan Mazur, "Believers and Disbelievers in Evolution," *Politics and the Life Sciences* 23, no. 2 (2004): 55–61, http://www.jstor.org/stable/4236748; Eric Woodrum and Thomas Hoban, "Support for Prayer in School and Creationism," *Sociological Analysis* 53, no. 3 (1992): 309–21, https://doi.org/10.2307/3711707.

22.   Joseph O. Baker, "Acceptance of Evolution and Support for Teaching Creationism in Public Schools: The Conditional Impact of Educational Attainment," *Journal for the Scientific Study of Religion* 52, no. 1 (March 1, 2013): 216–28, https://doi.org/10.1111/jssr.12007.

23.   "Religious Landscape Study," Pew Research Center, May 11, 2015, http://www.pewforum.org/religious-landscape-study/.

24.   Joseph O. Baker, Dalton Rogers, and Timothy Moser, "Acceptance of Evolution among American Mormons," *Journal of Contemporary Religion* 33, no. 1 (January 2, 2018): 123–34, https://doi.org/10.1080/13537903.2018.1408295.

25.   Jon D. Miller, Eugenie C. Scott, and Shinji Okamoto, "Public Acceptance of Evolution," *Science* 313, no. 5788 (August 11, 2006): 765–66, https://doi.org/10.1126/science.1126746.

26.   Baker, "Acceptance of Evolution and Support."

27.   Ara Norenzayan and Ian G. Hansen, "Belief in Supernatural Agents in the Face of Death," *Personality & Social Psychology Bulletin* 32, no. 2 (February 2006): 174–87, https://doi.org/10.1177/0146167205280251; M. Osarchuk and S. J. Tatz, "Effect of Induced Fear of Death on Belief in Afterlife," *Journal of Personality and Social Psychology* 27, no. 2 (August 1973): 256–60.

28.   1 Cor. 1:10.

29.   Daniel M. T. Fessler, Anne C. Pisor, and Colin Holbrook, "Political

NOTES

Orientation Predicts Credulity Regarding Putative Hazards," *Psychological Science* 28, no. 5 (May 2017): 651–60, https://doi.org/10.1177/09567976176 92108.

30. Laura Sydell, "We Tracked Down a Fake-News Creator in the Suburbs. Here's What We Learned," NPR, November 23, 2016, http://www.npr.org/ sections/alltechconsidered/2016/11/23/503146770/npr-finds-the -head-of-a-covert-fake-news-operation-in-the-suburbs.

31. Vidya Narayanan et al., *Polarization, Partisanship and Junk News Consumption over Social Media in the US* (Oxford: Computational Propaganda Project, February 6, 2018), http://comprop.oii.ox.ac.uk/research/ polarization-partisanship-and-junk-news/.

32. David Lazer et al., "Combating Fake News: An Agenda for Research and Action," (conference held February 17–18, 2017, Harvard Kennedy School Shorstein Center on Media, Politics, and Public Policy, Cambridge, MA), https:// shorensteincenter.org/combating-fake-news-agenda-for-research/.

33. Angie Drobnic Holan, "Sarah Palin Falsely Claims Barack Obama Runs a 'Death Panel,'" PolitiFact, August 10, 2009, http://www.politifact.com/ truth-o-meter/statements/2009/aug/10/sarah-palin/sarah-palin -barack-obama-death-panel/.

34. Frank Newport, "Many Americans Can't Name Obama's Religion," Gallup, Washington, DC, June 22, 2012, http://news.gallup.com/poll/155315/ Many-Americans-Cant-Name-Obamas-Religion.aspx.

35. *Last Week Tonight with John Oliver*, season 4, episode 19, "Alex Jones," directed by Christopher Werner, aired July 30, 2017 on HBO.

36. Dariusz Dolinski and Richard Nawrat, "'Fear-Then-Relief' Procedure for Producing Compliance: Beware When the Danger Is Over," *Journal of Experimental Social Psychology* 34, no. 1 (January 1, 1998): 27–50, https://doi .org/10.1006/jesp.1997.1341.

37. Dariusz Dolinski et al., "Fear-Then-Relief, Mindlessness, and Cognitive Deficits," *European Journal of Social Psychology* 32, no. 4 (July 1, 2002): 435–47, https://doi.org/10.1002/ejsp.100.

38. "Full Transcript: Second 2016 Presidential Debate," Politico, October 10, 2016, https://www.politico.com/story/2016/10/2016-presidential -debate-transcript-229519.

39. Timothy Snyder, *On Tyranny: Twenty Lessons from the Twentieth Century*, 1st ed. (New York: Tim Duggan Books, 2017).

40. "Bush: 'Leave Iraq within 48 Hours,'" CNN.com, March 17, 2003, http://www.cnn.com/2003/WORLD/meast/03/17/sprj.irq.bush.transcript/.

41. Mark J. Landau et al., "Deliver Us from Evil: The Effects of Mortality Salience and Reminders of 9/11 on Support for President George W. Bush," *Personality & Social Psychology Bulletin* 30, no. 9 (September 2004): 1136–50, https://doi.org/10.1177/0146167204267988.

42. Katie Benner and Hawes Spencer, "Charlottesville Car Attack Suspect Indicted on Federal Hate Crime Charges," *New York Times*, June 27, 2018, https://www.nytimes.com/2018/06/27/us/politics/charlottesville-death-hate -crime-charges.html.

43. Daisuke Wakabayashi and Scott Shane, "Twitter, with Accounts Linked to Russia, to Face Congress over Role in Election," *New York Times*, September 27, 2017, https://www.nytimes.com/2017/09/27/technology/twitter-russia-election .html.

44. Narayanan et al., *"Polarization, Partisanship and Junk News."*

45. "Defining Critical Thinking," Foundation for Critical Thinking, https:// www.criticalthinking.org/pages/defining-critical-thinking/766.

46. Geoffrey K. Roberts, "Political Education in Germany," *Parliamentary Affairs* 55, no. 3 (July 1, 2002): 556–68, https://doi.org/10.1093/parlij/55.3.556.

47. Stephan Lewandowsky and Ulrich K. H. Eckler, "Beyond Misinformation: Understanding and Coping with the 'Post-Truth' Era," *Journal of Applied Research in Memory and Cognition* 6, no. 4 (2017): 353–69; Elizabeth J. Marsh and Brenda W. Yang, "A Call to Think Broadly about Information Literacy," *Journal of Applied Research in Memory and Cognition* 6, no. 4 (2017): 401–404.

48. Guillermo C. Jimenez, *Red Genes, Blue Genes: Exposing Political Irrationality*, 1st ed. (Brooklyn, NY: Autonomedia, 2009); Robert Green and Adam Rosenblatt, *"C-SPAN/PSB Supreme Court Survey 2017: Comprehensive Agenda"* (Washington, DC: CSPAN/PSB, March 2017), https://static .c-span.org/assets/documents/scotusSurvey/CSPAN%20PSB%20Supreme%20 Court%20Survey%20COMPREHENSIVE%20AGENDA%20sent%2003%20 13%2017.pdf; Annenberg Public Policy Center of the University of Pennsylvania, "The Annenberg Public Policy Center of the University of Pennsylvania: Americans Are Poorly Informed about Basic Constitutional Provisions," news release, September 12, 2017, https://www.annenbergpublicpolicycenter.org/ americans-are-poorly-informed-about-basic-constitutional-provisions/.

NOTES

49. John Stuart Mill, J. B. Schneewind, and Dale E. Miller, *The Basic Writings of John Stuart Mill: On Liberty, the Subjection of Women and Utilitarianism*, 2nd ed. (New York: Modern Library, 2002).

50. Sebastian Junger, *Tribe: On Homecoming and Belonging*, 1st ed. (New York: Twelve, 2016).

51. Paul Leicester Ford, ed., *The Writings of Thomas Jefferson, Volume X: 1816–1826* (New York: GP Putnam Sons, 1899), p. 389.

INDEX